Istvàn Szabó

Screenwriter; film director

Filmography:

1961	*Concert* (short)
	Variations on a Theme (short)
1963	*You* (short)
1964	*The Age of Illusions*
1966	*Father*
1967	*Piety*
1970	*A Film About Love*
1971	*Budapest, Why I Love It*
	Dream About a House
1973	*25 Firemen's Street*
1974	*Premiere*
1977	*Tales of Budapest*
	City Map
1978	*The Hungarians*
1979	*Confidence*
	The Green Bird
1981	*Mephisto*
1982	*Catsplay*
1984	*Colonel Redl*

What film I would take on a desert island is very difficult to answer, but I should like to take one film of Ingmar Bergman's. It is very complicated to choose one of five or six

marvelous films, and that's why I would also take Fellini's *8½* or
Orson Welles' *Citizen Kane* or Kurosawa's *Rashomon* or Bergman's *Wild Strawberries* or *Fanny and Alexander* or *Winter Light* or
Cries and Whispers. You ask me to choose one film—it's a big
package, but maybe if I could have some video tape, then I
would have ten possible choices. But those are my favorite films
and filmmakers today. They are honest, truthful; they know
cinema has marvelous possibilities to speak with people about
important human considerations and they do it. The technique
of making films is so simple—anyone can learn this profession
now. I think the average filmmaker today all over the world
knows this profession and they have different marvelous styles
and techniques, but the philosophical or human values only
some people have, like Bergman, Fellini, Kurosawa, or Buñuel.

In my films I'm trying to say something about our experience: Middle Europe is something special. In this century we
have many important experiences in our history and from our
politics, and I think this also influences our private life. This is
very important. Maybe today you need to know it, maybe not.

It's very easy to give bad examples of how film has affected
people socially, politically, and I think now film is on a very bad
path. Film is in a big crisis right now because the major part of
the audience has been taken away by a daily struggle, the social
problems, and also by television, video, and cable. Children and
old people have been made the movie audience. It's the children's only chance to hold hands in the dark, and it's the only
chance the old people have to leave their homes, where they
feel very lonely. That's why filmmakers who want to make
money from these needs naturally want to please the audience,
the old people and the children. That's why silly little children's
stories that are all the same, like blue jeans and Coca-Cola, are
being made into films, or films for the old people somehow
imitate a certain style, an old style. They're not original anymore
because they're imitative and full of sentiment. So I really think
that film is in a big crisis and doesn't even see its future, whether
it'll remain alive or not.

I don't think it won't survive because churches and temples
have stayed open way after book printing started, and stadiums
have remained open although television broadcasts those

MOVIES
FOR A
DESERT
ISLE

Also by Ellen Oumano

Film Forum
Sam Shepard

MOVIES
FOR A
DESERT
ISLE

Forty-Two Well-Known

Film Lovers in Search

of Their Favorite Movie

ELLEN OUMANO

St. Martin's Press

New York

Library of Congress Cataloging-in-Publication Data

Oumano, Ellen.
    Movies for a desert isle.

    1. Moving-pictures.   I. Title
PN1995.085   1986   791.43'02   86-13494
ISBN 0-312-55051-0

First Edition

10 9 8 7 6 5 4 3 2 1

This book is dedicated to my parents,
Rose and Jack Shamis.

CONTENTS

Acknowledgments

I wish to thank Tom Allen and Emile de Antonio for their generosity and continuous invaluable help; Lee Fryd for her many contributions; Bob Miller, my editor, who thought of the idea for this book, and Lisa Di Mona, for her many helpful acts; Geri Thoma of the Elaine Markson Agency, for her support and encouragement; and, of course, most of all I wish to thank the people who were kind enough to sit for interviews and address this "impossible" question.

Introduction

The premise of this book is deceptively simple: Ask prominent and articulate people working in various capacities and at various levels in the film/art/business world what film they would take if they were stranded on a desert island—not the best film ever—but one they could live with. A deliberately "impossible" question, it echoes W. C. Fields' joke on Philadelphia: First prize is a one-week stay, second prize is two weeks, and the losers win permanent residence.

In fact, this desert island for movie lovers is not unlike one of Dante's circles in hell, probably somewhere near the circle reserved for the uncommitted. As Andrew Sarris reminds us in these pages, "Hell is doing the same thing over and over." After repeated screenings, a favorite movie (which is roughly how the question translates) could become boring to the point of being loathsome.

Of course, in the interviews the question of what movie to take to a desert island generated discussions ranging far wider than one's favorite movies. For example, the lack of repeatability of movies often led to a consideration of what role movies play in one's life and just how significant that role is. Would a movie be a priority for survival on a desert island? Probably not. Would viewing images of human beings, of whose company one is now deprived forever, not be a "sour and ironic" experience, as Emile de Antonio put it? Why movies are not important enough or even necessarily desirable for a desert island forces reflection on just what their significance is and for whom. What role do movies play in our lives, individually and socially? What would one movie be like if there were no others and if there were no work, no play, no friends, family, or lovers—not even strangers—to form a context for that single film? A new film can be as exciting as an encounter with an intriguing stranger, whereas an old favorite can be a beloved companion, guardian of secret fantasies, comfortingly familiar. A film can be a friend, but one's *only* friend? The question of which film inevitably narrows down to what kind of film is the right choice—tragedy, comedy, musical, and so on. Would it be a film filled with secret nooks, crannies, and winding passageways waiting to be explored, a complexity of sights, sounds, and rhythms offering surprises a few viewings beyond the average, pedestrian "story" movie, or a film soothing and familiar like a well-worn ritual, a guaranteed respite from the harsh facts of life on a desert island or anywhere else? Would it be *Citizen Kane* or *Duck Soup*?

Whatever effect we look for in our movies, their impact on the personal and national psyche cannot be denied. The Farrah Fawcett hairdos of a few years ago and the Brooke Shields eyebrows of today attest to the tremendous power of the movies—usually through those magnified images of human beings known as movie stars—to capture and embody our cultural and individual fantasies. Movies are clearly a collaborative art, but most people don't consider that the final collaborator is the viewer, and that the movie house is the place where a film's life really begins, where the filmmakers' and the viewers' dreams meet and bounce off each other, where we share an experience at the same time that we spin our individual fantasies.

If film is made from the same stuff as our shifting cultural life and our changing dreams, how lasting can it be? Many have suggested that a book has the advantage of timelessness, that literature is less rooted in a particular time and place, and that music and art exist even further beyond the confines of time and space. Perhaps movies have the transitory quality of words written in the sand of this hypothetical island. Even physically, film is rather fragile, made from stock that fades in a short period of time and strips of celluloid that are easily ripped and crushed. The real issue, however, is can a movie that inevitably reflects and projects back the images of a particular time and place have meaning for another culture and period beyond its value as a cultural relic, or is it merely fodder for the anthropologists of the future?

But something of any film experience is guaranteed to survive even on the desert island that many feel our culture has become, if not on the desert island proposed in this book, because movies are better than life. Finally, they are an instrument of enhancement: Things look better up there on the screen, and if they don't always work out better than in real life, at least someone else is doing the suffering for us. We will always need the movies.

We know that films can carry the burden of our psychic hobgoblins as well as communicate our hopes and dreams. They can entertain, educate, surprise, shock, sadden, and comfort. Movies can do all these things for us, but the question still remains whether any single film can do all or some or even one of these things for us repeatedly. Would the monotony of desert-island living only be magnified by the monotony of the same movie—the same narrative, the same characters, the same backgrounds?

Almost every contributor had his own way to confront this dilemma: Two wanted to make up a compilation film of their favorite clips; a few others wanted to take a work in progress to occupy the long empty hours and keep the creative juices from turning as dry as the sand. Some used the auteur theory to support their right to take a filmmaker's entire body of work; a few others preferred to rely on their imaginations rather than anything as stiflingly real as a movie, whiling away the hours under the hot sun making up their own movies in their minds. Although most shrank in horror at the thought of being on an island with nothing else for company but one of their own movies, a few chose to take one of their own, not for the movie itself but for the many memories of people, places, and circumstances involved in its creation. Not a few tried to bend the rules even further, hoping to exchange the finished film, projector, and screen offered in this deal for raw stock so they could film carefully, frame by frame, or exchange the film for video equipment so they might tape and erase, tape and erase for a lifetime. What does this say about the future of filmmaking when filmmakers want video, or when they say they prefer to take a woman, or at least try to bargain for a projectionist of the opposite sex? Perhaps it just attests to the flexibility, practicality, and ability to negotiate that are among the many talents required to manage a career in the film world today.

Almost everyone complained that they had too many favorite films to choose from, and, of course, the same stately eminences hover over these pages: Bergman, Fellini, Ford, Godard, Hawks, Hitchcock, Kurosawa, the Marx Brothers, Welles. How one related to these and other great filmmakers served in a way as a kind of Rorschach test on one's relationship to film in general. For example, for film writer and publisher James Monaco, Godard, born in December of 1930, is nonetheless the "poet" and the "future" of film; whereas for Marianne Faithfull, singer, composer, and sometime actress, who worked on Godard's film with the Rolling Stones, *One Plus One/Sympathy for the Devil,* he was "old-fashioned," trying to be part of something he didn't understand.

Once again, Jean Renoir's maxim applies: "Everyone has his reasons." There are no rule in cinema, the anarchist's medium. While *Citizen Kane* continues to fascinate and seduce, so do Harpo, Chico, Zeppo, and Groucho. Some want to penetrate reality, others want a magic show. Some want to laugh, others want to cry. Some want their intellect teased, other opt for porn. The choice really depends on individual needs, interests, and experiences working in film. For example, actors tend to relate to a good performance, whereas musicians tend to choose a film by the soundtrack.

Of course, the talk extends beyond the films one would choose or not choose for the desert island to the stories in these pages—often surreal, slapstick comedies of errors or tragedies themselves—of films that were made, almost not made, or never made at all. Many contributors wondered whether Hollywod would last much longer, whether the dinosaur had grown too big to survive a new age. How has the role of movies in our culture changed now that more and more people are staying home with their VCRs, watching movies they might otherwise have gone out to a theater to see? How does the fact that 1985 marked the first time the studios made as much money from home video sales as they made at the theater box office affect the future of movies as we have known them? Is Wim Wenders correct when he estimates that the cinematographic language of film has perhaps ten years left before the electronic language of video takes over completely? A great deal of talk centers around this relationship of Cain and Abel, the brother media. If filmmakers feel that the viewer sacrifices the communal experience of a large screen in a darkened theater surrounded by others when he stays at home in front of the tube with the kids running by, the telephone ringing, and the refrigerator and bathroom only a few feet away, how does it strike filmmakers to know that pre-video sales have opened up a whole new avenue of financing, especially important for low-budget, independent filmmakers, and that many more people will see their work via video systems than in the theater?

Everyone seemed to be in accord with the assessment that if the film industry isn't on the verge of disaster right now, it is certainly in the trough of a wave, as Richard Roud, director of the New York Film Festival, put it. There was much discussion of Hollywood's tendency to shoot for the lowest common denominator, with many wagging fingers pointed at "Ramboism" and "Spielbergian" movies as a major contributing factor. Most acknowledged, however, that the unhappy situation of today is not that easily explained. It is certain, however, that modern audiences have grown cynical in the face of the Niagara of images and sound that deluge them every moment. They have become blind in self-defense. The question now remains, what, if anything, can open their eyes and make them want to see?

Robert Altman

Theater, television, and film director; producer; writer

Filmography:

1957	*The Delinquents*
	The James Dean Story
1964	*Nightmare in Chicago*
1968	*Countdown*
1969	*That Cold Day in the Park*
1970	*M*A*S*H*
	Brewster McCloud
1971	*McCabe and Mrs. Miller*
1972	*Images*
1973	*The Long Goodbye*
1974	*Thieves Like Us*
	California Split
1975	*Nashville*
1976	*Buffalo Bill and the Indians or Sitting Bull's History Lesson*
1977	*Three Women*
	The Late Show (prod. only)
1978	*A Wedding*
	Welcome to L.A. (prod. only)
	Remember My Name (exec. prod.; dir. by Alan Rudolph)
1979	*Quintet*
	A Perfect Couple
	Rich Kids (prod. only)
	Health
1981	*Popeye*
1983	*Come Back to the Five and Dime, Jimmy Dean, Jimmy Dean*
	Streamers

1985   *Fool for Love*
         Laundromat

How about trading raw stock for the film and a camera instead of a projector, and then I can turn around and shoot a film while I'm on the desert island and never be able to process it. It will always be in my mind and then I can rerun it as much as I want.

I almost think that films, or at least the films I make, really don't try to tell stories. I like to watch films that tell stories— once. It becomes so linear that once you've reached the end of the line, it doesn't take you back to the beginning again. It just drops you there, and you do drop the experience; whereas if you can keep sending somebody around in a circle, and keep picking up new stuff all the way, they can watch it repeatedly. With story films, you've got it; there's nothing more to deal with after the end, unless it throws you back into it. It isn't important that the butler did it. What is the detailing now that the element of surprise is out of it, now that I know what they did? On the fifth, sixth time, each time you see the film, you should be able to say, "Oh Jesus, they did that, but *this* is really what was going on." That to me is the fun of it; that's the only way to do it. You should see something you haven't seen before because each time you view a film, you've changed, you've had other experiences from the first time you saw it. You look at it differently because you're different. And it's the same way with a painting, any painting. You say, "Oh, that's really . . ." and then you go back and you look at it and you say, "Wait a minute, that's not a goddamn still life, that's a landscape." Then you say, "Wait a minute, this guy's dealing in color." A painting, music, a film stimulates you, but not the same way each time.

One film that influenced me was *Brief Encounter*. I remember seeing it, and before that, movies were stories and that sort of thing. I thought, "What are they doing making this movie with this ugly broad, this old lady in this film with these funny shoes?" And then, suddenly, halfway through the film, I'm in love with her; I want to get in bed with her; I'm crazy about her, and the next thing you know, I'm crying for her dilemma. And suddenly I realize that this is really a beautiful lady and this isn't a story. I'm telling myself the truth about something through what I've seen. I felt the same way about *La Dolce Vita*, about *Persona*. They open up doors and bring out a bunch of computer information that you have. It just comes rushing out. Nothing else will open up the same number of doors at the same time. Each film is opening up a different combination of doors so it becomes different for every person. I read a piece a young guy who just died of leukemia wrote on *Come Back to the Five and Dime, Jimmy Dean, Jimmy Dean*. This friend of his was going to screen the picture and then read the piece to a bunch of his friends. It's almost his wake. He even says in it that he's running out of time. And, my God, he saw things in the film that I didn't even know existed, and yet they do exist and he was able to draw them out. But they certainly were never conscious in my mind. You might think, "This isn't true; this guy is reading all this into it." And then I have to think, "It is true because he *is* reading all this into it." You don't have to agree with it. What he did is valid, and I was amazed to see all the little coincidences that he took out of the film. It's like watching a magician on the stage. I saw Penn and Teller; it's a terrific show, all illusions. They take it one step further by showing you how they're doing the trick, but you're still amazed at the fact that they even thought it up and you still don't know how to do it. And this is the same thing. Sometimes the director doesn't know his own tricks either. He may think to go "this way" because we work in ways that become familiar, that are similar-looking paths. You tend to take them because they're a little easier, or you think they are, but they still get you into a density and you have to fight your way through it. So someone might ask me, "Why are you shooting that way?" And I might answer, "Well, I'm shooting that way because I want to get the feeling I'm way back there and this and this." That's all bullshit; I don't know why I'm shooting it that way.

The critics are the least qualified to understand the reasons because they're trying to second-guess what someone else is going to think, which they cannot do. So their critiques of the film are the least valuable, the least accurate, because they are not their own. Vincent Canby, for instance, does this constantly. He'll give a film a bad review or a good review, but usually a bad review, and then three or four weeks later, after he's killed the dog, he'll come back and say, "Well at the time I was thinking that people wouldn't understand it." He'll do these giant apologies and people think, "Isn't that great." But it's like a guy shooting your dog and then saying, "Oh listen, I'm sorry, I made a mistake." You've still got a dead dog. More important, what he's really telling you is he did not write his own impression of the film. I've had people from more commercial papers blatantly tell me, "I write for my readers; I don't write for myself. I'm writing for the way they think." It's not going to make any difference but it isn't accurate; it's not honest.

When somebody like this guy who died writes, he writes for himself. He knew he was dying, so he wrote a lot about death and sterility and found a lot of that in my films—in the ones he picked to deal with. He's reading those films from his point of view and having them serve his purposes. These opinions don't necessarily agree with my purpose or somebody else's purpose, but they express a truth. That's the reason for film and that's why it's an art and not a craft. If it's a craft, it's the same thing for everybody—the lanyard's got three colors and it's braided the same way. You just cannot account for people's perception of a film.

We had a screening for *Fool for Love* in Los Angeles and two well-dressed women in their fifties got up and walked out early in the film. They got popcorn and were hanging out in the lobby. I sent the publicity girl to ask them why they left and were hanging around, and they said, "Oh isn't somebody going to speak later?" (I was.) When she asked, "Why did you leave the film?" they answered, "We've seen it before." This was the first screening of the film anywhere. The publicist said, "Oh, you mean you saw the play." They said, "Was it a play? We didn't know that." So they had no knowledge of it. She asked again, "Why did you leave?" And one answered, "I knew what it is; I've seen it or heard about it, but I don't like Sally Field

anyway." "Sally Field!" said the publicist. "Well, it's like Sally
Field. It's one of those Norma Rae movies; I know how it's going
to turn out." There's no way in the entire world that I can ever
know or guess what the woman who was speaking perceived in
the first part of *Fool for Love,* but the truth of it is she did
perceive something about it that she didn't like or respond to
and she put it off into that category she didn't like.

Another person walked out and my editor went up to her
and asked, "Why did you leave the film?" She answered, "I've
had enough of this violent, personal sex life, this love relationship back and forth—I don't need to see anymore of it." That's
okay because it struck a nerve and it was a trip she didn't want
to go on—fine. *Fool for Love* made a lot of people angry, which
is encouraging.

Film truly is a collaborative art. I agree with Volker Schlöndorff—it's just like a circus, including the participation of the
spectators.

Vincent Canby did an article in *The New York Times* about
VCRs and what they're doing. He said you don't get the richness
from the VCR soundtrack of *Nashville* as you would in a theater.
The truth of the matter is you get a much better soundtrack on
VCR because you can get stereo, and in the theater most people
did not get stereo. The sound is much better on the tube. The
idea that the tube is smaller is also a fallacy. I have a six-foot
screen at home and I sit about nine feet from that, so I'm seeing
as much as my eye can handle. In the theater, I'm further back.
So it's all geometry and space. He's wrong. We saw *The Killing
Fields* the other night at home and it was a terrific film; visually
it was just great. I saw as much of the visual impact of that film,
maybe more, because of the content of it; when I saw those war
and refugee shots, suddenly it evoked memories of what was on
the tube in the sixties, for that's where I first saw them. You
don't have to have a big canvas. It works anywhere, and I think
people will see things they wouldn't go into a theater to see
because they know they can easily take the tape off and put
something else on. The distractions are nothing; you can easily
start again. Interruptions never destroyed a book. If you have
to get up and go to the toilet in the middle of a film, when you
come back, you've missed it. You can't say TV and movie the-

aters are the same, but when you go into a big store and look at a mural, you can't get far enough back to look at all of it, so you have to walk alongside and look at it in pieces. You're doing your own panorama. It's all geometry.

I don't know for sure, but I think when I want to do a certain kind of film I know the majors don't want to do, suddenly there seem to be more players out there. There are a lot of individual investors for the first time. If you have a real movie, a feature film or even shorter, and you have the negative and don't have much more than three or four million dollars in the thing, it's pretty hard not to get it out. There are just too many ancillary avenues for it now. I think it's the best of times really. I think we will see better films, although it's going to be harder to see them. The majors are still going to be searching for that *Rambo* and teenage dumbo, but the people are going to tire of that quickly, and I think that's probably what you see in the change at the box office. I think you're going to see more really interesting films being made because people can now do something that they follow with a passion; then they can say, "I want to be involved in this; I think it's great." They can also say, "I know I'm getting my money out of this."

Emile de Antonio

Film director; producer; writer

Filmography:

1964	*Point of Order!*
1967	*Rush to Judgement*
1969	*In the Year of the Pig*
	America Is Hard to See
1971	*Milhouse: A White Comedy*
1973	*Painters Painting*
1975	*Underground* (codirected with Mary Lampson)
1983	*In the King of Prussia*

The only film I could possibly consider taking would be one made by the Boy Scouts of America—hopefully a very long film—on how to build a lean-to, how to fish. But I know how to do all sorts of things that the ordinary city person doesn't know how to do. I know how to spear fish and make a bow and arrow myself. I'm an outdoor person.

The first thing you would have to do is define the desert island: How much space and how much vegetation, what sort, and is there water? And assuming the island is a decent size, let's say one-tenth the size of Manhattan, from the Battery to Houston Street, and there are fresh water and trees growing and that's it, then I would want no film of any kind, even if there washed ashore only one thing: a beautiful, absolutely waterproof projector with a film enclosed and, of course, a source of power. Most people wouldn't think of that. But let's say it had a super battery that would run forever, almost a divine instrument. Then there's still no movie I would want.

First of all, I know of no film I would want to see even five times. There would be something almost punitive, the ultimate irony, that I would be stuck with anything; that I would turn on the machine and on that flickering screen I would see images of people who are not real, doing things that are unreal, while I would be faced with the reality of being alone. It would tend to be an ironic and sour kind of experience for me. It's not that I'm unimaginative.

Marcel Duchamp said, "There's no art without an audience." I would be the audience, but I'm an artist and I don't really like anybody's films that much. But in addition to that, it's like Bishop Berkeley's famous question: If an acorn falls from a tree in the forest, and no one hears it, is there a sound? That's a very profound question; it has to do with the whole theory of knowledge, of sensory perception—all of that, because it takes a hearer to hear a sound and I don't want to be that passive person who is the viewer to begin with. The consumers of art are passive people and I'm just physically an active person.

Given the fact that I'm surrounded by an ocean and I have a stick, I would start writing my autobiography, even if the ocean would wash it away, because writing my autobiography would keep me alive. I would write with a stick: "I was born May 14 . . ." and all the rest of it. I would illustrate it—make big sand drawings tracing my feet and body in the sand. And I would think of some way to fix the drawings. I would get involved with those problems, and, hopefully, they would never get solved, because they would be the only thing to keep me alive—the hope of some solution that was never there, because otherwise the solution would bcome boring.

I like movies but I know of no movie that has enough emotional, historical, philosophical, visual substance so that I could look at it forever. Particularly not my own. I spend too much time on them. Those are the last I would take, though I may like them better than other films. People think I'm crazy because of the elaborate rules I make when I lecture and get paid a lot of money. One of the main things is that I have to have a place to stay that's comfortable for the two hours my film is on. They say, "You won't sit in the theater and watch it?" I say, "You must be out of your mind. I spent a year and a half working on that fucking thing! You think I want to sit there and look at it? I mean, I look at my films every five years and I'll look at the last three minutes as I wait in the back before you introduce me to the audience, but more than that, no way." I lie down in some hotel and then someone picks me up with all the time measured out so I can put some water on my face, put my shoes on, and drive back to where the thing's showing.

I would rather take a book because a book is something else. A film is a purely passive experience: You turn on a machine and all you have to do is open your eyes. Reading is even physically different—your eyes move in a volitional way. The average person just looks at the screen blankly like a dumb goat in front of a snake. I look at things within the screen but even so, once you've done it, it becomes boring.

I don't want any film, but there are some films that can stand up to several screenings, of course: *Birth of a Nation, Rules of the Game,* and because I'm perverse, I could look at a Marx Brothers film about once every three years. I've seen some of them about five, six times. I love them. I know what's going to happen and I don't care. One of the reasons I love them is they're so anarchistic and I'm an anarchist. Groucho always plays some important, significant character. He's always either a president of a university or a prime minister or a president of a country or a doctor, and he's always a fucking fraud: He's goosing the women; he's sleeping on the job. One time he comes down a fireman's pole and they're all blowing horns and saluting, waiting for the prime minister to come, and he's saluting too. Then they all look around and they find him.

Birth of a Nation is everything that's ever happened in film. American Marxists are all against it because of its position on blacks. But in the early days of the Soviet revolution, before it became the sour, ugly, monstrous fucking thing that it is now, Lenin loved it, Eisenstein loved it—it was what they studied. It's not only Griffith's use of the closeup; there have never been such crowd shots, horses, people on horseback, war. Everything you've ever dreamed of as a kid is all there and it's beautiful.

Frame by frame, it's better than most paintings. Remember those guys riding through town? The ambition to take that tacky medium at that time—the ambition to have Lincoln shot! I mean, that's as ambitious as Shakespeare; that's as ambitious as the death of Caesar in front of his senate. It's all the glory of history.

But you're talking about a man without history now. You're talking about a person on a desert island. I would have no history then; I would have no future. I would have to have something that consumes the present and tries to create a little bit of the future. And a film won't do that. My writing in sand would, even if it lasted three days, even if I somehow dig a place away from the high-tide mark where I can write, "My name is Emile de Antonio. I was born May the fourteenth. My father was a doctor; my grandfather was a doctor; my great grandfather never did a thing because he was rich; and my uncle was a general in the Italian army. He was a fascist, and I became a communist when I was sixteen. Why did I do this?" I'd start self-analysis, but what's the point of analyzing yourself when you're not going to be there finally? All these are monumental projects.

The main disease on a desert island is monotony. I could write in the sand different film scripts of how people survive on desert islands, including Buñuel's *Robinsón Crusoe* and any of the various versions of *Mutiny on the Bounty*. That's something that would keep you awake and alive, a script of the thing you're doing as you are doing it. Buñuel's *Robinsón Crusoe* is really good; you could think of different ideas around Robinson Crusoe and a desert island and start writng them down as you would do them. It would take you a year to write ten full scripts on sand using a stick. It's not like using a word processor. A stick on the sand is really slow.

If you had a Portopak with a ninety-minute tape, the real pleasure would be that you could erase it and do it over. But I think that would last about as long as looking at *Birth of a Nation*. You would then become Claude Bernard, and you could study the life of one ant through your life as it procreated and had children and struggled to survive and then you could play God and kill it. That sense of power would be very great.

The greatest film in the world is too trivial to spend six months with or even a year. I'd rather have a shovel.

*M*ichael *A*pted

Theater, television, and film director

Filmography:

1973   *Another Sunday and Sweet F.A.* (Granada TV)
         Triple Echo
1974   *Stardust*
         Kisses at Fifty (BBC)
1976   *The Collection* (Granada TV)
         21 (Granada TV)
1977   *The Squeeze*
         Stronger Than the Sun (BBC)
1979   *Coal Miner's Daughter*
         Agatha
1981   *Continental Divide*
1982   *Gorky Park*
         P'tang Yang Kipperbang (BBC)
1984   *Firstborn*
         28 Up (initially for Granada TV)
1985   *Bring on the Night*

I'd take *Belle de Jour* by Luis Buñuel. I just love the film, and I think it would be fun to have on a desert island: It's sexy, funny, and it would remind me of how entertaining and intelligent film can be.

I have no preference for working in documentary or fiction films. I just find it stimulating to work in both, to work in as many as possible. One should be able to turn one's hand to

11

different things. Each feeds the other. I think it makes what you do better if you're constantly searching out new things, new ways of doing stuff. That applies to working within different budgets, different sorts of material. I personally find that very stimulating. There's more freedom with a low budget. On the other hand, with a larger budget you do have more time and maybe you can take more care. Of course, some stuff benefits from being done roughly and quickly, and other stuff benefits from having a lot of money and attention lavished on it. I just get worried when I know I'm doing a wrong thing, when I'm doing a picture for a lot of money that should cost a little money, or when I'm doing a picture that is underbudgeted. I think you can smell what the right price for a film is. An example would be *Gorky Park*—we should have spent more money; and on other things, maybe we should have spent less. I only feel happy when I know I'm treating the piece of material the way it should be treated, and if I'm not, that's when I get uncomfortable. When the budget is higher, of course you have more obligations, commitments, more masters to serve. Invariably, I suppose if you're spending more, there's more attention being paid to it. One of the reasons *Coal Miner's Daughter* was successful was that it cost very little and no one paid any attention to it at the studio. They just let me go off and do it. Had it been an expensive film, they might have had more influence in the way it was cast, and so on. They didn't even distribute it that well; it just took off. It was one of those films that just caught on; it began to have a life of its own. The campaign was pretty bad if you ever look at it these days; it was just a picture that was in the right place at the right time, and it found its audience immediately; it generated its own, which is generally what I think happens with movies. I don't think a campaign has ever made a movie.

I was the research runner on *7 Up;* I found the kids. I took it over on the "fourteenth" year. By that time I was a fully trained television film director. I'd just left Granada, but I'd been there for seven years, so I was sort of known and favored there and the guy who directed the original had left and gone back to Canada. So it was natural for me to take it over and I've gone on since. The plan wasn't originally to follow these kids up; it was a single film about the English class system. I really don't like to keep in touch with them too much. If they want me, I'm there, but I don't want to give them the feeling of always being watched and observed. It's very interesting because I saw a film done by some German filmmakers who'd done the same thing. They got in touch with me—I'd though mine was unique in the world. But they weren't as rigid about the seven-year gap. They sort of kept popping back when something happened. If someone got married, they did it. But it made it very difficult to follow because there was no clear time span in it. It was very difficult to make coherent, to see people change their look and all that kind of stuff. So I thought when they showed me their film that I'd probably made the right decision to do mine every seven years, irrespective of what particular point it was in somebody's life.

I believe great writing and great acting can illuminate as well as a documentary does. I left documentary because of that reason. I was dying to say and express things and other people couldn't do it for me. I thought I could do this much easier and quicker if I could get a good writer and a good actor. I can say what I feel or express human emotions much more succinctly and precisely than I could in a documentary, where you're wallowing around trying to get someone to say something, wondering "Why don't they see this?" or "Why don't they see that?" I got very impatient with it. I'm not saying that documentaries can't be enormously illuminating, but I wouldn't ignore the whole of fiction and theatrical feature films. Both have a lot to offer. I personally think that well-made feature films can be incredibly illuminating.

I don't bother to try to be objective when I do a documentary. I try to get involved in the people very much, because I'm not an expert. I'm not an expert on sociology or whatever issues are brought up in the 7 *Up* films I do, and I'm not a documentary filmmaker really, so all I have to offer is my concern and affection for the people. I've learned that lesson from doing feature films. I've learned the lesson painfully that if you're not involved in a character or care about a character, then you come a cropper, even if the character is having a negative influence on the story or whatever. Those lessons I've learned have helped me with documentary. I can't see doing a film with someone for whom you don't have a care or feeling. I don't see any advantage in any work being objective. You need to be intelligent and truthful, but I don't think you need to stand away from it all.

I don't allow the actors to be disrespectful of what we're supposed to be doing, but if they come up with something better than what's there or more comfortable for them, then of course. We always rehearse well before we start shooting, and I need to get the best out of them; I need for them to identify as well as possible with what they're playing. If the writing isn't in their voice, then sometimes you have to make adjustments; I do this as long as I feel they're not doing a grandstand or just doing it to show how clever they are. But I've never, ever had an actor whom I didn't want. Sometimes I've been lucky. When I did *Stardust*, my English rock 'n' roll film, Columbia put a bit of money in and insisted on casting the part of the American manager—it was about an English rock 'n' roll band in the sixties— and they cast Larry Hagman, whom I'd never heard of. He turned up only the day before we started shooting, but I was lucky, he was great. In fact, he invented J. R. in that film.

Sting asked me to do his movie, *Bring on the Night*, because he'd seen *28 Up* in London, and I think he was intrigued by someone who had covered different bases, done documentary films, feature films, and musical feature films. We met and got on like a house on fire and so I did it. I tried to do something different from the usual music video, but I don't think in the eyes of the buying public I pulled it off. I was hoping to do a film about the process rather than just the end product. Personally, music videos disappear in a cloud of smoke. They don't mean that much to me, and I wanted to do a film about the serious side of putting music together—make it entertaining but at least deal with process. But maybe people just want the glitz and the presentation of images sometimes unrelated to what is being done. I don't know. I can't watch MTV for more than ten minutes at a go. It's stupid to put it down; a lot of very gifted people work in it, but it doesn't appeal to me.

I think we're going through a rough time in film. It's very difficult at the moment. We don't seem to be doing very well at making good films. There are a lot of reasons for that, but we must also blame ourselves for somehow not communicating. We're not putting intelligent films that people want to see in the marketplace. I think it's very disturbing, but I don't think you can blame the studios. I think you have to blame all of us who get the chance to do films. But people, for some reason, don't want to go and see good films. I find it very depressing. I don't know what the stuff this Christmas [1985] is going to be like at the box office. Christmas is always a time when serious movies get out there and some of them do well. There are a couple of serious films: *Out of Africa* and *The Color Purple,* and you just hope they do well. If you do things well you hope people go see them. But it's getting harder and harder to make intelligent movies and have them accepted. You know as well as I do how many films you want to see and how many times you're disappointed.

Someone told me yesterday that this year was a landmark year, that the studios will have made as much money on VCR's as they have on theatrical box office returns. Frankly, I'm thrilled that my films are seen. I would prefer that people see them in the theater and it always slightly pisses me off when people say, "I rented *Gorky Park* and I really enjoyed it." And I want to say, "Where were you when I needed you?" It depresses me a bit because it's so wonderful to see movies with an audience. There's a communal thing; you're not just sitting in your home, and you get the film well projected and sounding good. I hope people don't lose the habit, as they have in England, of going to the movies. That's always been the flagship, the driving force of the industry. My inclination is that it doesn't necessarily have to be a ride on the Big Dipper to go to the movies. If you can create an event, an intellectual event as well as a physical event, people will go. There are lots of reasons why people go to the movies. You can get people out, but you've just got to put stuff in front of people that makes it worth their while to put their six bucks down to go in and see. The studios are getting more and more nervous as films get more and more expensive and fewer and fewer recoup their money. They recoup their money in the end through various means—tapes, cable, and so on—but my perception here is that it's a pretty nervous time and if this Christmas isn't very, very successful, it'll get more difficult. They will be more nervous about doing films that aren't *Rocky* or whatever.

We're in a trap in a sense. Stuff is expensive; labor is expensive and unions have worked themselves into salaries, scales; guilds have worked themselves into protecting their members, You can't put blame; it's a natural thing that's happened, but it's having a very unfortunate cumulative effect. What happened with the British film industry wasn't so much that. People lost the habit of going to the cinema and that was that. But television in England is more agreeable. I think the English as a kind of racial thing tend not to go out as much and stay at home more. They lost the habit of going to the cinema and making films just became uneconomical—a simple equation.

HAROLD BECKER

Designer; stills photographer; film director

Filmography:

1963　*Eugène Atget*
1964　*Blind Gary Davis*
　　　An Interview with Bruce Gordon
　　　Ivanhoe Donaldson
1965　*The Birds*
1967　*Sighet*
1972　*The Ragman's Daughter*
1978　*The Onion Field*
1980　*The Black Marble*
1981　*Taps*
1983　*Vision Quest*

To have life reduced down to one film! One of the great things about film, like books, is how many there are out there, and you're always looking at the next one. To keep running the same movie, like running the same "movie" through your head, might drive you to madness. The only answer I can give you, because it springs to mind, is I might take one of Renoir's films only because the people in them are so human, and, of course, the thing you would miss most on a desert island would be human company. That might be the closest you could come to human company—a film like *Rules of the Game*. The wonderful thing about Renoir in that film, as in his others, such as *Grand Illusion,* is that to him there are no blacks and whites. The wonderful thing about his human beings is they are such a mixture of things. That's what makes them so human. So there are no good people, no villains per se, just as is true of the real world. It's very, very hard to accomplish that in dramatic form because dramatic form basically contains heroes and villains. Of course, in Shakespeare we do understand our villains and find them as interesting as our so-called good people. In fact, it's hard to define Shakespeare's so-called good people. It's that gray line. "Everyone has his reasons," said Renoir. In most dramatic form, the simplistic approach is to make people clearly vehicles for good or evil—the struggle between black and white —but in a work of art you get closer to being able to create shadings of character and still hold that dramatic intention of character. Of course, that's the dangerous part, because you can have a sympathy for Richard III who is a terrible villain, yet the other characters in the play all deal with him as a very human character, just as is true of the reverse.

Prior to doing *The Onion Field,* I couldn't imagine myself doing a movie about cops. I had built-in prejudices, as we all do, and, of course, as you get to know people, if you're open, you find that those prejudices need examination, and you can learn something from all that. I know I did.

I'm not that much of a student not to know that we haven't had *Rambo* with us through all of film. I don't know whether it's an invention of our times. The thing to say may be not that we have *Rambo* but that we almost don't have anything else. That's where the problem lies. There probably always were films that were more simplistic, that gave people a pure vicarious thrill without any qualifying conditions. What seems to be missing at the moment from the equation are other kinds of films, or enough of these. When the only diet becomes this kind of black and white cartoon movie, then the concern becomes, where are the other films? I'm not ready to give up on the fact that there is room for other kinds of films.

The Onion Field did well for what it was. It was a small film in terms of its costs and everything, so it made its money. It made a dollar but it certainly was no big hit. It was a very successful movie in terms of critical success, in terms of a certain kind of audience, but, by and large, it didn't fulfill that other thing for this type of picture. It would have fulfilled it if, for example, by the end of the picture the good guy blew away the bad guy, which is not the case in *The Onion Field* at all. It's almost the story of a triumph of evil. I have to give so much credit to Joseph Wambaugh, for whom this was, let's say, a life's work, and for his understanding, which was right there in the book. So the balance was struck already: It came from a book that already had a depth of characterization for all the characters, not just the Powell character. I think the important thing about *The Onion Field* is what we did was believable. You felt you were watching the truth. If there is one word for the film, I feel it is "truth." Maybe this sounds pretentious when I say it, but any kind of work of art attempts to get to some truth, and I think that's one of the things that makes *The Onion Field* special.

There was an attempt to tell the truth about all of the characters. That's what we came down to finally. We went to such great pains to be honest; we did nothing in that film that would in any way divert one from the reality of that situation. We didn't try to make moments more dramatic than they were. We just tried to arrive hopefully at what they really were. In other words, there was never an effort to exploit the reality of the situation. Joe said one thing to me at the beginning and that was almost a coda for the film: "The most important five words in this film are 'This is a true story.'" A lot of people put that on films, on television films, on books, and it's not necessarily carried out, but I think that becomes a mandate once you say it.

It was a work of dedication on everyone's part. Everyone who was involved in that film wanted to be in it, not because of the money—there was very little—and not because it was easy —it was hard. But it was one of those things that doesn't happen very often in a lifetime, where everyone came together because they wanted to be there. It's the kind of a thing you dream about on any film. Usually there are too many diverging things: One person is there for career, another person is there because it's a job, and so on. This film was a work of love on the part of all the people involved, and with that, it was enormously difficult. The film was shot in forty-two days on a budget of 2.4 million dollars. There are literally scenes on which we couldn't afford

to do more than just the master shot; in other words, where I
had to be able to accomplish everything I had to do in a moving
master, so to speak, a master shot that would take me into my
closeups and everything else. There simply wasn't enough time
to do more coverage and other things that could perhaps have
given me more insurance or security. Finally, it did work out
very well, but these were things that were mandates for our
situation.

Because it is so agonizing, the promising thing about *The
Onion Field* is that there was an audience for it and there *is* an
audience for it. If it had been distributed by one of the major
studios—it was distributed by one of the smaller ones—it might
have done better. If one looks back at the seven years since it
was made, it's certainly been seen by a great number of people.
So you have to say there is an audience for this kind of picture.
Of course, we don't even want to get into the fact here that the
marketplace is such now that people are only looking for the
big, big hits. It's all or nothing. That's what militates against
some pictures that might be made otherwise. There seems to be
a focus just on the home run. But I'm a great believer that the
pendulum swings, and the real issue is to just keep going and
plugging away. I believe, strangely enough, that right here in
Hollywood, which is so pilloried for causing this, there is a desire to do good things too. There are always people who want
to make a picture that is seriously considered. I do believe that
the saving grace of the business is that, unlike other businesses
where that's not a consideration at all, most people who come
into the movie business do want to do things of which they can
be proud. As in everything, people would like to have their cake
and eat it too. But I think that's where the chances exist for
making other kinds of films. There is an aspiration to do more
serious movies, movies that aren't just the lowest common denominator. Of course, the final analysis in this business is success measured in terms of box office.

The Black Marble didn't find an audience. I loved that film.
We're brokenhearted over it; we feel it never got any distribution. It was buried. That's the sad one. I did *Taps,* which did
find an audience, and I also felt it had something to say. That
was an interesting one because some of the critics claimed it

could never happen, that it was preposterous. One group of people I never heard that from were the people who had been through that experience. I actually had a camera operator on my last film who told me he went to a military academy out here in Los Angeles where he was on a firing squad that actually carried out mock executions at school. If they had had bullets, he said, since they had terrible conflicts with the townies, he's sure they would have used them. He said he found *Taps* a very true story, as did most people who had been in the military in that context or had been in a military academy. So often from critics you get a sheltered view of life that they try to impose on the rest of us.

I've been proud of the films I've done. Of course you're trying to make a film that's going to be interesting/entertaining. I think if it's interesting, it's going to be entertaining. Along with that I want to make films that are going to leave people just a little better when they walk out than when they walked in, or certainly not worse for the experience, whether they feel a little better about themselves, about being a human being, anything —just so there's some affirmation involved.

I don't really have a formula and when people ask, "What kind of film do you want to make?" I can't really put my finger on it. It's almost like saying I'll know it when I come across the material. I'll respond to it. I guess I respond to it out of my own feelings at the moment. But I do believe I want to care about the people.

One of my best shorts was something I did as a kid about the civil rights movement in the South—*Interview with Bruce Gordon*. It was a powerful fifteen-minute film. He was a black SNCC worker in the South in 1963 talking nonstop in a church in Selma, Alabama. That's all I shot. It was *cinéma vérité;* I had a camera on my shoulder. So there are no rules. At that moment, there was so much pouring out of him that it made for great image, great drama. If you were just to hear it on tape, it wouldn't mean half of what it does seeing it. And I've seen marvelous things that Bergman has done where someone is sitting foursquare in front of the camera, speaking, and you are getting an enormous power from it. So, there are no rules. That's the great thing about film.

TOM BENEDEK

Screenwriter

Filmography:

1985   *Cocoon*
       Orange County Red (to be produced)

It's very difficult. I don't think there's any movie I would like to watch endlessly, maybe *Dr. Strangelove*—that way I could imagine I was the last person left on earth. I would be a continuation of the movie; I would be able to laugh at my situation—dark humor—and I could act all the parts. I love Kubrick: *Paths of Glory, The Killing, 2001*—all of them. He's doing a movie about Vietnam called *Full Metal Jacket,* with Michael Herr, who wrote *Dispatches.* It should be great, and it's the right time for a Vietnam movie.

I'm into European films: Godard, Truffaut, Buñuel, Chabrol, and also into Hollywood films. I always loved Westerns when I was a kid: John Ford movies, Howard Hawks. As I learned about film and wanted to do it, I watched all of Kubrick's movies, Joseph Losey's, Elia Kazan's, Orson Welles', and the American independents—John Cassavetes' and Warhol's early stuff—a wide range. I really loved to watch movies until I started to have a career.

Now I don't watch movies as much. I watch my own movies and read my own screenplays because I'm writing five, six days a week, so I watch movies made by people I know, current movies, to see what people are doing. I just don't have the energy—I'm not out there making sure I see everything Bertrand Tavernier is doing. I also don't find it as interesting; we're not in the golden age right now. I feel we're sort of in this middle period and that so many European films are derivative of what was being done twenty years ago. Hollywood films are in some ways more interesting, but they're also redoing or improving on what was done before. They have their eye on their audience to such a great degree that the movies aren't as instructive as they used to be, maybe because I've seen so many. I used to learn a lot—I still learn, but I used to be trying to learn how to make them. Now I'm trying to *get* to make them and I realize there's more in terms of writing better screenplays myself in order to get to do that. So I'm working with my own stuff rather than trying to figure out what other people are doing.

I think the sixties *Nouvelle Vague* were filmmakers who were coming into their own and just happened to be extremely talented, and there was a postwar thing. There was so much experimentation with the technology of filmmaking, with how movies are made, how movies are perceived. Very talented guys were making films and there was also a market. There was the possibility to make films outside of the system's producers who were controlling the market in Europe before. There was more freedom, both financially and artistically. That excitement was an aesthetic experience that I really enjoyed, but I think the reality is that what most people want from the movies is something simple and they want to be able to identify with the characters. They want to go on some kind of ride with the story, so you're really back to the fundamentals of narrative storytelling. There used to be comedians telling stories, people sitting around and telling each other stories. Now it doesn't exist as much, so movies have fallen back to what they were doing before, which was trying to tell people stories.

For example, I don't think *Rambo* is a success because of its politics—it's a sort of heroic opera, larger than life. I think it's a success because it's this very broad action movie with this star who has a lot of charisma for a lot of people. It's sort of a fallback; though, it's not like a John Ford movie. The best of John Wayne's stuff is what he did with Ford and Hawks: *Rambo* is not up to that level. The storyline of *Beverly Hills Cop* is just a riff of Eddie Murphy—you know, the snobs and the slobs. I thought that was done in a reasonably witty fashion. That's the other thing—some of these movies have about twenty minutes of riff that delights people and the rest of it is negligible; it doesn't matter. If you're a star and you know you have an audience, you can try to make a movie out of *Beverly Hills Cop* for yourself, or you can make *Rambo*. As a writer you have to assume people want to see something better. *Cocoon* tells a story: It's in a framework that is very recognizable to people; it's almost a genre—extraterrestrials on earth. So people do know what they are going to see, but it does tell the story of some people who are involved in the situation. *Back to the Future* also tells a story. There are decent movies being made.

When I started writing screenplays, I found in Los Angeles there's a context for writing, since Francis Ford Coppola. There's a context for the young screenwriter. Everybody knows about him; it's very wide open; it's not closed. You just have to be civilized. In fact, you're better off if you're not civilized. But you can write screenplays and there are people to tell you what format to put them in, and everybody will read them because everybody in the industry is looking for a good screenplay. So I started writing screenplays and having little jobs in movies as a production assistant, other kinds of jobs selling pots and pans, clothes—all kinds of jobs over the years. I just continued to write screenplays. I wrote ten screenpays before I wrote *Cocoon*. The sixth or seventh I optioned to somebody, made very little money, and it wasn't even a studio deal. Someone commissioned me to write another screenplay. I did that and nothing really happened. It was nice at the time but it wasn't very solid—both those screenplays fell through the cracks very easily.

I stopped writing for a while and started thinking about writing. I just looked at movies again. Then I started writing again after a couple of years. I wrote a screenplay called *Orange County Red,* a spy thriller that takes place in Orange County, and a lot of people liked it. I got mixed up with Larry Kasdan and Bob Zemeckis; Kasdan wanted to produce it and Zemeckis wanted to direct it. It was before Zemeckis had directed *Romancing the Stone*—in between *1941* and *Romancing the Stone.* We were never able to get anywhere with it at all, except he was involved in a project called *Cocoon* and they were looking for a writer. He suggested that I work on it, so I was hired to do an adaptation of an unpublished novel called *Cocoon*. I did it and everybody liked it: The producers liked it; the studio liked it. But the studio was in the midst of throwing Zanuck and Brown off the lot, so they were moving from Fox to Warner Brothers, and it was very acrimonious. I handed in the script and everybody thought it would go over to Warner Brothers with everything else, but Fox liked it. They wanted to make the movie. They gave it the green light immediately, so Zanuck and Brown moved back to Fox, opened another office at Fox after vacating six weeks before, and I waited. A lot of other things happened: Zemeckis ended up making *Romancing the Stone* and being forced to drop out of *Cocoon,* and we got Ron Howard, who directed it. The movie finally got made two and a half years after I started writing it. It's not too bad. It was a dream after ten years. I finally entered the Writers Guild with *Cocoon.*

Before the shoot for *Cocoon* there was a fair amount of changes, but after he began, Ron took it as his own. The movie is basically from the screenplay I wrote and rewrote and rewrote. I wrote it and then worked on it with the producers while the then director, Bob Zemeckis, was unavailable. We waited a long time; then Ron became involved and I worked on it with Ron. It's very collaborative. When a director undertakes to direct a screenplay, hopefully he has his own ideas. Movies come to life, if they come to life, with the director, and the director has to re-imagine the whole movie in his head. A good director, I think, re-imagines the context of everything in his own head. The screenplay is the basis for that but it really gets mediated by the director. You really depend on the director to do it right. I was lucky with Ron—he really had a good sensibility about it, a good understanding of what it was supposed to be. I'm really delighted, overall I'm delighted. Seeing the rough cut was hard because it's impossible. It's never going to be the way the writer imagines it, but the writer has to imagine it so vividly that it's like seeing one movie in his head. When I saw the finished form, it was sort of one step away from that movie in my head. It took seeing it two or three times; each time I'd see it, I'd integrate and enter it. Now I go to see it every week and it's very symbiotic—it's part of me; it's part of the director; it's part of the producers; it's part of the actors; and it's all very moving for me.

Audiences also collaborate when they go to movies—it's a collective experience and there's such a limited amount of time to make a movie. It's not like a play where you can spend a week on a scene with everybody there and watch it with an audience. So with film, there has to be this common arena within which the show takes place as far as its narrative thrust, its characters, what happens. I think you have to accept that as a screenwriter. You have to say, "I'm part of this process." I do want to direct and that's what I started out doing, so I am working toward that. And as a writer-director you can see it through and see your version, but I think that along the way you end up giving leeway to the actors and your cinematographer, so it's the same thing but you're more in control.

When I think of writer-directors who only write and direct their own work, I think of Woody Allen, who's superb—I mean no one else could do his stuff. *Play It Again, Sam* is a great movie —it's one of my favorite Woody Allen movies—and he acted in it, wrote it, but he didn't direct it. Herbert Ross did. There are a lot of writers who become directors and end up working with other writers rather than just writing the whole thing themselves and then directing. I think you can make very individualistic movies, creating them in your mind and then translating them into film, but I think it becomes very difficult to dramatize things—you feel your way through it with the actors and with another writer.

I like to write by myself; I don't mind getting a lot of notes. In screenwriting in Hollywood you write and you get a lot of notes from the producer, from the director, and I think some things get better and some things get worse. It depends on whom you are working with. The thing about working with Zanuck and Brown is that their notes are so smart. I'm learning from this. I'm working more on characters; I'm making the narratives, the stories, more interesting. I'm understanding what you *need* to tell. There are a lot of things that I put in the first draft of a script that I think are essential for the people

who are working on the movie—the producers, the director—
to bring forward, and the actors should bring these elements
forward too. These are things they should know about the story.
There are also a lot of cases where once everybody who has to
make the movie knows these things, they realize that the audience really doesn't need to know them. So this can fall away
—this whole vast subtext of information about the story—and
the more you are able to exclude, sometimes the better off you
are. You tell the story with a little bit less, especially on paper.
You can write that an actor walks into a room and exhibits a
certain kind of behavior; you can describe that behavior in great
detail, but the fact is that an actor is going to be cast and the
chances are that within the time constraints, the director is going
to have to get that actor to represent that behavior in his own
way. That's an example of direction in the script that should
be as succinct as possible and then left. What is more applic-
able is pruning scenes that are *about* the story. These are good
to have in order to explain things, but then can be forgotten.
I'm always trying to think about my characters more and just
make them more real and try to tell a story in a compelling
way.

I've learned a lot from watching *Cocoon* every week, from
what the actors did, the way it was shot—where the camera was
put—the way it was edited. I just learned a lot about filmmaking. It was like this big class project that got taken to its final
form. Someone else was responsible for the final choices. I'm so
familiar with the framework for all those choices, but when I
see those choices, I really learn a lot. I can analyze what part of
the scene was used. As written, it involved too much stuff; the
script was much too long. So there are choices concerning which
scene was used and which wasn't, which part of the scene we
could get away with. After they've made a number of films, the
good filmmakers start to realize what they don't need to shoot,
where they need a lot of coverage, where they need to be very
specific about what they shoot.

I'm going to have to create some kind of momentum. Now
that I have done one adaptation that was successful, I am being
offered a lot of adaptations. I was offered *Winter's Tale* by Mark
Helperin, to be directed by Martin Scorsese, so I may do that.

It hasn't happened yet, but it's been offered. I'm working on an original now that I want to direct—I won't try to pitch it; I won't try to sell it. Once it's done, I'll say I want to direct this, and if they like it, it's the only way they're going to get it.

JOEL AND ETHAN COEN

Writers; directors; producers

Filmography:

1985   *Blood Simple*

Joel: We would probably take *Bring Me the Head of Alfredo Garcia* by Sam Peckinpah. We're fans of most of his movies, but we haven't seen that one. We thought we would take something we haven't already seen. That way, the first time we watch it, it's new.

Ethan: We're going to watch it so many times, that the first time we might as well see something we haven't seen before.

J: We've heard it's a good movie from a couple of friends who recommended it, and we just haven't gotten around to seeing it. I like some of Peckinpah's movies but not all of them. I didn't like *The Osterman Weekend* very much—that was pretty confused. To tell you the truth, I haven't seen that many of his movies. *Straw Dogs* was kind of interesting, although I must have seen it when I was twelve or thirteen. It seemed good to me then. *Bring Me the Head of Alfredo Garcia* sounds good. It's some guy carrying around somebody's head in a burlap bag on the back of a horse.

E: This guy is traveling around with his head through Mexico and he has to pull into service stations every few miles to get new ice to pack the head in.

J: It just *sounded* interesting; it was the first one that came to mind. There are lots of other movies, obviously, that we haven't seen that we'd like to. This was one, for instance, that we've been thinking about trying to rent on videocassette.

E: Also, another person who described it to us said one guy screams to the other, "Bring me his head, nothing else will satisfy me," and then the film cuts to Warren Oates playing the piano and singing "Guantanamera" in some honky-tonk in Mexico. That sounded good.

J: Like we said, we haven't seen the movie, so we could be wrong, but that's how it was described to us.

E: I hear they're planning a sequel called *Bring Me the Rest of Alfredo Garcia.*

J: We could make it but we should see the original one first.

E: I think it would be more interesting without seeing it.

J: We go to the movies a lot, so we're aware of things, but consciously *Blood Simple* wasn't influenced by other films and filmmakers, as much as it was by American pulp murder fiction —melodramas and mysteries. That's more what we were thinking and actually talking about when we were making the movie as opposed to other movies. I think most of the conscious influence was from fiction like Chandler, Hammett, and Cain, especially Cain. Obviously we were influenced by lots of filmmakers in some way or another, but I'm not sure how.

We like Hitchcock and probably were influenced by him. It is a murder story. I like Fellini, Kurosawa, Hitchcock—lots of Hitchcock favorites: *Shadow of a Doubt, Rear Window, Notorious.*

E: *Psycho.*

J. I like *The Birds* too. Roman Polanski is another favorite—he's terrific: *Knife in the Water, Repulsion, The Tenant, Chinatown, Rosemary's Baby.* I love all his films.

Those filmmakers all have a boisterous sense of fun, I guess.

E: They're all peppy.

J: Yeah, they're all peppy. I like all of Kurosawa's samurai movies. *Red Beard* is also a great movie, but my favorite one is *High and Low*. It's not exactly a detective story but it is sort of a detective story, because it's about a middle-aged man who owns a shoe company, played by Toshiro Mifune, whose son is kidnapped. Actually, it's not his son; somebody tries to kidnap his son and gets the chauffeur's son by mistake and then Mifune . . .

E: . . . has to decide whether he will pay a ransom for the chauffeur's son.

J: And he makes the right choice. He pays the ransom, ruins himself doing it, and then tries to find who kidnapped the kid in the first place. So it becomes a kind of detective story.

J: We storyboard our films like Hitchcock. There's very little improvisation because we're chicken basically. We don't like going on the set without a pretty fair idea of what we're going to do. Movie sets are real chaotic places, and I think we both think better in terms of conceptualizing the way things should be shot and the way things should be treated in a calmer, less pressured atmosphere; and you can do that before you start shooting a movie. Certain scenes are previsualized more exactly in terms of how they're finally going to be edited than others. It depends on the scene. With action scenes, for instance, you usually have a pretty good sense of how you are going to edit, whereas with a dialogue scene, you might not really know until you shoot it and put it together.

E: That's because the coverage is just more standard, so you've got your master and your coverage and you don't bother to plan out ahead of time.

J: You come out with an idea of how to cover the scene; it might be rather standard coverage in terms of the kinds of setups that you do, but then you put it together when you're editing it. We usually plan action scenes very specifically for the camera. And it's more economical when you've planned it out before.

J: We did work out weird transitions in the editing. We did them because they're more fun. You want to figure out something visually that's going to work with the editing to propel the audience into the next scene in an interesting way, so it's fun to work out transitions that accomplish that, have some sort of dramatic impetus.

I just saw *After Hours,* Scorsese's movie, which I thought was brilliantly edited. Thelma Schoonmaker, the editor, is really brilliant. It's just incredibly well cut.

E: It's peppy.

J: Schoonmaker also did *Raging Bull.* But I'm sure Scorsese works incredibly closely with her. In our partnership I'm credited as the director and Ethan is credited as the producer and we share the writing credit, but actually what we do is a lot more fluid than the credits suggest. We could share the credits, but our standard answer is that I'm bigger than he is. In actuality it's very equal in terms of what we do.

When we shot *Blood Simple,* we were thinking of the audience, but we didn't test screen. We consider that cheating. Other people, who do screen, play by their rules, and we play by our rules. It's our ball so we make the rules. We do go to the theater to see how *Blood Simple* is doing. I think we were pretty close to the mark. Certain things are pretty easy to tell actually. *Blood Simple* was supposed to be scary in parts and it's fairly easy to tell whether an effect is going to make the audience jump or squirm.

E: Humor is a little bit harder.

J: Yeah, it's harder to be sure in putting the movie together whether you're going to get a big laugh in a certain place as opposed to a big scream or a jump. People's reactions to scary stuff are less subjective and more universal, and it's easier to trigger what is sort of a formula.

E: Like the newspaper hitting the window or the screen door. You know you're going to get an enormous bang and everybody's going to jump.

J: Yeah, you know everyone's going to jump; but having Emmett say, "In Russia they only make fifty cents a day," we thought was funny and it never even gets a giggle.

The actors didn't have much input with dialogue, but we

rehearse and the actors had an enormous input, in terms of their interpretations of the characters, changing what we might have visualized when we were writing or even getting as specific as how certain scenes should be blocked. That all changes in rehearsals when you're working with an actor. A lot of stuff does change—the syntax of certain lines. You write something that looks good on paper but sounds stilted when it's actually said and that stuff changes, but that's relatively minor. We rehearsed off set and then ran it through for the camera.

We raised the money for *Blood Simple* through a limited partnership. Hollywood has been knocking on our door a little bit since we had a success. Let's say, they've been tapping on it. We've gotten a lot of interest from studios about doing movies. We happen to be making the next movie with Circle Films in Washington, D.C., who distributed *Blood Simple,* because they're interested in financing the next picture. We worked with them, liked them, and it's a comfortable situation. It's good for everybody.

The new film is called *Raising Arizona* and it's about a couple in Arizona who want to have a child, can't, and what they do. It's a comedy, no horror.

It's kind of depressing that films now will have most of their lives in video, because the movie loses so much of its impact, I would think. I don't know. I don't feel too great about it—don't mind me; I'll just sit in the dark.

E: He's not too happy about it.

J: Yeah, I'm not too happy about it. It's kind of depressing, but, on the other hand, it's kind of lucrative. It helped us to make *Blood Simple* a profitable venture. It's worth a lot of money now and it keeps going. So you can't complain about it from that score.

Even a process like Showscan isn't the answer; they'll figure out a way to project that onto video screens and people will get their Showscan cassettes at home, and we're back to square one.

E: What are you going to do?

J: Yeah, what are you going to do? It is interesting; I've never seen Showscan and I have no idea what it looks like. I think the impact of a movie is so much greater in a movie theater than it is at home that the argument that by making movies more spectacular for the theater, you're going to revitalize the theater business as opposed to the video, isn't a strong one. I think it's already much more dynamic in a theater. But, it's true that the quality of projecting films nowadays has become pretty depressing. The Castro Theater in San Francisco, though, is great. It's sort of a small version of Radio City Music Hall. It's an old movie palace that's been renovated and they show first-run movies.

It's true that the more successful independent films get made, the more it helps people who are trying to get their own projects off the ground independently. I really liked *Stranger Than Paradise;* it was fun.

Our film came in at around eight hundred thousand dollars. We were lying about it for a long time. We were saying it was more until we sold it off everywhere we wanted to sell it. If you can say it cost more money, you can ask for more from various markets without them giving you a hard time. We were saying it cost one and a half million.

E: For some reason we started with two and a half million and then we worked our way down.

J: Then we couldn't remember what we had told the last person. This next one will cost under ten million.

Another film we thought of taking to the desert island was one of our own invention: *Fanny Alexanderplatz,* the longest, artiest movie ever made. All we have is a title.

*R*oger *C*orman

Writer; director; producer; distributor; developer of talent

Filmography:

As director-producer:

1955	*Five Guns West*
	Apache Woman
1956	*The Day the World Ended*
	Swamp Women (director only)
	The Oklahoma Woman
	Gunslinger
	It Conquered the World
1957	*Not of This Earth*
	The Undead
	Naked Paradise
	Attack of the Crab Monsters
	Rock All Night
	Teenage Doll
	Carnival Rock
	Sorority Girl
	The Viking Women and the Sea Serpent
1958	*War of the Satellites*
	The She Gods of Shark Reef (director only)
	Machine Gun Kelly
	Teenage Caveman
1959	*I Mobster*
	A Bucket of Blood
	The Wasp Woman
1960	*Ski Troop Attack*
	The House of Usher

The Little Shop of Horrors
The Last Woman on Earth
1961   *Creature from the Haunted Sea*
Atlas
The Pit and the Pendulum
1962   *The Intruder*
Premature Burial
Tales of Terror/Poe's Tales of Terror
Tower of London (director only)
1963   *The Raven*
The Terror
"X" the Man with the X-Ray Eyes
The Haunted Palace
The Young Racers
1964   *The Secret Invasion* (director only)
The Masque of the Red Death
The Tomb of Ligeia
1966   *The Wild Angels*
1967   *The St. Valentine's Day Massacre*
The Trip
1969   *How to Make It* (director only)
1970   *Bloody Mama*
Gas-s-s-s . . . or It May Become Necessary to Destroy the World in Order to Save It!
1971   *Von Richtofen and Brown* (director only)

As producer only (partial list):

1953   *Highway Dragnet* (coprod.)
1954   *The Monster from the Ocean Floor*
1955   *The Beast with a Million Eyes*
1958   *Stakeout on Dope Street*
1959   *Crime and Punishment U.S.A.*
1960   *The Wild Ride*
1963   *Dementia 13/The Haunted and the Hunted*
1966   *Blood Bath*
1967   *A Time for Killing* (coprod.; some scenes directed by Corman and not credited)

1968	*The Wild Racers*
	Targets
1970	*The Dunwich Horror*
1972	*Boxcar Bertha*
1973	*I Escaped from Devil's Island*
1974	*Big Bad Mama*
	Cockfighter
1975	*Capone*
	Death Race 2000
1976	*Jackson County Jail*
	Eat My Dust!
	Fighting Mad
1977	*Grand Theft Auto*
	I Never Promised You a Rose Garden
	Thunder and Lightning
1978	*Deathsport*
	Piranha (co-exec. prod.)
	Outside Chance (coprod.)
	Avalanche
	St. Jack
1980	*Battle Beyond the Stars*
	Humanoids from the Deep
1981	*Smokey Bites the Dust*
1982	*Forbidden World*

I would take *Battleship Potemkin* for a number of reasons, two in particular: One, the film itself; two, its position in film history. I think it is a film that paved the way for much of modern filmmaking in the structure of the script, the photography, the use of realistic and natural locations, and, above all, in editing. Much of modern editing stems from that film, particularly the montage sequences, the Odessa Steps sequence in particular, but the entire edited structure—the unity. As for the film itself, I think it is one of the most powerful films ever made.

It deals with a major social issue on a major scale, yet, at the same time, focuses on a series of individuals, so you see the element of the mutiny, which was one of the major moments in twentieth-century Russian history, leading up to the revolution. You see and understand the motive for the mutiny, yet, at the same time, you emphasize with the individual characters, so it comes to life both on an individual, personal basis and as a grander statement of a political viewpoint.

I think *Birth of a Nation* is also an important film, but to me, *Battleship Potemkin* is somewhat more polished, and I was personally more involved with it.

There wasn't one film but many that stimulated my interest in motion pictures. By seeing a number of films, I became involved in the process. When I was in school, I saw a John Ford Western, *My Darling Clementine:* It was a Western plus; it was more than a Western, and that film may have been more instrumental than others in my deciding to make films.

I started in films as a messenger at Twentieth Century–Fox —that was the only job I could get—and I worked my way up to the story department. From the story department I went to Europe and studied literature at Oxford, came back, became a literary agent and sold a script I had written with myself as associate producer. That led to producing and then to directing.

I formed my own company purely for the independence. The first film I made was an independent film, and the majority of my work has been independently produced. I worked in the studio a couple of times, but I prefer the freedom of doing my films myself.

My films are really varied. They run from a film such as *The Intruder,* which though a low-budget film might be closest to *Battleship Potemkin.* William Shatner played a rabble-rouser attempting to tear up a Southern town. It was an attempt to deal with a major social and political problem and, at the same time, to tell it in a personal way. So I went from a serious film like *The Intruder,* which won some awards in film festivals, to a film like *The Little Shop of Horrors,* which is a tongue-in-cheek comedy-horror film. So it has been a varied output.

I'm not sure whether I could describe a single vision I have, but probably it would be to attempt working on two levels: first a surface level of entertainment and then beneath the surface level, a subtextual level that is meaningful to me and, hopefully, would be meaningful to the audience. *The Intruder* was a key film for me because it was the first film I ever made that, although the reviews were very good, lost money. One of the reasons it lost money was that I made my point in the film and abandoned my concept of working on two levels. I did not attempt to make it entertaining on the surface, but instead focused on the more serious subtext. And it was too serious.

I've never had trouble with distribution; I've always worked through a major studio and had an arrangement with American International for years.

I think we'll see a major shift in the way we distribute films because of the advent of home video, but I don't think the studios are interested now in low-budget films. However, there will be exceptions: Somebody in Laurel Canyon or Venice or Greenwich Village or Sioux City, Iowa, will make a low-budget film that will either be brilliant or have a combination of some lucky elements of exploitation that some studio might want to take a chance on. But, in general, I think the studios pay lip service to low-budget films while they are certainly committed to high-budget films.

When I started my distribution company, my idea was to look for developing, young talent that hadn't been exposed. Until then I was primarily concerned with making my own films and occasionally financing others. When I started my distribution company, I looked for young filmmakers with whom to work. A first-time director that I worked with was Irwin Kershner; others were Martin Scorsese, John Sayles, Bob Towne, Peter Fonda, Peter Bogdanovich, and Francis Coppola. As far as actors, there were Charlie Bronson, Robert De Niro, Bruce Dern, Jack Nicholson, David Carradine, and a few others. Mainly they would find me.

I think right now movies are at a low ebb. The cost of filming is so high—but these are generalities; it's important to state that there will always be exceptions to whatever I say. If I say the majors will not go for low-budget productions, there will be the occasional low-budget production. But in general what's happening today is the triumph of commercialism. The budgets have gone so high that the studios are going to the lowest common denominator to protect those budgets and increase their potential profits. As a result they are somewhat stepping away from a more significant type of film for which there is an audience if the budget is right. Admittedly it will not have the grossing potential of a *Rambo* or a *Star Wars;* on the other hand, it will cost less, still return a profit, and be a film of which one can be proud. But there aren't very many people in the studios who are interested in making fims of which they can be proud. The corporate takeover of the studios has something to do with this firm concentration on the bottom line of production. As far as the older days are concerned, in some respects it may have been better, but there is always a tendency to romanticize the past.

Wes Craven

Writer; film director; former professor of humanities

Filmography:

1972	*Last House on the Left*
1978	*The Hills Have Eyes*
	Stranger in Our House/Summer of Fear (NBC)
1979	*The Hills Have Eyes, Part II*
1980	*Deadly Blessings*
1981	*Swamp Thing*
1984	*Invitation to Hell* (ABC)
	Nightmare on Elm Street
	Chiller (CBS)
1985	*The Twilight Zone* (6 episodes)

I would probably take a film on how to build a ship out of a take-up reel, projector, and movie screen. If I took Charlton Heston as Moses, in *The Ten Commandments*, I could figure out how to part the sea. But watching movies by yourself is not much fun. It's very much of a communal thing, not like reading a book, where you have to sit down by yourself. It's enjoyable to watch movies with other people.

Strangely, I don't know what film I would want. How is that for an honest answer? Bergman would be too depressing over a long run; Fellini would be a little hard to pin down and frustrating. Maybe *It's a Wonderful Life* by Frank Capra—it's an upper and very well done—or some Marx Brothers.

The two filmmakers, actually three, I would cite in my early looking at films would be Cocteau, Buñuel, and Polanski. Polanski's *Repulsion* and Cocteau's *Beauty and the Beast* and Buñuel's films in general—there's just something about Buñuel, like *The Exterminating Angel*. I forget the name of the film with the sheep head and the characters just walking into the mansion. Those films have off-the-wall images in a very civilized setting that were very poignant and powerful for me. I think those three guys were really the godfathers of film.

It's interesting: A film is not as dense as a novel. You can think of spending a year with *Anna Karenina*. There's a great deal more information put into a novel. Novels are much more dense than film, and can certainly go into the interior workings of a mind much more clearly and lucidly than a film can, because they're much more controlled. First of all, they're specifically the voice of one single person rather than passing through a million filters, marketplace considerations, and everything else. Second of all, they're able to deal with the interior of the mind by specifically conveying invisible images, allusions, parallels, and comparisons—fantasies that are not necessarily visual. You can't burn Moscow on film like you can in a novel. There are certainly limitations of scope and expanse in a novel. Everything has been done, but I think your mind can put characters into very real situations much more easily in a novel than in a film. It's not that I want to put down my own medium, but if I had to spend a long time with something, I would rather spend it with Shakespeare or some form of literature than a movie.

Actually in *Nightmare on Elm Street* I felt that I was working with the strongest points of the medium in presenting subjective viewpoints—that is, the ability to distort reality visually very easily, because you can manipulate what is seen so easily. For instance, through the creation of a room that can spin upside down, you can alter gravity. The basic tricks of cinema have been around since Méliès and the French guys figured out that those tricks worked very well in alliance with a story about dreams. In a sense, the marriage of the subjective view and film was on from the beginning of the very concept of cinema. It's something that lends itself very well to cinematic treatment. But cinema was dealing with images rather than interior thoughts, which is another form of subjectivity that's very hard to deal with cinematically. Conceptual things such as valances of truth, falsehood, or anything else are very difficult. But the dreamlike images that cinema deals with are also obviously what dreams deal with. In *Nightmare on Elm Street,* I could open up the whole Pandora's box of dream images because this was a film about dreams; it is itself sort of a dreamlike state.

I spend time with movies rather than with writing now because not that many people read. But I also enjoy being with people, I enjoy images, and I think my greatest skill is in images rather than in specific manipulation of language. I think I lay things out better in images and situations than I do in exact exposition of words, although I'm a good writer and, from the first, my writing has been noted for its imagery.

I guess I have to begrudge conceptual expression to literature. I think it's the fountainhead of conscious thought; music is certainly of the unconscious. I think film flows out of literature. My roots are in literature. I started out as a writer and studied literature long before I studied film, so my important exposure to thought was in literature. I haven't seen anything expressed in films that wasn't expressed years before in literature, with the exception of horror films, which is part of the reason I enjoy doing them. They were the cutting edge of something or other—nobody was ever able to express what. But they didn't have real parallels in literature. You do have horror in literature, obviously—you have *Frankenstein*—but it's not like a modern horror film. I think modern horror films deal much more with conveying images, violence, and the actual frailty of the human body. There's a preoccupation with that in horror films. Hitchcock's work was more of the suspense thriller. He's an anomaly, certainly not what horror film has become. *Psycho* was about as close as he got to it.

Sound is immensely important in films and, probably until recently, terribly ignored. I know I was attracted to it immediately when I made my first film. I had an unusually large amount of tracks running. At the mixing studio they said they'd never had a low-budget film come in there with thirty-five tracks at once. I'm very much an advocate of the acoustic environment;

in many ways it's much more evocative than the visual one. It's unlimited, except by the imagination and the associations of the hearer. I would include sound effects in music, and there's always some musical composition that lies alongside of or beneath or around the visual. But the visual can be very, very explicit, and I like dealing with ambivalent images and a lot of shadow so that you allow the imagination to fill in the blanks.

The horror genre was a way in for me, but it was a long way in. I certainly became established in the horror genre as somebody who specifically did that, but I am now turning in some ways away from that because I want to expand.

The budget for *Nightmare* topped out at 1.7 million with thirty-two days of shooting. It was well planned and it was made by two people—the producer and myself—who both come from low-budget backgrounds, so we knew how to get a lot on the screen for very little, and there was very little bullshit. It was done basically half union, half nonunion. It was storyboarded and everybody who worked on it was totally committed to making a mark in film. Most of them were young and starting out and ready to make their first really good film. It's just that mentality rather than a bunch of union professionals showing up for just another movie. It was a bunch of young people who gave it everything they had because they wanted to make their mark.

We rehearsed various scenes on and off in preproduction, but a lot of that stuff you can't rehearse. You can't rehearse a scene where you're being chased down an alley. We talked a lot about the basic concept of the movie and what I thought the characters were like. We rehearsed enough to get a feel for the lines—which worked and which didn't work. And we just went out and did it.

Robert Englund, who played Freddy, the nightmarish figure I named after my worst enemy when I was a kid, has been around for a long time with a lot of different roles, a lot of practical training and Shakespeare, so he's very experienced. He's a very different choice of villain for me. Before my villains were stuntmen or people who could do very physical things and were very large. But in this case, I went for somebody who didn't have to be big but who would project an immensity by his acting.

I didn't sit down and figure out psychologically what I was trying to do to the audience. Basically I was just following instincts and old fears from my childhood, what frightened me as a child. I think if you go back to childhood rather than teenage time, it was really the bogeyman. There's something very, very potent about that fear of the old man who is out to get you, so I based it on my early fears of the bogeyman and also classic nightmares that I had as a child—and those I read about, like fear of falling, fear of not being able to run fast enough. Those that I can remember it seems everyone else has had too. I had a dream when I was a kid of running from a neighborhood bully. I was much younger than he was in the dream and he just kicked a can—a flat can—and it sliced right through my Achilles tendon. I couldn't run after that and he just loped behind me. I can't remember the rest of the dream. Afterward I found that many different people had dreams about being crippled or being in mud or in quicksand. The original thing in the film dream is that Nancy's legs become elephantine—very large and heavy; and when it came down to it, it turned out that we couldn't attain that on our budget. Then I thought that she would run through a wet cement sidewalk and sink up to her knees. It turned out that we couldn't find a place where we could afford to do that either, because we would have had to light a whole street. So, at the very last minute, I said, "All right, the stairs are going to turn to goop." It was the last night of shooting and it was a matter of two hours before we were going to shoot it. I had a carpenter take out three steps and replace the carpeting with oatmeal. That's literally what we did. We did it very, very quickly with one take. We just knew we wanted to get a shot of her not being able to run and sinking into some sort of goop.

Typically my films have been financed by distributors: New-line Cinema, which produced *Nightmare,* is a distributorship; they pieced it together with other distributors—foreign distributors and a videotape distributor.

At the moment, the production-distribution situation is certainly better than it was two years ago, when it was just the pits. It was the economy in general. I watched the film business really diminish during the recession and come right back as soon as money was flowing and the stock market started coming back.

It's almost directly linked to the prime lending rate. It's just a direct result of the economy, and if we go into another recession, it will be just as hard to get small films going again. A small, independent guy can pay ten or eleven percent for his money as opposed to twenty percent, which was what it was costing us when we did *Swamp Thing*. It makes an enormous difference and more films can be made now. The studios are different critters entirely. There's a huge difference between the studios who think of a ten-million-dollar film as medium-priced or even low and an independent person who tends to want to make a film for a million dollars, or, at the highest, two million, and that's about it. So in between that ten million and two million there's a no-man's-land where very few people are making films. Those one- and two-million-dollar films are financed from much more limited sources, such as doctors and small investment companies, and they are much more fragile and dependent on the marketplace. Now is a very good time to be breaking into the film business.

Nightmare has gone platinum, which means one hundred thousand sales out of the box. The inital order from the video company who makes the cassettes was for one hundred thousand. But films lose a lot being seen on video rather than in a theater. The only thing you can say is that it's better they're seen that way than never seen at all. I won't make any adjustments for video in the way I shoot. That road is just too much for me to take. I know that when I was making films early on, the producer would say, "Don't start with a dark shot, because when it's showing in drive-ins, it'll still be light and people's headlights will wash it out. So you start with a day shot." I would never do that either. With video, everyone says "This will be too dark—they'll never see it on video." There's a certain point you can't do that anymore—you just try to go ahead, hoping the core audience will see it in a cinema, where it should be seen.

Of all the art forms, I think film is the most vulnerable to its own technology: The print itself—the medium—begins decaying; the colors wash out; people snip at it and drag it across editing-room floors. It's dependent upon its technology to be pristine as opposed to a novel, which you can put on the floor, step on, rip up, and if you can still make out the words, the images get across with no change.

The trouble with something like Showscan is that it's out of the means of the average filmmaker to shoot in; it's out of the means of the average theater anyway. I could shoot in 70 mm with Dolby stereo, but the fact of the matter is that the people who finance my films can't afford that either. The technology is around but the economics . . . I think the most important thing about a movie is the story itself—and the movie is the star, not the technology of the movie. If I had to, I would make my films on video or 8 mm, and I think they still would be tolerable. My films don't stand on the technology. The script, the story, the play's the thing. If I could, I would like to make films in people's living rooms, so it would really be happening in front of their faces. I hate the fact that you're dependent upon the prints being correctly timed, and then they get scratched and start to fade, and someone opens a door at the back of the theater and washes out the screen, and people are talking. As a filmmaker you want everything to be in perfect transmission; you want no static. You want people to see it in the perfect situation with great sound, no lights on, and everybody paying attention; but the fact of the matter is that eighty percent of the people are going to see it in their homes on a faulty television set, with the kids running through the living room. That's the nature of the medium.

Griffin Dunne

Actor; producer

Filmography:

As producer:

1979   *Chilly Scenes of Winter/Head Over Heels* (coprod. with
        Amy Robinson and Mark Metcalf)
1983   *Baby, It's You* (coprod. with Amy Robinson)
1985   *After Hours* (coprod. with Amy Robinson and Robert
        Colesberry)

As actor:

1979   *Chilly Scenes of Winter/Head Over Heels* (bit part)
1980   *The Fan*
1981   *The Wall*
1982   *An American Werewolf in London*
1983   *Johnny Dangerously*
1984   *Almost You*
1985   *After Hours*

The kind of movies that first occur to me would be big
ones, epics. I'm very interested in family relationships, but the
first one I was thinking about was a film with lasting appeal that
I saw on television last night, *Giant*. I would think of movies that
spread out over long periods of time, that have a sense of his-

tory. I'd keep dwelling on other people's history, since I would have none on that island. *The Godfather* and *The Godfather, Part Two* would keep me entertained for a nice long time. *All the King's Men*—I like movies that start at an early point in time and go all the way through. *Splendor in the Grass* also—I wouldn't have any love on the island, not even unrequited love, so I would watch someone else's unrequited love. *Baby, It's You,* which Amy Robinson and I produced, was influenced by *Splendor in the Grass.* John Sayles, Amy Robinson, and I saw the movie several times, and it was Amy's favorite movie as a child, so she thought of it when she thought of the story of *Baby, It's You.* As a matter of fact, we had a reference to *Splendor in the Grass* in the movie.

But I could never choose one movie! One movie—that's a killer. I jotted down my favorite movies of all time: *The Magnificent Ambersons* is one. I like the relationships within a family that are always changing. The sense of history—who else do you know from the time of your birth until you die but at least one member of your family, hopefully, and, in some cases, six or seven? You go through periods of hating somebody more than you could possibly hate somebody else and love somebody more as well. The emotions are so extreme in families, and spread out over sixty or seventy years. There's just something very moving to me about people who stay together; they have no choice but to stay together and the ones who don't amaze me. And it says so much about who you are and what you're going to be like, unfortunately or fortunately, or what you resist being like. If you believe a lot in heredity, the lengths people will go to break that process are such confining, restricting things. Families can have such highs and lows. It can be a powerful financial structure one week and then they can lose it all. It's not just one person being affected, but perhaps two or three generations of people getting used to being without and trying to get it back again. I've always been interested in generations who have the same purpose or who are at cross-purposes but have a name to protect. Our family is always falling in and out with each other, although we're a family on both sides—my mother's and my father's. There are a lot of members. Some get along with each other and some don't, but they're always talking about each other. Why people never get sick of talking about their fourth cousin is amazing to me.

Originally I wanted to act. Right after high school, I wanted to be an actor. I did plays in high school, some television in Los Angeles, and then I decided to go to New York to study at the Neighborhood Playhouse. When I got out, I didn't get any work at all. I couldn't get a job. Every now and then I'd be in an Off-Broadway play with ten people in the audience. That's all part of the process. I was a waiter and had a lot of different straight jobs, but I was very frustrated. It seemed that everybody was working except me and my two friends, Amy Robinson and Mark Metcalf, and the three of us spent a lot of time out of work together. During this time we optioned a book, Ann Beattie's *Chilly Scenes of Winter,* and quit acting for two years to make this movie. I was so obsessed with acting that I became more obsessed with the rejection of acting, the odds of getting work. I would read the statistics of how many actors in the Screen Actors Guild were unemployed. I was dwelling more and more on the negatives of acting—how hard it is to get a job, how low I was on the acting totem pole. And there is one. The cycles of unemployment do tend to go up; there's a climbing progression. I see people who really did start off as actors doing eight-house theater, Off-Broadway plays, and worked their way up and up. There is an actual progression possible as you get to know more and more people. I gave myself a tiny part in *Chilly Scenes of Winter,* and when the movie came out I started getting acting work because of that small part. I played a guy named Dr. Mark; I had only eight lines, but at the time the scene got a lot of laughs. I played a real officious prick who corrects his fiancée on how to pack a suitcase. A director saw it and then I got work from that and some sort of progression began to take place— little breaks were happening with an upward motion.

But I still produced because producing was sort of stable and I really thought I was doing something. Optioning requires very little money. At that time we didn't even have very little money- -or I didn't—but Mark Metcalf had just been in *Animal House* and he had the two grand we needed. We did our work out of our apartments until we raised the money from studios. Twentieth Century–Fox developed the script and United Artists made the movie. We got the script written, and Joan Micklin Silver approached us. She'd read in *Publishers Weekly* that we'd optioned the book, and it was her favorite. It just appeared without our knowledge. We didn't even know enough to plant it in the trades. The title, the ads, the distribution—all these were areas that we were very naïve about and are less so now. At that time we thought the hardest part was the work: making the movie, casting it, getting the finest cut, and delivering the picture. We thought that with what's called "delivering the final answer print," the studio would then take over with their distribution. We thought because they paid for it, it meant they couldn't wait to get it and see what they could do with it. We didn't realize that distribution is a whole different cast from the people you were selling to in the first place to get the picture made. Now you have to sell your picture to get them to distribute it. Unless they see something immediate about it that they can sell, you have to show them what to sell. We were sort of like, "Well, we wouldn't have made this movie if we didn't like it. I mean, we like it, why wouldn't anyone else like it?" That was a little simple. We didn't know how to sell it and thought it was their job. And we found ourselves really thinking about that —how to sell this movie. Exactly who is the audience? But it was too late.

If we could do it over, we wouldn't have changed the title. Even though they said we didn't have a choice, we might have called their bluff. The marketing people thought "Chilly" and "Winter" in the same title was too cold. How they came up with that, I don't know. What do you mean too cold? Chilly, winter? Where did they get that idea? I don't know why cold is bad for a movie. *Head Over Heels*, the final title, is too "footy" a title for me, too anatomical, the research people would have said. Everything is always "too" this or "too" that. It's either too dramatic or too visual. Criticism in the movie business is oftentimes couched like that. You take a positive thing and put a "too" in front of it and suddenly it's a criticism: It's too funny, it's too dramatic, it's too visual, and it's a way of getting out of making the movie. "'We just feel it's too brilliant."

Baby, It's You was kind of loosely based on Amy Robinson's life, which she told to John Sayles. From what Amy told him, he wrote a script, which was developed at Fox, but we ended up doing it independently and Paramount distributed it. After Fox developed the script, we went into what's known as "turn-around." When it was finished, Paramount paid for the cost of the movie, about three million dollars. We got to do the movie through a bank loan, not a loan like you take to buy an apartment. It was really an agreement: The bank gave us the money because Paramount had an option on releasing the film and picking up the cost of the movie.

We did a very similar thing on *After Hours*. We wanted to do it that way because we knew how to make the movie for that amount of money—a little over four million—and we wanted to use our crew, and they're not signatories to the studio. So to do it independently meant we could do it cheaper and use people we wanted to work with. We paid a different union to make that movie—NABIT.

The script of *After Hours* was at Sundance Institute, which was started by Robert Redford in Utah. Amy was up there for a seminar where filmmakers go to trade scripts and ideas and talk about movies. Amy was handed this script by Dušan Makavejev that was written by one of his students, a sort of "Why don't you read this, it seems interesting." She read it and told me about it and said there was a great part for me. The script was so original —we'd never read anything like it—that we optioned it right away and went to Martin Scorsese. Amy had been in *Mean Streets* and Marty and our company had the same lawyer, Jay Julien. Marty was looking for something to do right away. There was a hole in his schedule and he was looking for something to *go*. He liked the script a lot; we met with him, and we all wanted to make the same movie. It went very quickly after that. We sat down and he said, "Well, what's attached to this movie?" We said, "We would like to produce it," and I said, very quickly, "And I would like to play Paul." And he said, "Fine." We went on talking about other things in the movie. It was just a "fine" and we went on. I didn't know whether he had seen my work or not. I'm still an actor and actors are always riddled with insecurity—so are many other kinds of people—but when you're acting it's so much more up front. I was thinking, "He hasn't seen my work. Maybe he doesn't think Paul is very significant to the script. I don't know." We did a reading of the script a couple of times with actors who weren't necessarily going to be in the movie, but we did it just to hear how it sounded. And I was never really sure he knew I could do it until after those readings, and then I knew he knew. *I* always knew I could do it. I didn't know how he could.

The motivations of the character were very clear: Get out of this crazy girl's apartment and get home, and then something else would distract him. The movie is about surprise and expecting one thing to happen and being surprised by a completely unexpected turn of events. So whenever Marty and I were talking about a scene, we would talk about it as if we didn't know the bartender wasn't going to be at his bar or the set of keys would now be somewhere else. So I'd always go into a scene expecting something else, and then there'd be a whole other event. It would always be "all you have to do is go into that bar, get your keys, and you can go home." And we would play all of that and we would talk about that. If I didn't have the keys, I'd be thinking, "As soon as I get home, I can get a locksmith." And Marty'd ask, "Well, do you think the landlord will be up?" So we never talked about what was going to happen, but what was happening right at that moment. He approached it very collaboratively. Marty acted like he was in the same boat as Paul Hackett. He'd get as harried and frenzied as I was when we were talking. That was unusual as an actor to have a director act as though he was in the same predicament as you were in—without it being contrived. He thought about the overall circumstances as much as I did, and it put him in a very similar state to mine. It was great.

Scorsese took a lot of takes. There's a misconception about an actor doing a lot of takes—that if you take fifteen takes, it's because fourteen were wrong: "Okay, let's do it again" because you're screwing up. We would usually get it right the first one or two, and then the rest were just to see what else we could get. It was sheer greed for getting the best work. We just tried it and something different would happen, and if you get to take twelve, it means you have to get to take thirteen, and if you get to take thirteen, you go on; you do take fourteen, and then you do fifteen for the hell of it, and take fifteen was so great that you just have to do take sixteen. We didn't do sixteen takes every time, but it wasn't unusual. I really like doing it that way. People always have this feeling about their work that they wish they had done it differently: "If I had it to do over again, I would have kept working on that." Sure, there are things I look at and wish I had tried this or that, but this is the first time as an actor that when they turned the camera on to shoot the other person, I felt I had tried everything I could, every possible avenue.

When I first saw *After Hours* it was over two hours and twenty minutes long. Marty doesn't cut while he shoots, so it was everything—a whole range; there was really nothing taken out —the whole body of this entire one night. It wasn't an assembly, but a very long rough, rough cut. It was unbearable for me to watch, not only because I was in it, but because the evening was so excruciating—everything was going on. The more Marty cut it, the rhythm started coming into it. It got to a point where you could feel whatever didn't work. It was like an alarm going off. The movie would just be clipping along and he'd trip over something. Scorsese would smooth out that rough spot and then the movie would just clip along again. If you didn't take the film away to mix it, he would still be cutting frame by frame. I think he could cut a movie for years and years if he wanted to.

I've seen the movie so many times now that I don't have as strong a reaction to seeing myself as I first did. When I first did, my heart was beating so fast I couldn't concentrate on what I was saying. I couldn't look at the other actors; I could only look at myself. It was the most solipsistic way of viewing a movie ever, and now I see the bigger picture.

I was afraid of being terrible. The reason people don't like to watch themselves on film is because they're so terrified that everybody knows they're acting, because you see yourself acting and it's so embarrassing. You know the difference, and what if everybody sees you as you see you, where they see you pretending you're in that situation? It always amazes me that people don't see it. It takes a while getting used to seeing yourself, so that you can say, "That's okay; that's what your job is. That's what's called acting, making your job as believable as possible." Now, I'm much less hard on myself.

I've been getting a lot of offers, but nothing that I'm dying to do. It's probably always like that. They want me to do guys who are definitely jerks: they want me to play good-natured jerks in love with a girl and unable to get her. They do kooky things for a living—window dressers or own hot air balloon stores—and a kooky girl comes in and disturbs his kooky lifestyle. So I'll wait until something with a little more edge comes along.

MARIANNE FAITHFULL

Songwriter; recording artist; concert artist; actress; writer of soundtracks for film scores

Filmography:

As actress:

1967   *I'll Never Forget Whatshisname*
1968   *The Girl on a Motorcycle*
1969   *Hamlet*
1973   *Lucifer Rising*

Soundtracks:

1969   *One Plus One/Sympathy for the Devil*
1985   *Trouble in Mind*

I would like several movies—a Marilyn Monroe movie,
Some Like It Hot, directed by Billy Wilder, or another of the Billy
Wilder movies, because they fit in with my idea of life. They do
say that life as you see it is what you create. You know, existen-
tialism: You only see what you can. You only see three sides of
a room and you never know what is behind you. That's what
those Billy Wilder movies are like to me. They are like the bits
you see and also the bits you don't see.

I do love *Blood of a Poet* by Jean Cocteau because it's so
strange and unlike any other film. It was the first film I saw on

LSD. I was with Christian Marquand, Terry Southern, Robert Fraser (the art gallery owner), Christopher Gibbs, Michael Cooper, Paul McCartney, and Keith Richard—all these wonderful people. We were all at Robert's. I love *Blood of a Poet* because I love the soundtrack, which is the only area of feature filmmaking I've worked on apart from doing a movie as a starlet with Alain Delon years ago—*The Girl on a Motorcycle*—and *Hamlet* with Nicol Williamson. I also did *I'll Never Forget Whatshisname* with Oliver Reed. That was one day of work for which I was paid four hundred pounds, which seemed wonderful at the time.

I know there are musical films I would also want to take, like *Guys and Dolls*, and Charlie Chaplin movies—*City Lights* or *Modern Times*. I would also want to take Lang's *Metropolis* and a modern musical—*Gigi*—because I saw it during another highly emotional moment, like when I first saw *Blood of a Poet*. I think I saw it when I was thirteen or fourteen. *Gigi* gave me my vision of sophistication, especially the two old ladies.

I could also take *The Magnificent Seven*. I love the music for it and that leads me into Japanese movies, which I really like. Just before I did the movie with Alain Delon, I went to see these films of wonderful Japanese ghost stories. And the director of the film I did with Delon was a wonderful man named Jack Cardiff, who used to be Marilyn Monroe's lighting cameraman. I'm afraid the movie I did with him wasn't good, but one of the wonderful things that happened—I was very young, about twenty, and I was very grand with all my own ideas—was that I took Jack Cardiff to see these Japanese ghost stories because I wanted him to film English adaptations. I was also seeing Kurosawa movies, Antonioni movies—that was my film experience, my background for movies: cool, foreign movies. After I split up with Mick Jagger, I didn't continue acting in films. Obviously, it was a very good commercial thing to be living with Mick Jagger, and when I split up with him, the quality of my parts went down—luckily not the quality of my life, but certainly the quality of my parts. It totally destroys one to live in a goldfish bowl, but one brings that on oneself, so you can't complain. You get what you ask for, baby.

Actually almost all my music is created as if for soundtracks, because I think of my music cinematically anyway. I do see sounds in visual terms, not very clearly and perhaps a bit dated. I hear sounds in colors, but I don't *see* them as such. I don't make great videos—at least I haven't made the definitive video of my work yet, although I've worked with some very interesting filmmakers like Derek Jarman.

I only consciously started doing film soundtracks recently. I'm working on a movie, *Trouble in Mind,* titled after the old blues song that's been covered about ten times. They wanted me to sing another version, but I wrote a song for the movie, "Locked in Glass."

The first soundtrack work I did was with Jean-Luc Godard. Working with Godard was interesting. I worked on *One Plus One.* He was old-fashioned, hooking up with something he didn't know that much about.

A lot of us do film music that is never *actual* film music, but is nevertheless film music. One of the most interesting things I ever did was the music for *Hamlet* with Nicol Williamson. I had to sing all the songs, which was one of the reasons I was hired —to sing those Ophelia songs, those real victim songs. That was my image at the time. I did them really beautifully and I'd like to take that with me, too—me doing Ophelia with Nicol in *Hamlet,* definitely. Singing those songs, "How should I thy true love know from the other ones."

HENRY JAGLOM

Screenwriter; director; actor

Filmography:

1970   *A Safe Place*
1976   *Tracks*
1979   *Sitting Ducks*
1983   *Can She Bake a Cherry Pie?*
1985   *Always*

I think I would take *Swing Time*. It's somehow between that and *The Life and Death of Colonel Blimp*. The reasons for that have to do with this perfect dream of romantic love and a life that doesn't really exist, the life we fantasize about that is reflected in those films of Astaire and Rogers. I think *Swing Time* is the best version of that. The other side of it is those films of Powell and Pressburger, like *Stairway to Heaven* and *The Red Shoes* and *The Life and Death of Colonel Blimp*. They reflected another kind of fantasy. But on a desert island where I had to look at one thing over and over, I would want *Swing Time;* I would want to enter that world. To take a great piece of art that reflects the pain of being alive and the pain of existence would be pointless, because on an island, in that situation, you would not be forced to confront it; you would not need to deal with it; you would not have to reflect on this world because you'd be alone. You wouldn't reflect the outer world; you would have to reflect the inner world of your dreams, of the landscape of your childhood, the fantasies that come from total innocence. There's no starvation; there's no war, no suffering—you don't have to have art reflecting life that way, so art can lie back and just reflect the truth of our dreams. All those films deal with the dream of the perfectibility of love. *Stairway to Heaven:* You die in an airplane crash, but on the way to your death you hear a voice over the radio. It's the girl on shore you've never met and her voice makes you fall in love just before you die. That issue suddenly confronts the cosmos with whether love or death is more powerful. Therefore there's this trial going on in heaven, while on earth you are on an operating table. In heaven you are being subjected to a huge courtroom trial, attended by everyone who ever lived and dreamed and flew, as to whether you should live or not. Remember, in the film, one tear in a rose turns the whole black and white movie red and confirms that love is stronger than death and, therefore, that you should be able to live. It fulfills this dream that love will triumph over everything, even over death. And the same thing with *The Life and Death of Colonel Blimp,* which, for me, is in some ways the most perfect movie ever made. Not the greatest movie, but the most perfect encapsuling of our romantic dreams. You keep falling in love over and over again with the same woman—they're all played by Deborah Kerr. It sees life as a dream of love. In another way, the Fred Astaire–Ginger Rogers movies do that. Orson Welles was really horrified when I told him I would want to take an Astaire-Rogers movie to a desert island, because to him they're just kitsch, just junk. They're the pop culture of his youth, and he thought they were garbage. But to me they're not garbage— they're the dream of life, the dream of romance. They're what we grew up thinking life was going to be; they're what the whole issue of our life is, which to me is what my films are all about: Trying to figure out why life didn't turn out the way it was supposed to.

I could take my film *Always,* with me playing the lead, be- cause it's the perfect mirror of the truth of my life, if I wanted a mirror of what life was really like. My ex-wife and I costar; it was shot in our home; and it's about the end of our marriage. It encapsulates all of my feelings. But I don't know if I want to look at that over and over. It's bad enough that I made it and have to look at it now. If I were on a desert island, I think I would rather look at a dream, because as long as I was on the island, I wouldn't have to deal with the fact that the dream couldn't be perfected. Being on an island is like being on another planet, so you can imagine there is a world without wars, without suffering, and starvation, and oppression of all kinds, and that if the boat could just come and pick us up, it could take us over to Fred Astaire and Gingers Rogers' island and everything would be okay. You can just keep on inventing the real world you need, falling in love, and know that it's fine.

I keep going back to *Always* because *Always* is what we wanted to happen, but then it doesn't happen right. I was trying to exorcise the disillusionment in some way I wanted in all my films, and now more directly than ever, to reflect my life on screen and the lives of the people around me. What I like so much about *Always* is what Orson said when he saw it, that it was the greatest film he'd ever seen. I said, "My God, why?" He said, "No masks. You're not wearing any masks. I wish I could make one film as brave as that. I've never done it. I'm so envious of this film. I've always hidden behind a mask, and to show yourself, to really reveal yourself this truthfully, this fully, and not try to endear yourself to us like a lot of people do in that process, but to uncover who you are and just share that. Just once in my life," he said, "I'd like to get up on film, really me as I am." He did it completely in *F for Fake,* but he did only one aspect of himself. I know what he means: to share that vulnerability, fragility, the degree to which you're out of control of your own existence, to show the degree to which your dreams do not come true, to not hedge that, not to cover that, not to try to make yourself look better. I purposely didn't let anybody, including me, wear makeup in this film, and that was a symbol of what the whole film was about. I think the job for me, at least, is to try to subjectively communicate the truth of my existence and what I see and feel and what the people around me see and feel, and what our life is like. If somebody else took this film to a desert island and wasn't aware of twentieth-century life in America, in my particular strata, they would really be able to see what our life is like by looking at my films.

What's wonderful about the image of taking a film to a

desert island is that you don't have to take a great work of art; you don't have to take the great, socially responsible film. It doesn't have to be significant. It's what you want to see over and over again, and what you want to see over and over again is the stuff of your dreams, the stuff that makes you happy, that makes you feel certain things are possible. I don't think you should have distance. What I like about combining all these activities of writing, directing, acting—making my own film and using my own life—is that I try to forget about it as a conscious act of re-creation, and I try to plunge back into the chaos of existence. I don't see why art should be any different from life —in the sense that we don't know what we are doing in life. We are just being, and I want my films to reflect that truth. I don't want to have an objective overview; I don't want to have distance and say, "I see, that's what I'm going to do," because then I'm giving more knowledge to my situation than my real life has. Then I'm shading it; then it's not truthful; then I'm making things work out in a certain way. I purposely leave certain things open in this film, because life is constantly about things that change and that are open and that we don't control.

The first day shooting *Always* I did a terrible thing. I'm a little overconfident. It never occurred to me that it would be a problem directing and acting. I always acted and I knew how to direct, and so I thought, "What's the problem doing them to-gether?" I had a terrible first day because I found that while I was acting, I was trying to watch the others out of the corner of my eye and make sure they were doing well. Of course, that negated acting spontaneously and being there as an actor, which means forgetting where you are. As a director I had to remem-ber exactly where I was and watch everything to make sure I was getting exactly what I needed. So I called Orson up com-pletely nuts and asked, "What am I going to do?" He said, "You've got to separate the two, totally separate them. Never act when you direct. It doesn't matter, you're there on the screen; fine, it'll work out. Just pay attention to what you're directing, which means as much as possible act in singles so that the cam-era is only on you and you don't have to worry about anybody else. Set everything up and then forget about everything else. Just act." And he said those films that had worked best for him were where he had forgotten about directing and only concentrated on the acting. When I got all the pieces together, I saw stuff that happened when I was distracted, but I didn't need to use that in the final film. Where I was acting, really giving myself truthfully to the situation, I had all those pieces. It was a question of finding the way to put them together. That's the editing process.

I think Woody Allen to some extent does it when he is allowed to. I think his most successful version of that is the one film nobody likes but I loved, and I think is one of the greatest films ever made—*Stardust Memories*. He really, truthfully, surrenders to the truth of his life, to revealing who he is, what he feels, what he's experiencing. It may be an unattractive truth; it may show that he really has an attitude toward his audiences, toward critics and so on, which is going to make the film automatically unpopular, but if that's his vision, that's his vision. He was so honest about it that I was moved and excited and impressed. The same with Bob Fosse and *All That Jazz*, where he choreographs his own death scene. That's an astonishing film of self-revelation and an honest giving in to what you're doing. I just saw Susan Seidelman's *Desperately Seeking Susan;* I think she gives in to it completely, and it's a wonderful vision. Scorsese, as black as his vision is, constantly has a need to reveal the truth of his life. Fellini has always done it. He started off doing it, and may have been the first person to do it. Certainly *8½* is the great example of that. I love the films that force you to recognize the author behind the film, within the film, that force you to know you're not looking at someone hiding behind conceptualized visions of themselves, but that you're looking directly into someone's heart, feelings, needs, and fears, and that they're revealing them to you. I may not want to enter their lives, but if they're telling me the truth about what their life is like and the life they know about, there's something important about the film. There's never been a Scorsese film that's not been important, and some of them have horrified me. *Taxi Driver* and *Raging Bull* were some of the most disturbing and unpleasant things to look at, but in them he reached into himself. He was able to touch women's fantasy in *Alice Doesn't Live Here Anymore*. And he's truthful all the time. Cassavetes has been truthful all the time, as has Woody Allen. They're always reaching for some kind of admission.

We all share certain dreams and losses and fears and anxieties and hopes and wishes, and it's really exciting to try to capture those. This is why I work with actors the way I do, trying to get the essence of who they are up on the screen mixed in with the character I give them, rather than imposing a character on them. That's why Karen Black in *Can She Bake a Cherry Pie?* has never been more herself, and Tuesday Weld's never been more who she is than in *A Safe Place*. Jack Nicholson says in interviews that if you want to see who he is, take a look at *A Safe Place*. As a continuation of that idea, I now reveal myself more fully. I ask everyone else to do it; the least I can do is peel that off myself as well. For me, it's just taking it a step further to actually play what is basically myself, though I have created a fictional story line. But everything I say in *Always* and everything my ex-wife says is emotionally truthful. That, I think, is the ultimate fulfillment of what film can be.

I don't want to work with anyone I don't know well emotionally and who I don't find emotionally complex. I would like to think what I'm capturing is some reflection of the truth of what our lives are like, and yet, on that desert island, I don't want to see that truth. I want to see the dream of what life could be like. I want to see Ginger Rogers' dresses and Fred Astaire's feet move—see him dance the night away and keep falling in love with the same perfect woman—and never have it go wrong because we never get to the sixth reel.

As far as filmmaking now is concerned, I think it's the best time in history for independent filmmakers. One, the big commercial filmmakers have all become obsessed with childhood. They all make these gigantic comic books about cute little space creatures or weird children's events. That leaves twenty, twenty-five percent of the audience, the adult audience, hungry for films that really reflect something about their lives, their relationships. This has produced an ever-growing group of independent distributors who have more power than independents ever had in the past because they're aiming only at that twenty-five percent. It's like the Samuel Goldwyn Company who bought *Always* and gave me a million dollars, which is unheard of. Nobody gives one million dollars for an independent film. That would have been impossible a few years ago, but that's largely due to a second factor—the existence of cassettes, VCRs, cable, and a technology that is sufficient so that if you make a movie under a certain amount of money, you are going to make money on that film. If you aim a film at that twenty-five percent of the audience and the American population is 250 million, twenty-five percent is more than 50 million people. It's more than any film needs to ever get. At five dollars a person, that's more than 250 million dollars, so you don't even need that. You only need ten, five, two percent if you're aimed sufficiently and say, "Okay, there's a grown-up market out there; we're not going to make films for every twelve-year-old in Dubuque. That we'll leave to the Spielbergs and the Lucases, and the people who are wonderful at it." But the rest of us can really feel very empty when looking through the pages of the movie advertisements trying to find a movie about people.

Now, suddenly, there's a clear division in the audience—in a way it's good, and that's been taken up by a whole new brand of distributor. Seven, eight years ago I couldn't get anybody to distribute *Tracks*. Now I would have a choice of four, five, or six really good distributors. It would have a real shot. In Europe it's a big film. Europe has always had a tradition of films for adults. It has also always had a tradition where their critics told audiences not just what they would like or would entertain them, but what they should see. They have a tradition that has to do with the level of the work, which they take seriously; film is art for them. They don't treat it as mass entertainment. *A Safe Place* played for eight years in Paris because there were always a few people to fill up a one-hundred-sixty-seat theater. There were always one hundred and sixty people who want to see something stimulating.

If you're not interested in millions of people and millions of dollars, you can really be happy. I'm the most lucky person I know in this town. All my friends who are in mainstream commercial filmmaking are complaining. They don't get to make the films they really want to make; their dreams aren't being fulfilled. They have to compromise if they are directors and use actors they don't want or submit to other people cutting their films; or if they're writers, they have to watch other people chop up their material; if they're actors, they don't get to play the parts they want to play. Then, if they're studio films, the studio takes all the profit with all that creative bookkeeping crap. I'm the only one I know who makes exactly the films I want to make and makes them inexpensively so that nobody is looking over my shoulder, nobody tells me what to do. I cast them, shoot them, edit them the way I want, and then I look around for who I want to distribute them. Nobody has interfered with them. And then I make enough money on each film so that every one goes into profit. I'm astonishingly lucky.

Jim Jarmusch

Screenwriter; film director

Filmography:

1980   *Permanent Vacation*
1984   *Stranger Than Paradise*
1986   *Down by Law*

It's an impossible question. The answer would change every hour. I think I would take *Out One: Spectre,* a film by Jacques Rivette. The original version, *Out One,* was made for television and is thirteen hours long. It was made in 1970. I was asked this question before and that's what pops into my head only because it's a film you could watch a hundred times and have a different reaction to every time. The traditional kind of narrative is not of any interest to Rivette and therefore his films make a lot more sense several days after you've seen them, rather than when you've just emerged from the film—for me, anyway. I don't understand exactly what I've seen or what I feel about it; it's something that's an accumulation of thought about his films that makes them interesting for a longer period of time after you've seen them. That's probably what I would take with me, although, as I said, my answer could change every half hour; there are so many people I like.

I like Dreyer's work a lot; I like a lot of Antonioni's films— they're something I could see over and over again, like *L'Avventura.* There's something similar to Rivette in that for Antonioni often the meaning of a scene is implied more by the way it's photographed than by what actually happens in the scene. What kind of landscape it takes place in will frequently affect the emotional importance of a scene more than the dialogue. I also like Sam Fuller's films, Nick Ray's films, Douglas Sirk's, a lot of Fassbinder's, and most of Godard's, so it's very difficult.

I think another film I'd be tempted to take would be *The Mother and the Whore* by Jean Eustache, which I like a lot, but I don't want to come off sounding like a Francophile. That film amazed me. I wish I could see it again. I've seen it twice, but the last time I saw it was probably six years ago. It's a film I think about a lot, that affected me very deeply both times I saw it, and emotionally, I sort of need to see it again. It's nothing more specific than that. I was involved in different relationships each time I saw it, so it affected me and applied to me differently each time. It's something that's universal—jealousy and love and how we react to people we love. I'm also very interested in it in terms of the way it was scripted and directed and in terms of the acting. It's something I think I could learn a lot about acting from by seeing it again. There are a lot of Nick Ray films I also like to watch over and over again, particularly *In a Lonely Place* and *Bigger Than Life*. For some reason I see different things in them.

Asking me what films I've seen the most times is probably not a fair question because I was an usher at the St. Marks Cinema and I had to see a lot of bad films eight or ten times. Oddly enough, I've probably seen *L'Atalante* by Jean Vigo, *Rebel Without a Cause* by Nick Ray, and *The American Friend* by Wim Wenders the most. *The American Friend* is one I like to see all the time. There's more tension in the acting between Dennis Hopper and Bruno Ganz than in any of Wenders' other films. Something happens between them. From the point of view of watching the actors work, it's maybe Wenders' most interesting film. There are other films of his that are more interesting for other reasons. I like *Kings of the Road*.

Yesterday, I finished the script, or the newest draft, for *Down by Law*, my next film. It will be in some ways a similar style to *Stranger Than Paradise*. It won't all be in master shots and it won't have a blackout after each scene as in *Stranger*. Economy and style sort of went hand in hand in determining that style. I thought the style suited both the story and the means in which we were able to make the film. This new film will be similarly austere in certain stylistic ways. Right now I'm planning on everything being in master shots and medium closeups—face and shoulders—with no intermediary shots, no medium shots. A lot of films are told basically in medium shots—TV and most Hollywood films. I want to eliminate what is used most often, but I want to have closeups. The three main actors, Tom Waits, John Lurie, and an Italian actor, Roberto Benigni, have such incredible faces, so I want to have their faces more prominent, but I also like wide shots to play scenes out in. So it will be cutting between those kind of distances from the actors without the intermediary level that most stories are told in. I'm going to eliminate the most frequently used distance, but I will have closeups. That could change next week, but that's the way I'm thinking now. I'm doing it less to make a statement than because I think it's the best way to tell this story. It's also because I think people become too reliant on a certain kind of language, film language; but most importantly, it suits the story. We're shooting it in and around New Orleans. It's also black and white, but it will be very fine-grain film, not open grainy as in *Stranger*. Robby Mueller will shoot it. I'm real excited. Tom, John, and I were together last night for a while and I got really excited watching them interact with each other.

After *Stranger,* I had a lot of widely different offers to direct films that were very bad, like teenage sex comedies. It made me wonder whether the people who were offering these films to me had even seen my film. There's no nudity or virginity jokes in it. I tend to be obstinate and avoid certain things just because I think they've become clichés, like virginity jokes in teenage movies. I had offers to produce my own work through studios and also offers from various levels of producers from Dino de Laurentiis to Arthur Cohn. A lot of people expressed interest, which was very flattering, and I learned a lot. At first, I used to say a lot of things about what it is to be an independent filmmaker, which I now have learned doesn't exist. You are never independent of the money, of obtaining the money, but I'm still very obstinate as far as compromise. I would much rather walk away from something immediately than compromise. I'm very stubborn, so my independence is based on that rather on what kind of money it is or whose money it is or where it comes from. I've learned a lot about that; I don't think independent film-makers really exist, because you have to get money to make the film, and where the money comes from is not important. It's what's on the screen and how it's presented that counts.

I'm still not interested in making a studio film where some businessman is going to tell me how to cut it or what kind of music or what actors to use. That I would never do, even if I was starving. I just would rather do something else to get by. This film will have a negative pickup deal from an American distributor, where they will have distributions rights in English in advance. That will be the major part of the financing and the rest of the financing will come from Europe and deals there. None of these deals are made; we're negotiating them at the moment. So I can't say from whom, but it will be an American-European coproduction, executive-produced by the same German producer who produced *Stranger Than Paradise*. So it won't be a studio film, but it will have a distribution presale. The budget is around one million dollars.

Other films have such high budgets because a lot of bankers, executives, agents, and lawyers get their money, and that takes a lot of it. Fassbinder made a lot of films, but he had it all figured out that he would burn out working at that rate. There was no way around that, but he made more films than a lot of people do in a much longer lifetime. That doesn't mean a lot to me anyway. I mean, Nick Ray didn't make his first film until he was thirty-seven or something, and Jean Vigo only made four films although he died at twenty-nine.

I went to graduate film school at New York University, but I don't have a degree. I went for two years, but I didn't complete the program because I made a feature-length film as my thesis project and used some of the funding that was supposed to pay my tuition to make *Permanent Vacation*. I got out with my first feature, but I didn't come out with a degree. I worked with Nick Ray and met Wim Wenders through Nick. Wenders' company helped me make the first part of *Stranger*, and then the feature was produced by a different producer.

I met Tom Waits in January of 1985 just by hanging out a bit and we became friends. I was writing a different script, a love story, which I wasn't able to finish for emotional reasons. It was for a specific actress when I started writing it—a close friend of mine who died last October. Right around the time I first met Tom, I was still trying to complete that somehow but was not able to. I started writing a separate script at the same time, writing a character for Tom and one for John Lurie, and somehow it just became easier to take up this story. Then I met the other actor in Italy, Roberto Benigni, and the whole story sort of snapped into place based on thinking of these people as characters—I invented characters for them. So in a way meeting Tom started *Down by Law.*

I don't understand the process of writing a script and then casting for the main characters. I start with the actors with whom I want to work and then try to write characters for them, which is how *Stranger* came about. Essentially John Lurie was the most important. He was somebody I'd known for six or seven years before making the film. He's briefly in my first film also. I'd wanted to do something with him and then *Stranger* came about from that.

I'm really interested in acting but not in the sense of having personalities or actors who just play themselves, although some people thought in *Stranger* that these people were just playing themselves. I'm interested in working really closely with the actors. First, I write it with them in mind, but I don't base the character completely on their own personality. I find things in their personality that suggest a character. Then the process that's most interesting to me is to work with them individually and decide with them what parts of this character are parts of themselves and what parts are not; how can we eliminate those parts of themselves that are not; how can we accentuate those parts that are and make a character that's not them. Once the cameras roll, it's their emotions that are responding, not the character's, but they are the character at that point.To me the most exciting thing about filmmaking is working with the actors and getting to the moment where their own emotions are really reacting but they're in character. They're in this removed, abstracted story that's not real life anyway, and yet they're reacting to the emotions. That's what interests me. I'm not interested in camp acting or just personality acting, where they just play themselves. It's a delicate thing and working with the actors is really exciting.

The difference is that I've written it with them in mind, so right from the beginning I've been developing it in my head for that actor. I know them personally; it's not like some stranger that I want to be zapped into character and when the camera stops then they're out of character. It's more intricate than that. The script does change once I start working with the actors, but the essential idea of every scene I write doesn't change. The dialogue sometimes changes and sometimes doesn't. In *Stranger* probably eighty percent of the scenes are exactly as I wrote them and twenty percent of the dialogue changed through rehearsals and making decisions on characters as we worked. It depends, but one thing I believe in, that I learned from Nick Ray and from watching Wim Wenders work also, is that film for me is dead if it's finished by the time your script is finished. That, for me, is completely uninteresting. The script is a blueprint and from there you make a piece of architecture, but you're going to get ideas for new rooms as you go along. I think it's different for everyone.

That's why Jean Eustache amazes me and why he was one of the most important film directors. Yet he was someone who, from what I've learned from talking to people who worked with him, had everything completely scripted. The dialogue—even Lea's long, rambling monologues—was totally scripted. It seems completely improvised, and yet it was the opposite. So I think it's just how you work best, and not only does every director work differently but every actor works differently, even if it's with the same director. It's always a matter of finding the right way of communicating with each person.

I think there's a need for all different kinds of cinema. What Douglas Trumbull is doing sounds very interesting to me, but it's very unrealistic. They had some questionnaire in *American Film* about the future of cinema and the effect of video. There was something Scorsese said that made so much sense to me. He said he was composing his films for the small screen as well as for the big screen, because twenty years from now probably the only way you will be able to see his films will be on video. I think that's realistic. That, to me, is a more realistic stance than to go after whatever technology can do, when people are not going to have access to it. I hope that people keep exploring technology and that people like Trumbull can find out what can be done so we can have that spectacular kind of experience with cinema. But for somebody like me who wants to tell basically small stories, that's not a viable pursuit. It would bother me a lot to have my films shown exclusively on video, but a lot of things that are reality bother me a lot. So you have to make a decision about who is going to see your films, who you are going to make them for, and how they will be seen in the future, or whether they will at all.

I feel optimistic, which is against my generally cynical nature, but for some reason I feel optimistic. *Rambo* exists—that's a problem both politically and aesthetically because so many people like it, but, at the same time, there are enough people now who are saying, "We're tired of this kind of crap. What else is going on?" That makes me optimistic.

Stanley Kallman

Attorney for the Cannon Film Group, Inc.

I guess the film would have to be something I could watch over and over again, not the best film ever made. I would have to take *Richard III* with Laurence Olivier, and I would probably want to take *The Odd Couple* with Walter Matthau, and then I might also pick a new movie I just watched on VCR, *Carmen*, directed by Francesco Rosi with Placido Domingo and Julia Migenes-Johnson. It's an excellent movie. If I could throw a fourth one in, it would be *Barry Lyndon*. I could watch them repeatedly for different reasons. In the case of *Richard III*, it's the performances, especially Olivier; *The Odd Couple* is probably the funniest movie I've ever seen; and in the case of *Barry Lyndon*, it's a combination of the photography, the music, and the way it's all put together—not necessarily Ryan O'Neal, although he's okay in it, but there are so many smaller performances in it that are excellent. I remember when I first saw it; I hated when it was over, having just been told by a friend of mine who I didn't respect that it was boring. I can't imagine how anyone could have thought that. I thought it had so much visual action; it's such a beautiful movie and Kubrick is such an excellent director. In the case of *Carmen*, it's the best visualization of the opera I've ever seen, and Migenes-Johnson is so great—this role was made for her. Cannon is possibly using her in a new movie we're making, *Tales of Hoffmann*, with Placido Domingo. There are four soprano roles in the opera and we're hoping to get her to sing all four.

74

Being an attorney for a movie company is perhaps more interesting than other types of practice, but it's not any different. You have to negotiate deals with the artist, but in a sense it's the same as negotiating with a company for the purchase of a product, a building, or whatever it is. It's not that I think of an artist as a product, but it's essentially the same thing. Norman Mailer is selling us his book, his product, and we have to negotiate for that product.

Some films such as *Heaven's Gate* are expensive, but we, Cannon, can make a movie for five million dollars and you wouldn't know whether it cost five, fifteen, or twenty-five. It all depends on the ability of the producers. You can run up the cost of a movie tremendously by paying too much for your talent—that's your first big problem—and then by indulging the director taking twenty shots of the same scene when possibly five might do it. If he wants a special effect, he might blow up a whole town instead of doing it a cheaper way; but except for the talent, it's basically a question of how much you're going to indulge the moviemaker and allow him to spend of your money. Of course you have problems with the strong unions in places like New York, where it costs more to make a movie than in New Orleans or Atlanta, and it costs more to make it in Hollywood than somewhere else. Our company, for instance, makes its movies all over the world, for example, in Israel because it's very cheap to make them there and because we have the facilities there. But unions play a part in it, and if you're going to make a movie in a union town like New York, you're going to pay more than in a nonunion town.

The studios have made as much money from home video sales as from box office returns, but only with movies that haven't been that successful. If the picture is successful at the box office, it will never generate as much from home video sales as it will from the box office. But the picture that isn't that successful, that did maybe ten million at the box office, which means that when the money gets to the producer of the movie he might get four million from that, can make that much or possibly more from the home video sale. If the picture does fifty million at the box office, the producer might get twenty million from that. And you're not going to get that much from video sales, with exceptions such as *Rambo,* which was on a commission basis—the amount of money it got for video being comparable to its box office. Of course, *Rambo* did two hundred million, so its video ran up to forty, fifty million dollars only because of the very strange deal it had. But normally video does not equal box office; there may come a time when it will. But it's a wonderful additional revenue, something we didn't have before. On the other hand, it's probably cutting into box office revenues, so it's a mixed blessing. I'm not sure yet whether it's a plus or minus, and I'm not sure the industry knows yet either. In certain areas abroad, video is becoming so pervasive, it may very well be threatening to the box office. For instance, in Bermuda, there's no theater, there isn't even a movie house open anymore.

If you think that the studios will become more and more interested in producing and distributing pictures that will not necessarily do well in the theaters but should make money on the video market, you're assuming that the home video market will someday turn the same way that network television has turned. Network television used to pay large sums for theatrical movies, and then suddenly they came to the point where they stopped buying theatrical movies altogether and started to make made-for-TV movies. And now they get better ratings for the made-for-TV movies than they did for the theatrical movies, only because the theatrical movies have been seen so much in other media. What you question is, will the time come when the video market will be a market all for itself and people will make movies just for it? I doubt it. The thing that makes a movie popular in the video market is its sale in the theatrical market. I'm talking about the purchase of tapes. People will pay thirty dollars for *Beverly Hills Cop* because it was so popular. They won't pay thirty dollars for a title of which they never heard. They certainly won't pay eighty dollars, as they are doing for *Ghostbusters,* if they never heard of the title. They may rent it, because after a time, you've rented *Beverly Hills Cop, Ghostbusters,* and there's nothing else to rent, so you rent something you never even heard of because you want to see something different that night. You'll buy a *Carmen* because you want the opera for your collection, but you won't buy a picture that you've never seen that was advertised in the paper: "Oh well, I didn't

see that when it played at the Coronet. Maybe I'll buy a tape."
So I doubt if people will ever buy tapes made just for the home
video market.

Cannon is the largest producer of motion pictures in the
world. This year, 1985, we made twenty-five motion pictures. I
think the next largest studio was Warner Brothers, which made
fifteen pictures. We had a picture, *Breaking*, from which we
grossed forty million dollars box office. That could be termed a
blockbuster in that it cost us a million dollars to make. If it cost
thirty million to make, then forty million wouldn't have been a
blockbuster. We would have needed one hundred million. Cannon thinks in terms of making a movie that, hopefully, can be
presold to television, to video, to the foreign markets—even
before it opens theatrically in the United States, so that it's covered its negative costs. If the picture turns out to be a big success, a blockbuster, that's just great, but we don't start out
saying, "We're going to make a blockbuster." I don't know that
anyone does. *Back to the Future* is a blockbuster, but if you'd read
the script, you'd never have dreamed it was going to be one.

If it was up to me, if anything, we wouldn't make so many
films, but the people in the company [Cannon] are so energetic
that they work twenty-eight hours a day, and we just have so
many projects going all over the world. So it just happens we're
making more films than anyone else. Until very recently, the
critics have felt that ours have been mostly schlock movies, but
now *Runaway Train* has been nominated for three Golden Globe
Awards. *Fool for Love* is not a shoddy movie; we just completed
Othello with Zeffirelli directing and Placido Domingo singing;
and I've just signed Godard to do *King Lear*. We've signed Coppola to direct a movie with Dustin Hoffman, and, of course, the
next two movies Stallone makes, he's doing for us, whether
that's a plus or a minus. He's making a movie for us right now.
He'll be making *Over the Top* for us very shortly, for which we
paid him twelve million dollars flat fee. At the time we paid this,
it sounded like a lot of money, but considering what he made
on *Rambo*—because he had a percentage deal—we got him
cheap.

Akira Kurosawa

Screenwriter; film director; producer

Filmography:

1943   *Sanshiro Sugata*
1944   *The Most Beautiful*
1945   *Sanshiro Sugata, Part II*
        The Men Who Tread on the Tiger's Tail
1946   *No Regrets for Our Youth* (also coscripted)
        Those Who Make Tomorrow (codirected with Yamamoto and Sekigawa)
1947   *One Wonderful Sunday* (also coscripted)
1948   *Drunken Angel* (also coscripted)
1949   *The Quiet Duel* (also coscripted)
        Stray Dog (also coscripted)
1950   *Scandal* (also coscripted)
        Rashomon (also coscripted)
1951   *The Idiot* (also coscripted)
1952   *Ikiru* (also coscripted)
1954   *Seven Samurai* (also coscripted)
1955   *I Live in Fear* (also coscripted)
1957   *Throne of Blood* (also coproduced and coscripted)
        The Lower Depths (also coproduced and coscripted)
1958   *The Hidden Fortress* (also coproduced and coscripted)
1960   *The Bad Sleep Well* (also coproduced and coscripted)
1961   *Yojimbo* (also exec. producer and coscripted)
1962   *Sanjuro* (also exec. producer and coscripted)
1963   *High and Low* (also exec. producer and coscripted)
1965   *Red Beard* (also exec. producer and coscripted)
1970   *Dodes'ka-den* (also coproduced and coscripted)
1975   *Dersu Uzala* (also coscripted)

1980   *Kagemusha* (also coscripted)
1985   *Ran*

The first film I saw that made me feel I wanted to become a film director was Abel Gance's *La Roue,* so I think that would be my first choice on this desert island. It's a movie; it's cinema; it's well done. But I don't think I would settle for that condition. If I were condemned to such an existence, I would want a very large number of films and I wouldn't mind at all sitting and looking at them over and over again.

The furthest thing from my mind when making a film is to teach anyone anything. I have no desire to impose my personal philosophy on my audience. I do feel that the world as a whole has come to such a pass that our situation is desperate. I feel it is of grave importance to encounter this desperate situation face to face and not turn away from it—in order that we find a way out, to find a light at the end of the tunnel. My film, *Ran,* may appear to be a tragedy, but my intention is simply to look at our own situation. In the course of my filmmaking, I have portrayed people's deaths many times over. For example, the death of the gangster in *Drunken Angel,* the death of the samurai in *Seven Samurai,* the Macbeth character's death scene in *Throne of Blood,* the death of the shadow warriors and the general in *Kagemusha.* But I think in comparison with all these other past deaths in my films that the death of the lead character in *Ran* is perhaps the one that contains the most hope.

The character of Hidetora is one that begins at the pinnacle of worldly power and confidence—a result of having carried out unspeakable deeds throughout his life to attain it. What happens to him in the course the film is that he is forced to pay for these unspeakble deeds. It is only at the point where he has fallen to the depths of misery and desperation and has been treated not like a great warrior but like a beggar, that he arrives at his first understanding of what is important in life. Through his downfall he attains a kind of purity and has his first glimpse of clear, blue sky when he realizes that all he really needs is the love and understanding of one son. So his destiny to me is the most pitiful and, at the same time, the most magnificent that I have been able to conceive in my films. If there are gods and angels at that moment, they're probably coming forward and putting a halo over his head. I don't know whether this is how the audience seeing the film interprets this scene, but, for me, that is the meaning.

There is an element of Shakespeare in my work. I have done an adaptation that was not a straight adaptation of *Macbeth*, *Throne of Blood*. As compared to Macbeth, my view of Lear is that he must be the opposite phenomenon. Macbeth begins as a fairly good person, and over the course of the play, with the intensification of his ambition, he becomes a very evil person. But, as is stated in *King Lear*, I feel he starts out at the point where the Macbeth character finishes. The evils have all been done and the development of his character is toward the good. This comparison is something that interested me greatly in making the film *Ran*. In *King Lear,* the character of Lear never reflects on his own past. He doesn't seem to understand why things are happening to him the way they do; but I feel the probable reason for his madness in the play is that the evil past is coming back to him. Unless I interpret it this way, I can't justify what's happening to him in Shakespeare's play. Speaking about these causes and effects, I brought all of these elements into my view of the character of Hidetora. His madness derives from the pain of confronting his own past and the betrayal of his children. In this respect I feel my film is very different from Shakespeare's play.

I didn't intentionally avoid closeups in this film. It came about that way naturally. The problem with closeups is that if the actor is aware that the camera is only going on his face, he tends to act only with his face. So when I do closeups, I do them in a way that the actor doesn't know that only his face is getting into the frame. For me it is extremely important that he act with his whole body and his whole soul. For example, in *Ran* I felt the essence of the nice leading female character was better expressed through her posture and movements than through her

nerally believed that a closeup can show the most
.ear-cut expression of a person's character, but I'm
..ut in agreement with that prevailing notion.

There isn't less camera movement in this film than others,
but the reason you may not feel the camera movement is because almost all the scenes are shot one scene, one take, but with
three cameras, and the cameras are in constant, very violent
movement. But the footage from all three cameras was then
edited together, so that it's very difficult for the spectator to be
aware of camera movement. Every time the actor stops moving,
the camera stops moving, because I do not want the spectator
to be aware of the camera and to be distracted by the camera
movement.

The title I really intended for this film was *Chaos*, but there
isn't any Japanese equivalent that expresses that, so as a poor
substitute I used the word—the single character—*ran*, and in
the course of the production of the film all the Japanese who
were involved became accustomed to the Japanese title. So by
the time it was finished, the producer and everyone who was
involved in producing it abroad decided that it would be better
to keep the Japanese title, although I still don't feel that it quite
expresses what I wanted. The reason I feel the Japanese title is
not all that appropriate is that its meaning is more narrow. It
has a very strong connotation of historical nuance. For example,
looking at the period before that when the film is set, various
revolts, rebellions, have been named something or other *ran*,
the name of the place, the names of the clans involved—that
sort of thing. Where there are references to a time of warfare
within a particular province, *ran* is used in those circumstances
that are rather narrowly defined, so I don't think *ran* has the
breadth that the word *chaos* has. *Chaos* means a state of great
confusion. What I meant to express is something within the
human heart that I feel still exists today in terms of the conflicts
that we all face, these internal contradictions that I wanted to
bring out.

My viewpoint is not pessimistic or tragic at all. I think the
pessimistic view of the world would be to refuse to consider the
kinds of problems I'm asking you to consider. In Japan I have
found the audience doesn't want to think about these things.

It's very hard for me to think about them myself, but it's essential that we do. I've even made films about the problem of atomic bombs, and it's true that the audience has a resistance to thinking about it, but we mustn't turn away. I would consider my own viewpoint in those terms to be the opposite of pessimism. I would say I'm rather positive in my desire to find a solution to those problems.

Ron Mann

Writer; filmmaker

Filmography:

1981	*Imagine the Sound*
1982	*Poetry in Motion*
1983	*Echoes Without Saying*
1984	*Listen to the City*
1985	*Marcia Resnick's Bad Boys*

First of all, I wouldn't take a film; I would take a laser disc because you can put so much information on the disc itself with a stop-frame action, so you don't have to look at the film in a linear way. You can break down the narrative. The laser disc has the capacity to zip from the beginning to the end of the film in split seconds; it's interactive, and it has the ability of cataloging information. You can access it by a menu, a format, or by pressing up any frame you want. The reproduction of images is amazing, absolutely fantastic. There are a lot of discs that are available: One has plants and animals on it and you can access up to fifty thousand photographs. The Museum of Modern Art has a disc. That would be one I would take because you could get their complete archives. Kodak also has their entire archives on disc. And you can put two tracks on it, like French and English, so if I was going to be on this desert island, I could learn French. If you have a computer attached to this system, you interface the computer with the archive.

I did a disc for my film *Poetry in Motion;* that's why I'm familiar with it. The laser disc was invented when the military gave M.I.T. a ton of money to develop this system, and I started getting into it about two years ago. Laser discs are the future, and they're virtually indestructible. so if a coconut falls on it, no problem. It looks like a Frisbee, but if you hold it up to the light, it gives you that rainbow reflection and looks like one of those compact discs. There are a lot of distributors in software for laser discs that have put a lot of quality into the work by using an original struck print. A good example is the Criterion Company, who made *Citizen Kane* and *King Kong* on laser disc. At the end of *Citizen Kane,* Ronald Haber wrote a visual essay on *Kane.* You can stop on any frame, go back and watch each section as many times as you want—study the film. Haber gives an audio portion, narrating as you go through, but you can also tune that out because you have access to the stereo track. The essay lasts about ten minutes, but you are directed to go back to frame so and so. The disc on *Poetry in Motion* has electronic publishing at the end, so it's similar to the *Kane* disc—it's two hundred and twenty pages of text, so you can key in the performance of William Burroughs and then see the actual typed text electronically. You can go back and forth. It's a new medium that's catching on and developing. Its value is that it's a new medium, a new way of film, and a new way of looking at film. You can shoot it on 35 mm; it goes to one-inch video, and then it's pressed onto the disc. So you can get a 35-mm image with incredible quality. They're very cheap, about twelve bucks. Every thing about that medium interests me now tremendously.

Even on the disc, there's not one film I would take, but I would want to take de Antonio's work in its entirety because it's the history of American politics, culture, and life. It's his politics, but it's really America's politics. That would give you an incredible scope of who you are, where you are—art and politics —and he invented non-narrative filmmaking. I owe everything to Emile de Antonio—that is to say, my style, my thinking, my reflections, my views. He's my mentor, and I don't do anything without his advice. I'm just trying to emulate his style. He's the most important documentarian. Others made important contributions, like the Maysleses, but they haven't made significant documentaries for me. I'm Canadian and come out of the Grierson legacy in a way, too, but I'm more influenced by de Antonio's work, just because of the way he thinks. His thinking comes out of art, from the notions of John Cage to Rauschenberg. He looks at the world and at film as art; not many people consider that. People usually do things for money. There are films he admires that I like, for example, *Salt of the Earth*, which I just found out today is going to be put on laser disc by the same people who did *Kane*. You can imagine everyone is telling them, "You're crazy, *Salt of the Earth* on laser disc?" But they don't care either; they have real conviction.

There are a lot of people in the States who have real concern for filmmakers, a concern with films, who care what's going on. There are a lot of independent films people struggle to make and a lot of independents are out there—Edith Kramer at Pacific Film Archives; Karen Cooper at Film Forum; Dan Ledley in Nebraska. It seems that most of these people don't want to be on a desert island, or maybe they feel that they're on desert islands and they want to do something about it, to irrigate the wastelands. Most theaters don't want to take chances. There are film festivals that have the ability to bring in these struggling filmmakers, who are virtually stranded on islands, and make the bridge for their films to reach a community that is in danger of drying up.

I grew up watching films. I started when I was very young. There was a cinema called the the Roxy in Toronto and I used to trade records to get in for free, even though it was ninety-nine cents to get in. I used to see all the European films and American films. I couldn't go a day without seeing a film. I used to stay up late at night and watch the midnight films on television. *L'Avventura* by Antonioni was one of my favorite films, along with Godard's *Weekend,* Truffaut's *400 Blows*—all the foreign films—but I also liked *Truck Stop Women.* I wanted very much to expand my knowledge of films. I was in love with filmmaking. I didn't go out and play football with everybody else. Then I got too busy to see so many films, and that's when I started making films of my own. What de Antonio taught me was to go out and do it. I never went to film school. You can just go out and do films on your own. When I was sixteen, I worked all summer, then went out and made a sixty-minute film about the seventies. It's called *Flack*, about how people couldn't do anything about a problem except to talk about it. It's about complacency in the seventies. I learned from Antonioni, as a matter of fact, especially from *L'Avventura*, that boredom can become a very powerful emotion.

I try to deal in my films as a kind of cultural historian, making films you don't get to see on television or in movie theaters, on subjects such as jazz, poetry, unemployment. When you switch dials on television, it's all the same, so I'm looking between the dials. A film with Cecil Taylor, Archie Shepp, Bill Dixon, and Paul Bley has incredible importance in documenting what the art is, what the music is.

Alan Rudolph is another filmmaker I admire. He does his films his own way. Buñuel and Marx Brothers movies—those films really move me. Their world was so screwy, growing up in a screwy time. The ability to laugh is important, the ability to put your life into perspective in a scrambled-up, madcap, surreal world.

Lewis MacAdams

Poet; performance artist; journalist; video writer; director; producer

Filmography:

1979   *California One* (PBS; cowrote and coproduced)
1985   *What Happened to Kerouac?* (cowrote and directed)
1988   *Fun House* (one-man show, starring Eric Bogosian; directed and coproduced)

Wim Wenders' *The American Friend* related very much to my own life at the time I saw it because I was moving back and forth between America and Europe a lot, and I'm a very political person. The film talks a lot in a very indirect way about what America is now and what Europe is now. It is also about the friendship between two men. As I began to see Wenders' work, I began to realize how much of a basic theme friendship was. These were things I hadn't really considered. I'd seen a lot of movies, but I hadn't really thought about filmmakers' themes or I hadn't been touched in some personal way by the work so that it really mattered to me other than as an entertainment. I had been touched by all of Stan Brakhage's movies and all of Godard's movies. I liked them as puzzles, as ideas, and as thoughts, but I realized that Wenders was making poems—stuff that was really heart work, but not dumb, sentimental heart work—and really trying to talk about what was true as far as he could see it, in a way I never really related to in movies before. I don't have that sense of movie stars that I loved in childhood or any of that. Maybe because I read books. I leaned much more toward that.

I started out as a poet—that was my main thing for many years—and it wasn't until I was in my late thirties (in the late seventies) and I had ten, eleven books of poems and stories out that my poems were getting more like stories. I'm a performer and punk was happening, so I started doing these performances in a club called the Mabuhay Gardens in San Francisco, which was a punk fountainhead at that time. I wore a tie and stuff like that. I wasn't thinking about being punk; I was thinking about taking my poems off the page, because I was always really into performance. When you're standing up in front of people and making up a poem, basically you've got to tell a story—that's the only way it has any meaning. That's when I met Wim Wenders and saw *The American Friend*. It was all sort of tying in together. I had lived in northern California for fifteen years and I'd never been to Los Angeles and was never even curious about it. I just went to the movies occasionally, but when I saw *The American Friend,* I just knew what I wanted to do, that for the rest of my life I was somehow going to make movies. Wenders opened the door.

Lately I see it a little differently. I know slightly the girl who was Wenders' former girlfriend and who also stars in *The American Friend.* They were together for a long time and when Wenders married Ronee Blakley, she made a big suicide gesture. I didn't know about all this at the time I saw the film, but I could sense there was all this story, this passion. Grown-up love is deeper than romance. What the Dennis Hopper character was able to draw out of these two people related to real life in a way that most movies never do because they're too stylized or just entertaining.

Another film that really influenced me a lot—it seems it was around the same time—was *Renaldo and Clara* by Bod Dylan. I love that movie. I aspire to making movies like that because I think they're huge and messy and incredibly, intensely real and personal, and they're also symbolic on a zillion levels. I like the richness of a film like *Renaldo and Clara.* Dylan was really exposing himself and hiding himself. The scenes between Dylan and Baez are just amazing. There's nothing else quite like them in movies that I've seen. So that was a real influence on me. But you can't find anyone who likes that film. I was with a guy who was an assistant director or production manager on that. Everybody didn't like it, he said. But I think it's a film that will last. I didn't like the two-hour version; I like the four-hour version. I wanted the whole story, everything. Another thing I liked about *Renaldo and Clara* was that it was in real language.

I like words, but I also liked *The Road Warrior,* which probably had eleven pages of dialogue in the whole movie. I like really good language in movies, such as a movie that is traditionally, icily made, like Harold Pinter's *Betrayal.* I love that just because the language is so beautifully put together. Poets have never made movies in America—or at least very rarely. Wim was a painter—that's how he started—so his is essentially a visual craft, even though he has an incredible ear. I think now even more so.

Andy Warhol's movies are also amazing. If I were to think of three films for the desert island, they would be *The Chelsea Girls, The American Friend,* and *Renaldo and Clara.* They form this weird triangle in my mind.

I love *The Chelsea Girls* because the people in it were so incredible; it was a real vision of hell. I always thought Warhol's attitude—that to make interesting movies you just have to put interesting people in front of the camera—was completely true and it still is. That's one of the things I loved about *Renaldo and Clara.* Although there's a beautiful story and an incredible sense of Hamburg in *The American Friend,* I think the people in it are extremely interesting people. I don't like the overbearing sense of the director, especially in documentary films. I don't like people to be in between the camera and the people who are talking to you. I love Les Blank and my favorite documentary work of all time is TV TV. They were the first hand-held documentarians and the only ones who got some support from public television. Michael Shamberg, the producer, is the most famous one out of that gang. He's produced a lot of commercial movies, but there are a half dozen people from TV TV living around Los Angeles, such as Hudson Marques, who's a topflight soundman, and Wendy Appel, a documentarian who just did a movie about the porn movie scene here in Los Angeles.

They did pieces like *Maharishi in the Astrodome, Gerald Ford's America,* and *The Shah's Birthday Party.* They did about ten pieces that were really funny and daring for the time. Those kinds of works are what I'm interested in.

As far as structure is concerned, the thing with poetry and plays is that they depend on dialogue. I'm still a young screenwriter in terms of experience. But it's just a craft like any other. The best work I've put out was edited by me, *What Happened to Kerouac?,* a kind of documentary that was the first video theater piece. It opened in January of 1985 at three video theaters in Los Angeles and at the video theater in San Francisco and sold out every show for six weeks. It's done as a true work, but built like a fiction. It doesn't attempt to be a complete biography, but goes straight to Kerouac's heart. We're expanding it to seventy-five minutes and transferring it to film.

I'm not that interested in Hollywood. It seems almost dinosauric, but I am really interested in Los Angeles. The word "Hollywood" needs to be retired; it's Los Angeles movies. For sixty years they've been drumming out this name to sell movies, but it don't mean shit. A Hollywood movie doesn't tend to mean anything to a lot of people. Very few of the directors I deeply care about or respect are Hollywood directors. Hollywood's just a machine, like the Wizard of Oz, cranking it out. It's not this work that touches me, but Wim Wenders and the people in Wenders' crew of a few people—who make movies a million times more powerful to me than anything Twentieth Century–Fox put out this year—that does. That's what I care about. I've been to Wenders' company, Road Movies, in Berlin, and it's basically a desk—at least when I was there five years ago. It was in a shambled, raggedy two-story house and there was a desk in one corner and on the other side there was a playpen, and that was it. There are a lot of people in Los Angeles who are like that, but when you're in the belly of the beast, people are afraid to talk like that. There are an awful lot of people who want to make movies and television, but even though I'm forty and most of my contemporaries are pre-video and tend to look down on shooting in video, I'd just as soon shoot in video. People say video can't do what film can, but film can't do what video can.

JAMES MONACO

Author; journalist; president of Baseline, Inc. (provides advanced video-text communications and information services; deals in electronic publishing), president of New York Zoetrope, Inc. (a book publishing company)

Books:

The New Wave (Oxford University Press, 1976)
How to Read a Film (Oxford University Press, 1977, 1981)
Celebrity (Delta Books, 1978)
Media Culture (Delta Books, 1978)
Alain Resnais (Oxford University Press, 1979)
American Film Now: The People, the Power, the Money, the Movies (Oxford University Press, 1979, 1984)
Who's Who in American Film Now (New York Zoetrope, Inc., 1981)
The Connoisseur's Guide to the Movies (Facts on File, 1985)

Journalism, criticism, fiction:

The New York Times, The Village Voice, American Film, The Christian Science Monitor, More, Cinéaste, Take One

The thing you want to do if you're taking one film to a desert island is to pick the film that's going to be the most useful to you. Probably the first thought is to take some kind of compilation film you've made up of all your favorite scenes. That's if you're prepared for this disaster. Then you'd have a whole film history right there in one can. Somebody should do that for the video cassette market anyway. You'd need an anthology, because if you were taking one book to a desert island that's what you would do. There's something really great about those literary anthologies because everything's there: You can read a little Alexander Pope, a little Ernest Hemingway. But that doesn't exist on film yet, and anyway, that's cheating on this desert island. There is a critic, named Richard T. Jameson, who has to get credit. He ran a little magazine in the seventies called *Movietone News*. Every year he would do a thing called "Moments Out of Time." He would make an enormous list of all the great moments from all the movies he had seen that year: A look, a piece of dialogue, a shot, a cut, a *mise en scène*, a movement, a song, and he's absolutely right. That's what movies are all about —those little moments. The more moments a movie's got, the better the movie is. You could probably almost computerize it, assign values to those moments. There's a score of moments I can think of: There's a look Robert Redford gives to Gene Hackman in *Downhill Racer* when he's in the hospital that's terrific; there's a film John Wayne made with Don Siegel near the end of his life, *The Shootist*, which is really about Wayne, where they start off with a bunch of clips from Wayne's early Westerns. The list just goes on and on.

But if you have to pick a single movie with the most hooks, the most resonances, the most moments, then the best all-around movie that you could take to a desert island is, believe it or not, *A Funny Thing Happened on the Way to the Forum*. It has a reputation for being a bad musical for some reason that I've never understood. It's a superb musical. First of all, it's got Stephen Sondheim's music; the lyrics are the wittiest this side of current Sondheim, and I believe Leonard Bernstein worked on it too. It's based on a play by Plautus, of course, so it's classic farce, real classic farce with a capital C—Latin and it's also contemporary. Richard Lester used not only Zero Mostel, but Buster Keaton, Phil Silvers—a particular favorite of mine— Jack Gilford, and Michael Hordern—another favorite of mine, a British actor who always worked for Lester and is now Sir Michael Hordern. It's got a nice ingenue, Annette Andre. I don't think she ever did another movie, but she's pretty enough to look at. It's also got great settings.

Because it's Richard Lester, it's also very evocative of the mid-sixties and the Beatles and the rock videos that came after that. It's got a very lively style. It was criticized for being too cinematic, for being Richard Lester's kind of jazzy, mid-sixties style, for being like a rock video. They start a song in front of the house and the next thing you know, the four of them are dancing in a long shot on top of the aqueduct, and then two of them are on the roof and two of them are downstairs.

I don't think people really looked at it. The more I think about it, the more sure I am that anybody who criticizes it just hasn't seen it. It's really a great movie. And you can just listen to it. In fact, I've done this. You can compare the soundtracks of the movie and the Broadway show, which I saw, and see that Lester did the music better. The songs he did faster are better faster, and the songs done slower are better slower, and those he left out are better left out. It's just a better musical production all around. Of course, it's a musical and it has to be a musical that you take with you. I don't know what the rules of the game are, but I assume you're not allowed to take a record collection as well. You have to make this do for everything: It connects you back to the past with a farce; it connects you to the heart of the twentieth century with Buster Keaton through Phil Silvers to Michael Hordern—great comedians. And Michael Crawford, a young guy, is brilliant in it. He hasn't done much since, but that was one great role. *Forum* connects you to something that was important for the people of my age, which is Richard Lester and the Beatles—it's got resonances there. It's got brilliant dialogue: I've seen it ten, twenty times and I'm still discovering little things. It's got a little Joycean touch because it's Sondheim. There is a little word play that you don't get right away. So you've got this depth of dialogue you could probably get from Godard too, but I can only take one movie and this movie is going to remind me of Godard. It's going to remind me of Fellini, of Buster Keaton, of Plautus and Latin comedy, of the Beatles and Richard Lester, of musicals and of Broadway and adaptations. It's going to give me an awful lot to think about, and I'm still going to be enjoying the songs for another twenty years just as I have for the past twenty. So I know I'm not going to get tired of the songs.

As for structure, who did structure better than Roman farce? *Forum* has magnificent structure: They've got all of these doors and they go in and out of them just like it tells you in the textbooks that you have to do in farce. It's also acrobatic; there's dance there—so you're watching something that's visually interesting. It's also an outdoor film. An awful lot of it was shot outdoors in Spain, so there's some scenery to look at. And it's got to be color. Anyone who takes a black and white movie is either color-blind or crazy. Remember, this has got to be the all-purpose movie, the one I can live with for the rest of my life.

I also love *2001*—that's a monumental movie. It's certainly a masterpiece. John Lennon said he thought *2001* should be played continuously in a temple where people could go and visit it, and I think he's absolutely right, but I don't want to live with that. It's got some good music, but not enough laughs. By the way, this must be a comedy as well as a musical that you take with you, because life is too short and art is too long, also because of the Norman Cousins factor [Cousins cured himself of a degenerative disease by taking megadoses of vitamin C and continually running films of great comedians. He laughed his way back to health.] So I'm not only taking a movie; I'm taking penicillin.

Film is so much else, so evocative and resonant. There are probably better movies, by other criteria, than *Forum*, but I can't think of one that's got more hooks in it. You're talking to somebody who spent the last year and a half worrying about this very topic. I wrote a book, *The Connoisseur's Guide to the Movies*, that included 1,450 movies, and on every one I had to decide "Should this be in the book or not?" "Is this really worthwhile?" The introduction was based on Truffaut: He used to tell *The New Yorker* how many films he'd seen since he was last in New York, and by the end, it was probably about 12,000. The idea of the *Connoisseur's Guide* was to make your life a little easier than Truffaut's. We're all overwhelmed with a wealth of culture. Life is too short. The book is a gimmick; it's got ten symbols like the *Michelin Guide:* "Masterpiece," "Minor Master-piece," "Landmark in Film History," "Classic Film," "Personal Favorite," "Overlooked and Underrated," "Overrated," "Rec-ommended for Kids." That's another thing—if I get a spouse on this island, then we're going to have kids, so I want a film that's good for the kids too, and *Forum* is good for the kids. Other categories in the book are "Outstanding Music or Sound-track," and "Comedy: Good for Your Health." The 1,450 mov-ies boiled down to forty masterpieces. Sure it's tongue-in-cheek, but that's what I came up with. So I looked over this list: *The Big Sleep*—sure that's great, but if that's the only one? You have to do this negatively. You have to make a list of your top 1,500 favorites and then stare at each title and say, "That's the only one I'm taking with me. Can I live with it?" In many cases you're going to say, *"North by Northwest*—that's one I love, but not every day. *Modern Times*? Well, I don't want to see that again so soon." *The Sorrow and the Pity* is on the list too.That is a masterpiece, but I'm not taking it. *Potemkin,* no thanks. More recent films on the list are *Reds*—terrific—and *The Tree of Wooden Clogs,* a mag-nificent movie. But in the last couple of years, I don't know, none of the big blockbusters.

I wrote *American Film Now* in 1979 and then in 1984 we wanted to put out a second edition, so we read through it. All we had to add were two short chapters. Other people might disagree, but we tried to come up with important filmmakers in the last five years and the candidates were John Carpenter, John Sayles, and today I would say John Hughes. I guess you have to be named "John." Hughes is the most interesting of those three and Sayles is sort of interesting; I don't have much interest now in Carpenter. And who else? You're still talking about the same people as star filmmakers as five years ago: Coppola, Scorsese, Spielberg, and Lucas. I guess people don't talk about Peter Bog-danovich so much anymore. He's been replaced by other Bog-danoviches. They're talking about Jim Jarmusch because there's nothing around. He was around five years ago. My list was limited to the Hollywood orbit anyway. If you get into indepen-dent stuff it's much more complicated. In 1979, one of the things that excited me was the potential of video, because you can then make movies that appeal to much narrower audiences.

You don't have to appeal to the mass market all the time with *Star Wars VIII*. You can do regional films. In the late seventies, regional films from Boston, Seattle, Atlanta, were very interesting. There's still an occasional movie that comes up that way. Some guy gets an N.E.H. grant and a little money from Public Broadcasting and puts together something really local. But that promise hasn't really been fulfilled yet. I guess that's because there's so much wealth of film material that can be used on video cassette that it's probably going to be another three or four years before they start having to be more creative and productive in terms of the cassettes themselves. They're just recycling all the back lists and the front lists and making money hand over fist, so the industry has to shake out first before people start producing especially for cassette or developing specialty interests and specialty distribution companies.

Nothing significant has happened over the past five years, even in terms of the business. Conglomerates get bought and sold. Marvin Davis moves in and out, but who cares? I guess we didn't know five years ago that Coca-Cola would buy up the entire film industry. The only thing really new is pop video, but the problem is they would be great if there was some good music on them.

I think the role of the movie critic is to turn people on, like a teacher, but they think their job is consumer reports: "Stay away from this one. See this one." I guess that's a function for people. But I don't think they should bother to write about uninteresting movies; just write about the interesting ones. The less you know, and the more they find for you, the more valuable they are. I don't need them to tell me that a movie everybody else is writing about is an interesting movie, because I'm overwhelmed with information. I want to read someone who's found this little film I've never heard of. That's the really valuable information for me. The other thing a critic should do is entertain. The French know this. Criticism is just an excuse for writing an essay that should be entertaining. It has nothing to do with the subject. The French do that very well. The Americans don't know that. They think they have to say something about the subject. Renata Adler was very interesting as a critic because often she would review the movie house, not the movie, or she would go out and watch industrial or commercial movies, or she would review film product that wasn't feature film, which is really important.

Watching films at home doesn't usually disturb me, but it disturbed me greatly watching *Forum* because the filmmakers used the screen so well that you couldn't see anything on TV. *Forum* is wide-screen and TV just shows the middle, so you miss half the movie. It's like a test of how well the filmmaker used the screen, but video people will eventually bring them out so you get the full screen. Aside from that, I think the advantages greatly outweigh the disadvantages. Critics tend to forget that they're the only ones in the country who see the films in focus in the theater. For most people, the television set has better resolution than they get in their local theater. Most people have living rooms that are larger than most triplex theaters, and it's not necessarily true that the audience will be larger in the theater than it is in your home. Plus, you've got more control over it; that's really important to me. You can turn it off; you can watch it again. Video discs are even a whole step forward from that because you can do so much with video discs. You can go back to an exact frame; you can run it slowly—it's a whole experience. It's just the power to the viewer. Bob Stein is on top of this; he really knows what the future is. He's important. You still want to go out and have an overwhelming experience with an audience and a huge screen. That's Trumbull's Showscan, and I think that will develop in terms of spectacle. That's important, too, but I can go to the store and pick up six movies tonight. The availability is so much greater, and, frankly, the majority of the movies I see now are on tape. Partly that's because I have kids and a lot of people have children. For them to go to a movie is fifty bucks. Forget it; once a year you do that.

It's specious to make differentiations—who cares if it's a film or a tape? Most people can't tell the difference anyway. I don't think the language is going to change that much. I think it's going to settle down. Look what happened with the novel and most other arts. You get to the point of total abstraction, total experimentation, and it's a dead end. That was the past. Now you shouldn't care that much. I think you want to focus more on people, on humanistic concerns—stories and people.

Less of the artsy-fartsy thing because that's been done already. I would say if you had to pick a model for the future, it's a poet like Godard. The man is fifty-five years of age, but we won't tell. He's a real poet and he has a wonderful sense of humor.

On the subject of movies for a desert island, my final words are "Tragedy tomorrow, comedy tonight!"

PAUL MORRISSEY

Screenwriter; film director; photographer; producer

Filmography:

1963	*Taylor Mead Dances*
1964	*Civilization and Its Discontents*
1965	*Space* (with Andy Warhol)
1966	*The Chelsea Girls* (with Andy Warhol)
	More Milk Evette (with Andy Warhol)
	**** (Four Stars) (with Andy Warhol)
1967	*I, a Man* (with Andy Warhol)
	Nude Restaurant (with Andy Warhol)
1968	*The Loves of Ondine* (with Andy Warhol)
	Lonesome Cowboys (photographer, editor, exec. producer only)
	Bike Boy
	San Diego Surf
1969	*Flesh* (also wrote and photographed)
	Blue Movie/Fuck (exec. producer only)
1970	*Trash* (also wrote and photographed)
1971	*Heat* (also wrote and photographed)
	L'Amour (codirected and coscripted; exec. producer)
1972	*Women in Revolt* (also wrote)
1973	*Andy Warhol's Frankenstein/Flesh for Frankenstein* (also scripted)
	Andy Warhol's Dracula/Blood for Dracula (also scripted)
1977	*The Hound of the Baskervilles* (also cowrote)
1979	*Madame Wang's* (also wrote)
1981	*Forty Deuce*
1983	*Mixed Blood* (also wrote)
1985	*Beethoven's Nephew* (also cowrote)

When I was in school, I saw a film over and over again; it was my favorite film. I always felt it was the best film ever made, and I still do: *Richard III* by Laurence Olivier. I don't think there could be any question that it is the best film. It's the best script ever done, the best play Shakespeare ever wrote. The movie is fantastic: It has the greatest actors of the twentieth century; it's filled with wonderful performances. It's a three-hour film that I've seen over and over and could still see. It has the best direction, music, actors, photography.

The thing I caught onto then, which I still totally believe in now, is that what makes a good or great film is great dialogue and great actors. Characters are dialogue. Characters who go around without speaking are really not too much of a character, except for Clint Eastwood and Charles Bronson, who might be exceptions that prove the rule. But basically, characters only exist in dialogue; and to be good, movies need good dialogue. *Richard III* has the best dialogue.

I liked all the English films of the late forties, early fifties. They made the best films then. Hollywood had already made its great films; and after the middle to the late fifties, the Italians started to make the best films for about fifteen, twenty years; and for the past ten or so years, I don't think anybody has done too much of anything. There might have been a couple of good films from the French, but they're not on the level of the English, Americans, and the Italians.

Other than that, in Hollywood terms, the best movie is *Gone with the Wind,* and of the American films of the fifties, definitely *On the Waterfront.*

I've always avoided creating characters that are black and white. All my characters are of two natures: The more terrible things they do, the more likable they become, I hope. I must have inherited that from my liking of *Richard III.* I've always felt a character can't be all good or bad, and I've never had one in a movie that is. It's something so ingrained in my psychology that sometimes I see a good actor in a part and I say, "That poor actor, what a horrible part. He had to play a goody-goody." Or he had to play an awful pig, a degenerate slob without any nice qualities. The tradition of writers of the nineteenth century, when all the best writing was done, created characters with more than one nature. I think Rita La Punta in *Mixed Blood* is not so far away from Richard III. That type of character gives the really good actor something to play and captures the audience's imagination, without giving it all so easily. You have to think twice about who they might be. Some people make these foolish remarks that I don't have likable characters, but all I'm interested in is likable characters.

Andy Warhol and I became associated because I was doing some little experiments at the time Andy was doing some experiments. He had more equipment and we saw each other's things at the Cinemateque, a sort of fly-by-night operation thought up by Jonas Mekas, which was a very cute, useful thing. I'm surprised in this day and age, when there are eight million people running around in film schools and trying to make films, that nothing like it exists now. This was twenty years ago. Mekas kept an open house and said, "Bring in your films and I'll show them to the people, whoever comes." Everybody was curious to see what the other people were doing, and it was written about in his *Village Voice* column. Without him doing that, I don't think Andy would have made his experiments and I don't know whether I would have made any. My experiments weren't really experiments, but simple old-fashioned silent narratives. I've never believed in any kind of experimental anything.

Andy was the first one in that period and the only one to buy a sound camera, like a newsreel camera. His films would certainly qualify as experiments, but they were experiments not in anybody's remote sense of avant-garde; they were experiments in retrogression, back to Edison's simple, uncut, "Isn't it wonderful, somebody's moving in front of the camera, looking at somebody else and eating a cup of soup or something." He simply went back to the most elementary beginnings of film and then when he bought the sound camera, he tried to do something that had been missing. When films began, they were extremely primitive and simple: People looked at one another, or they kissed, or they turned their heads, or got up and walked across the room. That was always silent, but by the time the sound picture came in in the thirties, people had advanced in cutting, and so on. But Andy took the sound film and put it back in 1895, 1900, and said, "Wouldn't it be remarkable—" I don't think he *said* this—but it was as if in theory film was just beginning in 1895 and it had sound; this may be what it would look like. But the basic premise that motivated him came from the art world—the idea that modern art is something that the artist *doesn't* do. The tradition is that art is a personal experience transmuted into something called "art." If that's what traditional art did, then in modern art, the artist has nothing of himself recognizable in the work. The work would exist all by itself. So Andy was trying to subtract the efforts of the film director from the film. That was all Edison could do at the time because things were very different.

It's a kind of a complicated, peculiar way of thinking, but it's very interesting because what it did was put this enormous emphasis on characterization, and characterization became the thing that would make one of these experiments work or not. If it was an interesting character in an interesting situation and the character could make the audience like him without any directorial anything—not one cut, not one change of angle— then it was interesting. And it brought film back to where the novel began, the epistolary novel (heaven knows where the theater began): the idea that communication of a character is worth paying attention to; it doesn't have to be in a dramatic narrative. A very good letter from a wonderful person is worth reading and a person in front of a camera talking with the camera or with some other person is worth watching if they're good characters. In my mind I see the whole experiment connected with the good Shakespearean plays and with *Gone with the Wind*. *Gone with the Wind* is a great movie because it has that extraordinary character at the center of it, Scarlett O'Hara, and that wonderful performance by the actress that makes it come to life. In every way, for a man the great role is Richard III and for a woman it's Scarlett O'Hara. When someone tells me that someone in a movie is a great actress, I ask, "Is she as good as Vivien Leigh as Scarlett O'Hara?" I compare everything to those two roles.

With a great artist you can't tell whether they are acting or whether they are identical to the character. Joe Dallesandro had a wonderful quality or presence within his range, which was a type of range similar to a person like Charles Bronson. Dallesandro would project strength and a kind of intelligence in his face that you wouldn't find if he verbalized a lot. This was a quality I used a lot with other people who would verbalize, like Holly Woodlawn or Sylvia Miles. I always contrasted those quiet and verbal types. With a great actor or actress, there isn't a distinction between the actor and the character. Vivien Leigh wasn't Scarlett O'Hara, but in the public's mind she always will be. There is only one actress other than Marilia Pera who is remotely great in my mind, and that is Vanessa Redgrave. Like Redgrave, Marilia Pera's whole life has been in the theater, as well as that of her parents and grandparents. When she goes in front of a camera, she is such a great actress that you think she's a person off the street who doesn't even know the camera is there. Her technique is so extraordinary, but it was never so incredible as it was in *Pixote,* where even I was fooled. I couldn't believe she was an actress. That was one of the finest performances in the history of the screen. She improvised all that.

I find the professional actors and actresses today uninteresting. I think some of the older people like Clint Eastwood, Charles Bronson, even Paul Newman are interesting—all the people who come from the fifties, when they hung onto the idea of what a movie star is. That notion has all been lost now. It seemed recently to come back for a few years with people like Brooke Shields and Matt Dillon and these really young kids who have put fresh personalities in front of the camera and who have the benefit of not remembering all this acting class garbage that stunk up the screen in the past twenty years. But Brooke Shields doesn't get the opportunity to work anymore, because they don't want beautiful girls who are twenty-one or two, intelligent, nice, and with whom they don't know what to do dramatically. I find most of the big successes of recent years are people out of the New York acting class syndrome who take themselves deadly serious, who scream and holler, who pant and whine, who are neurotic, and, who don't give me ten seconds of recognizable reality. All I see is acting class effort. It's deadening, and people are staying away from movies more. It's critics who've invented these people and said that they're great actors, and yet there's no audience affection for them, as there certainly is for Clint Eastwood. As for women, there's Jane Fonda, but she's almost fifty. She has a certain dignity and class and doesn't suggest the New York acting school.

Great human personalities exist in every corner of the globe during every second of life on the planet. I think that journalists who don't know very much have encouraged a kind of stupid, forced, phony, artificial acting. They have bought the sincerity effort thing and totally underrate the natural personalities who are sometimes no different off than on screen—like Robert Mitchum, who makes life more interesting just seeing him in a movie. People like him are not posing, are not thinking of their character. They're reacting the way they would because they're artists. To me those other people are boring and belong in a second or third or fourth part at best. But even if you look at *Gone with the Wind*, everybody in the third or fourth part is almost a genius. There's a quality of acting that went out— where you had to begin as a personality in your own right and you weren't finding people who were copies of others. Now everybody is just like everybody else and it's intentionally so. In real life, if you bother to open your eyes, you find people with their own distinct personalities.

Basically movies are no different from theater or video. There's nothing all that different about cinema. All that is garbage from critics. It's not different. Dramatic fiction is dramatic fiction, whether it's on paper, on film, or on television. Even television talk shows and news programs are in a sense dramatic, because they involve the human personality in a kind of posed, unreal way. All those media depend upon interesting human personality; and if a film cuts angles and goes outdoors with beautiful photography, it's still not that different. Every once in a while you read some critic saying someone has found a new film form. That's garbage because films are the same now as they ever were. A good book or movie is good because you like the characters. If I go to a movie and say I didn't like anybody in the movie as a character, I can't like the movie, even if the story is not offensive. Even in a well-made movie if the characters don't catch your fantasy as real people, I feel there is no point in having wasted the time. So it doesn't matter to me whether my films are viewed on video, because I think they depend on characterizaton and characterization comes across on video as much as it does on film and as much as it does in theater. To me it's all the same: theater, film, video, books— fiction. Is it worth paying attention to? Is it worth reading? Is it worth watching? And what makes it worth watching? Interesting character. You start from that.

I think in terms of the characters first and then I think of a story to go with the characters. In many cases I have an actor in mind when I write. Most of the people I cast have sort of theatrical personalities that blossom in front of a camera.

ROBERT MUGGE

Filmmaker; producer

Filmography:

1976   *Frostburg*
1977   *George Crumb: Voice of the Whale*
1978   *Amateur Night at City Hall*
1980   *Sun Ra: A Joyful Noise*
1983   *Cool Runnings: The Reggae Movie*
        Black Wax (portrait of Gil Scott-Heron)
1984   *The Gospel According to Al Green*
1985   *The Return of Ruben Blades*

It's a valid question, but I'm not sure my answer could be limited to one film. I couldn't even pick my favorite Fassbinder film or my favorite Godard film, because with both of them I see every one of their films as contributing to a larger vision, whereas there are some other artists in film and other fields who have made one great film or who have written one great book and you remember them for that. Maybe because of the auteur theory having come about, so many filmmakers seem to care more about creating a body of work than they do about making one great film. You almost have to wonder these days about how many great films there are. Back in the days when I was going to film school, late sixties, early seventies, you could say, "Okay, here's your *Citizen Kane,* your *Battleship Potemkin, Seven Samurai* or any number of films by Kurosawa." But as you see more and more films and you make films, you start to find smaller pleasures in the details of lots of different films, and, of course, that leads to the whole French film critic thing of raising very minor directors to the level almost of those great directors of whom they've grown tired. And so I almost might tend to do that because I've seen *Citizen Kane* so many times. I'd probably, as so many people do now, pick a different Orson Welles film as my favorite. Or I'd probably be more likely to pick a Sam Fuller film or a Nicholas Ray film as one that would give me pleasure in seeing repeatedly.

Because I make music documentaries, one of the biggest influences on me is almost a heretical notion, but it's Ken Russell. I love his BBC music biographies, some of which started out to be documentaries, but he was at the BBC pushing the edges, bringing more and more fiction material into them, being audacious both in the crossing over of styles and genres and also in bringing fiction together with documentary. Unfortunately, he got used to shocking people and he began to shock people in silly ways, but some of his really influential films for me were his *Dante's Inferno,* about Dante Gabriel Rossetti, *Isadora Duncan,* and *Song of Summer,* about Frederick Delius. And then I followed him into his early feature films to the point where I got to a film like *The Music Lovers,* which a lot of people put down. I loved the film despite its having by some standards some tasteless moments. I found in that film and in some of the other films he made at that time, a real richness of expression, a simultaneous romanticism, and a criticism of romanticism implicit in the material. I just found enough things directorially going on that I was able to watch the film twenty-five times and still enjoy it. So if I say the film I would take to a desert sland with me is *The Music Lovers,* on the surface it sounds like an abominable bit of taste on my part; but in terms of music-related filmmaking, that was a very important, informative film for me, and so it would certainly be one of the films I would take.

In fact when you go with this whole idea of a film on a desert island notion, your choices tend to be almost more emotional than they are intellectual. One of the interesting things that happens is no matter how much we study film, no matter how much we think about it, analyze it, and all that, there are always films that we like for emotional reasons, that we feel passionate about, and we don't know quite what it is.

The notion of intellectual reasons versus emotional ones is interesting. With Kurosawa, I would pick maybe a film like *High and Low* for purely intellectual reasons, because I love the sense of formal composition, the sense of a very logical mystery at work, and the logic of plot. I especially love the stylistic use of the black and white film that suddenly has this dab of color, right in the middle, and then the whole style changes after that. Intellectually, I love that. But to take a film to a desert island, I'd probably take *Red Beard,* which is a wonderful, emotional, humanistic experience. If I were to take the best Godard film, intellectually, I'd probably take *Numéro Deux,* but emotionally, I'd probably take something a lot easier, maybe *Breathless* or *Two or Three Things I Know About Her.* If I were picking one film in terms of greatness, and, again, it's totally subjective, God! Even that is tough.

I think the combinaton of motion and idea and music in film gives it some of its most overwhelming moments, even in films where you don't think about it. What would *Kane* be without Bernard Herrmann's score? It'd still be a fascinating film, but it would not have that immediate emotional impact. Nor would many of the Hitchcock films without Herrmann's scores.

My cameraman's father is a well-known writer, James McConkey, and he usually thinks of the most important art films as being those without any music. He comes out of a kind of neorealistic film tradition. I think those were the kind of films that were big when he was in college, and the American films that were connected with that—Cassavetes and all that. But Larry McConkey, his son, and I both look for creative use of music with image. We both studied with Slavko Vorkapich, who was responsible for many of the finest montage sequences in the Hollywood films of the thirties, films like *Mr. Smith Goes to Washington.* All of a sudden, the plot stops and all these pictures go by, time passes, there's an earthquake, and so on. He made all those sequences. He had a theory of cinema that was this real intense picture, motion, sound, and music all together—that was pure cinema. He used to give lectures illustrated with film clips at the American Film Institute in which he'd take these excerpts from films and show you the lyrical heights that film could reach with the combination of picture, motion within picture, camera angles, shot changes, music, and sound. That was very influential for both Larry and me. Like Jean-Pierre Gorin said about Godard, in every one of his films there's this one ten-minute section that he really cares about. All the rest is almost a kind of filler to get people to come to the theater to see the ten minutes he really cares about, as in the first ten minutes of *Contempt.*

I have moments in my films too. There's a moment in the Ruben Blades film where Ruben reads lyrics to a song by a Peruvian composer, a song that means everyone returns. I have a series of shots, almost dreamlike, of Panama, that go over that. And, for me, what I see and hear, the rhythmic, almost musical sounds of his voice reading the lyrics, the meaning of what he is saying, the nostalgic look back along with these dreamlike pictures is a moment of visual and aural poetry. That's one of the reasons I work with music, because there are a lot of opportunities to play with those things.

Most of my films are not entirely performance; they're what I call portrait films. What I usually do is pick an artist I really care about and find ways, whatever ways I think are pertinent, to project what it is I think is important about that artist's work —the old dialectic between art and life and the intercutting between them. That is pretty obvious, but there's some less obvious ways to do that. In *Black Wax* with Gil Scott-Heron, what I did was have him play his music at a place called the Wax Museum, which is a club that until recently existed in Washington. It had been built out of a former wax museum, and, in the back room, they had all these life-size figures covered in dust of past presidents and historical figures, including black historical figures. We built a fantasy set in which he walked through, and, of course, we had him walking through the streets of Washington singing the song "Washington, D.C.," along with a ghetto blaster that had the backup tracks on it. That was a way of communicating some complex social and political ideas, which most of my films try to do, while also presenting his art, his ideas.

Ken Russell, whatever he may have done in his later films

—flipping out in certain ways—was making films that were about music and art and culture but also were often saying things about related issues in society. In fact, I now organize all of these music films of mine into a larger grouping that I call "Vox Americana," different voices, not just from this country but from the continent, this hemisphere—people talking, usually eccentric, fascinating people who are sort of on the periphery of what's considered commercially important in music, but who are right in the center of what's important musically in the larger picture, music that will last when all the stuff that's making millions now fades.

I've also written half a dozen fiction screenplays. Twice I've gotten halfway toward raising the money for the budget and then ended up in near starvation with things falling through. In 1975, Ford closed all the tax loopholes for film and that killed me halfway there. All our investors dropped out. Under Jimmy Carter, the interest rates got so high, all our investors dropped out and put their money in money-market funds.

But this has become comfortable because there have been people like Britain's Channel 4 who are willing to fund me to do the sort of film that I can do very cheaply, between $100,000 and $150,000. But, yes, I want to do fiction films and part of the progress toward that is promoting these music films.

[Robert Mugge evidently gave this question further and considered thought, as the following excerpt from a letter he sent me will illustrate.]

I've thought more about this "desert island" idea, and I think that the only way I could deal with it would be to make a compilaton film out of sections from a *number* of my favorite movies. Included would be scenes from Max Ophüls' *Letter from an Unknown Woman*, Sam Fuller's *Pickup on South Street*, Fellini's *Amarcord*, Ernst Lubitsch's *Heaven Can Wait*, Welles' *Citizen Kane*, Ken Russell's *The Music Lovers*, Kurosawa's *Seven Samurai*, Bergman's *The Seventh Seal*, and Truffaut's *Jules and Jim*. And if there were still a bit more room on the reel, I'd stick on all of Chuck Jones' *What's Opera, Doc?* as well. I suppose I'm attracted to each of these films for essentially the same reasons: (1) each is beautifully crafted; (2) each provides an intense emotional experience while also stimulating the intellect; (3) each displays a romantic, even bittersweet view of life; and (4) each uses music brilliantly. Not that I think these are necessarily the qualities that make a film "great"; they are simply the qualities which so endear the film to me that it becomes almost a part of my flesh. Take these movies to a desert island? I take them everywhere I go.

DAVID NEWMAN

Screenwriter, film director

Filmography (as writer only, unless otherwise noted):

1967   *Bonnie and Clyde* (cowrote with Robert Benton)

1969   *There Was a Crooked Man* (cowrote with Robert Benton)

1971   *What's Up Doc?* (cowrote with Robert Benton and Buck Henry)
          Bad Company (cowrote with Robert Benton)
          Oh! Calcutta! (Newman, Benton, and others)

1975   *The Crazy American Girl* (cowrote with Leslie Newman; directed)

1978   *Superman I: The Movie* (cowrote with Leslie Newman and Robert Benton)
          Superman II (cowrote with Leslie Newman)

1981   *Jinxed* (cowrote with Burt Blessing)
          Still of the Night (story by David Newman and Robert Benton, screenplay by David Newman)

1985   *Santa Claus: The Movie* (story by David and Leslie Newman, screenplay by David Newman)

I would take *Rio Bravo*—no hesitation—it's almost a religion. I've seen it forty-two times; I've studied it on a moviola frame by frame, getting to look at things running backwards, starting and stopping. I've learned a lot from it, but now it's like an obsession or passion, it's long past learning; I just love that movie. It comforts me. It's everything I think a movie ought to be, and I like the movies better than anything in the world anyway. It's by Howard Hawks; it stars John Wayne, Dean Martin, Ricky Nelson, Walter Brennan, and Angie Dickinson in her first leading role. Everything I love about Hawks, I love best in that film. First of all, there are all those classic Hawksian themes about doing your job right, men at work, and what happens when a woman walks into that private world, and that whole chemistry between men and women that Hawks has done time and time again so wonderfully in *The Big Sleep* and *To Have and Have Not*. It's better in this movie than it's ever been. The relationship between John T. Chance and Feathers is, I think, one of the great love stories of our time, and the movie is about that incredible creation of an artificial family, which is a subject that has always interested me since *Bonnie and Clyde*. The people you work with and strive toward some goal with become your real family, and within that family there are ups and downs. People fall off the deep end and you have to save them, and there are times you have to be selfish. In that movie, I just love the family; I love the situation: the whole relationship between John Wayne and Dean Martin, having to do with giving. Martin is a drunk when the film opens; he had formerly been top gun. He's become an object of derision and has to be put back on his feet, so there's this kind of inspiring aspect to it. The relationships between Walter Brennan and Wayne, and Brennan and everybody else, are some of the great delicious relationships, involving a kind of cantankerous, curmudgeonly old grandpa with a wicked sense of humor. The plot is intriguing enough that Hawks remade the film twice, using basically the same plot in *Rio Lobo* and *El Dorado*. It's common knowledge that they're all versions of that story: They all have John Wayne in them; they all have to do with a prisoner held by John Wayne and the bad guy coming and saying, "We want him in exchange for something else." It's the same story about people who have to hole up and defend a little parcel of territory and draw upon each other in order to do it. And it's all the same characters: The Ricky Nelson character in *Rio Bravo* is called Montana. The same kind of role played by James Caan in *El Dorado* is called

Dakota—the young, brash kid who thinks he's as good as the big boys and he's not, but he's going to learn and is taken in in a kind of avuncular relationship with Wayne. All the dynamics of father to son, to grandfather, to brother, to wife—they're all there in *Rio Bravo*. Plus, there's a lot of joy in it, a lot of warmth. It stops dead three times—I don't mean pejoratively—for music entertainment. There's a scene where Ricky Nelson gets out his guitar and sings "Cindy" and everybody dances. There's a scene where Walter Brennan plays a harmonica, and a scene where Dean Martin sings a dreadful song that I rather like called "My Rifle, My Pony, and Me." For years I searched for a copy of the record and finally found it. There's a kind of classical element to the film in terms of this force from the outside that's constantly threatening—it's got mythic elements. It's a great film and it's a film that I don't even look at now as a movie but as part of my life. If I'm depressed or down, thanks to the invention of VCRs, I can put *Rio Bravo* up and feel better two hours later.

I made a list of ten or eleven films, all of which are almost equally important to me—films I can't do without, the way you can't do without your favorite book. It's always hard because there are certain directors like John Ford—which one of his films do you take? Finally, it becomes personal. I know *The Searchers* is the classic, but if I could have one Ford film, for me it would be *The Man Who Shot Liberty Valance*. The Hitchcock was really tough, but my choice is almost a sentimental one—*Strangers on a Train*, because it's the movie that got me into movies. It changed my life. I saw it when I was a kid. Up till then I used to go to movies all the time, but after seeing *Strangers on a Train* I couldn't talk for three hours. I realized that this was something I had to get involved in and it made me understand what could be done with cinema, with motion pictures. It still has this almost visceral, atavistic effect on me, because it's my first movie movie. It's just as Resnais said of *Rules of the Game*. Although there are Hitchcock films more brilliant and wonderful, *Strangers on a Train* is *my* Hitchcock movie. I hate to say something awful like it showed me movies are an art form because I don't like to think of them as that only, and, at the time —I was a kid—I still didn't think of them that way. But I had an emotional, visceral, aesthetic experience with that movie that I never had before, except when I saw *Pinocchio* when I was three years old and went running down the aisle screaming. I was trying to get the character off the screen because I knew Pinnochio was going with the bad guy and his father told him not to. I guess that's when I was destined to become a movie person. The next one is one that means almost as much to me as *Rio Bravo,* Godard's *Pierrot le Fou.* Again, all of Godard's films are hard for me to choose from because I love Godard's work with a sort of passion that to certain people defies sensibility. But *Pierrot* is one of the great films of all time, and it acts on me every time I see it again, and I always see something more. I think it's profound and great, and I love that film a lot. Fellini's *8½* is a movie I can't do without for all the reasons everybody has. I don't know whether it's fair to say that this is a movie, but I love *Berlin Alexanderplatz,* of all the Fassbinder films. I love Fassbinder a lot and I think I know almost every Fassbinder film, which is saying a lot since he made so many, but *Berlin Alexanderplatz* is having an effect on me that I don't understand because I've seen it now three times. I don't even know why. I just know that it's an extraordinary piece of work. I'm not even sure it's a movie. It's not television; it's not a movie; it's not a novel—I don't know what it is. I think it's something new and extraordinary. And I don't think it's like the other Fassbinder films either. If I had to take one that was the length of a normal movie, it would be one of the obscure ones, *Chinese Roulette.* Ermanno Olmi is a director that I love; one of his early films was called *The Fiancés,* and I just love that movie a lot. The Renoir film I picked—because there would have to be a Renoir film on any list of ten—is not *Rules of the Game* or *Grand Illusion;* it's a film called *A Day in the Country,* the most loving movie I've ever seen—the humanity that is the essence of Renoir—that film is just beautiful to me. The next film is one that oddly enough sounds like the diametrical opposite but has just as much richness and humanity in it—Sam Peckinpah's *The Wild Bunch.* That movie is very important to me. Then *Seven Samurai,* next to *Rashomon,* Kurosawa's most popular film. It's the great action movie of all action movies. It had a lot of influence on my own work. Finally, a Preston Sturges film, and, again, it's hard to pick out of Sturges' films. For me, they have so many delights. The one I like the best I know is probably not the best, the perfect work of art; that is probably *Sullivan's Travels;* but the one I love the most is *Miracle of Morgan's Creek.*

But if I had to pick one for this mythical island, I know it would be *Rio Bravo* because it has so much life, and the life in it never seems to date or change for me. For a long time I did see something new in it each time I viewed it, but by now it's the familiarity. Certain phrases from that movie have become a part of my family's and my way of speaking, like "Sorry don't get it done dudes," which someone in my house ends up saying at least once a week.

For a screenwriter, having directed as well, I subscribe to the auteur theory more than almost any other screenwriter in the world. But there's no question about the fact there are certain directors, like Hawks, Hitchcock, Ford, and some others, where it is clearly their film, their work. There's such a similarity, a consistency in the body of work, even in the kind of characters, kind of story and construction, in the kind of mood they create, that I think the fact that Hawks uses Leigh Brackett as a writer so many times is further proof that it's a Hawks film. If you've ever read interviews with Hawks, it wouldn't be fair to call *Rio Bravo* anything other than Howard Hawks' film. I feel that even though I write screenplays that are very often directed by other people, there are certain movies that are mine. In any case, the director is always the boss when it comes down to the final making of the film, and if it's a director who has a certain consistency in his career, then, I think, that should be noted.

Almost never am I disturbed by what happens to my screenplays. I've had such good luck with that, starting with Arthur Penn on *Bonnie and Clyde.* I always have tried whenever possible to be as closely involved with the making of the movie as I could be. Sometimes you can't be as closely involved as you want because you're busy on the next thing or because the production is off somewhere and no one is going to pay you to hang around the set having a good time for three months. But very often I've been closely involved with the shootings. I've had a couple of bad experiences like everyone else has. In the dreadful case of *Sheena,* I wound up with four lines left in the entire film, maybe five minutes of my story, and, unfortunately, motivated by greed, I didn't take my name off it because I had points that I didn't want to lose. It turned out to be a pyrrhic victory since the film was a disaster and my points amounted to zero. The only good thing is that almost nobody saw the film and nobody knows I had anything to do with it. That was a terrible experience because there was another writer who came in afterward and, in league with the director, turned the movie into something it never was. That was the only time I ever sat in the screening room in a cold sweat. I thought, "Oh my God, what am I going to do? My name's on this thing." Otherwise I've had a lot of very, very good experiences, *Santa Claus* being the latest and maybe best example. I was present all during the making of it, and I spent a year in the preparation of it. That picture, with maybe one or two minor exceptions (one having to do with something that was cut after a sneak preview, a few little things like that) is on the screen exactly as I envisioned it, the way it was written. That's happened a lot. It happened on *Superman II* and *III*, which my wife and I wrote together.

Some films I've written alone, some in partnership with Bob Benton, some in partnership with Leslie Newman, and the films I've done with Richard Lester have been done just as written because we worked so closely with the director. For example, the opening of *Superman III* illustrates a good point about directors. The opening of that film was a series of sight gags: a Rube Goldberg device where one thing falls down and knocks down another thing that causes a lady to let go of a leash that causes a dog to run down the street that causes a blind man to trip over the dog and so on. It's a series of disasters into which walks Clark Kent, who has to become Superman. A lot of people thought this was classic Richard Lester stuff, because Richard is a great master of sight gags, one of the few left in the world, and some people assumed that he must have done that sequence. The fact is that Leslie and I conceived and wrote that sequence exactly as it was filmed; however, if Richard had not been the director of that film, we would not even have thought of it. What we wanted to do was give him what we knew he could do wonderfully. And, of course, he did it wonderfully and added lots of little touches of his own. That's why I think the director is still the director.

I don't view the relationship between screenwriter and director as an adversarial one. When I directed my own film, *The Crazy American Girl,* I found myself overruling myself all the time as the director, but never arguing with myself. It always had to do with practical matters—the fact that you couldn't move the camera the way it was written because there was a door in the way, that sort of thing. There's a screen right between my eyes, and I'm sitting at the typewriter describing the movie that's playing in my head. Then, once it becomes a real production, that initial vision is always compromised by everybody. That doesn't necessarily mean it's sullied, but it's certainly always compromised, because suddenly the director comes in and he's got creative ideas of his own; the producer comes in and he's got ideas, and so do the actors. You had imagined that a girl had red hair and walked a certain way and they cast it with this brunette actress, so suddenly it isn't the movie that was playing in your mind, but then you had a different actress who brought a different quality to it. The only pure version of any movie is the first draft written by the screenwriter. From then on, it's just a series of compromises and it's just a question of whether they're the kind that do violence to something or very often improve it.

When Bob and I wrote *Bonnie and Clyde* and it won a lot of prizes, we were hot stuff. We won two Writers Guild awards and went out to Hollywood to receive them. There was this big screening followed by an onstage question and answer period. This was 1967 and, at the time much more so than now, screenwriters were really the low men on the totem pole and labored in obscurity. Most people didn't know who wrote the movies and some still don't know what a screenwriter does. We were taking questions and a lot of people got up—sort of the older generation of screenwriters who, as I say, had been laboring in obscurity in the field for years and years and had lists of credits as long as your arm, yet no one knew who they were. They were bitter and angry people, and we were getting a lot of personal publicity then. They said, "You guys have a great opportunity to tell the world about these bastards, these directors, who ruin our fucking work." We said, "Gee, we just had a wonderful time with Arthur Penn. He's a lovely man, a great friend; he made the movie that we wanted to make and he made it even better."

And they were really annoyed with us that we wouldn't put him down. Heaven knows, I know people have had bad experiences —I've had one or two myself, but I try not to have them.

After working with Arthur Penn, Benton and I worked for a long time with Joe Mankiewicz on *There Was a Crooked Man*. Joe still is one of my mentors. That was the most wonderful learning experience in the world because Joe's background was as a screenwriter first. Just working on a script with Joe was like going to school. The set was a joy because he's such a wonderful man.

I don't believe that the talents of screenwriting and directing aren't found together in one person. Benton is a great example, and I can think of so many others. Billy Wilder started as a screenwriter, so did Mankiewicz. I would say more than half the directors whose work I really revere are sometime writers or ex-writers. I don't think that those are incompatible skills at all. I write in a lot of camera directions. Some directors don't like it when you do that. I'm incapable of not doing it. I have every closeup shot and long shot and traveling shot that's in my mind on the page, whether or not they end up in the final movie. I try to do less than I used to because I've seen scripts where you can't see the movie because there's so much jargon. That's crazy, but somebody said to me early on, "Go ahead and do it, because whether or not I use your camera directions, it lets me know what you think the movie should be and you're the writer." It's certainly true. If I had a shot of you and me sitting across a desk and we were shooting it in singles and two shots and so on and, at the moment we were talking, I suddenly indicated a tight closeup of your eyes, what I'd be trying to say was that I wanted the audience to look at you at that moment, not at me even though I was talking, because what you'd be doing was more important. The only way I can do that is by writing "closeup" in the script. The director may shoot it five different ways, but then he knows my intention of what the subtext of the scene is about. The scene isn't about my talking and your listening; the scene is you pretending to listen and thinking about something else. So I just do that and the director will use it or not. I really think that a lot of screenplay is in one way or another directing on paper.

On the film I'm working on now, the producer and I have a deal with the studio for me to write and direct; and the studio has just undergone an upheaval, as they do all the time. The executive at the studio whose project this was is no longer there, so now I'm in the hands of somebody who may or may not give this film the green light. One of the reasons he may not—since I would like to think it's a wonderful script—is that it's not his baby. That happens all the time. Bob and I, when we were partners, had at least two experiences when screenplays we had done that were really good—one of them was set to go—didn't get done because the whole studio changed hands. One of the first things the new hierarchy does is to sweep the slate clean and begin all over again, because they don't want to inherit their predecessors' stuff. Unfortunately that happens so many times to projects. They don't get put aside because they're not good, but because of stuff like that. That's the most frustrating part of this business. I know that one of the best screenplays I ever wrote was for a film that never got made, and everyone said, "This is one of the best screenplays I've ever read." The film never got made and the screenplay still gets written about. It's just a bizarre thing.

I've been asked to speak to various screenwriting classes, and they always ask, "What do you recommend I read?" I always recommend that they go to the movies and that they read published screenplays. I can't recommend in any conscience any book on how to write screenplays. They tell you what kind of margins to have and to use capital letters for the camera movements and stuff like that. The only book I've ever read that I think is useful is by James Monaco, *How to Read a Film*, because the second half of the book has all the film terms, and that tells you all you need to know as a screen-writer. If you want to know what a tracking shot means or what a dolly-in means, you look it up in Monaco's book and that will explain it to you.

When Benton and I wrote *Bonnie and Clyde*, which was the first screenplay we'd ever written, we thought we knew a lot about movies because we went to the movies constantly. We went to the Museum of Modern Art at lunchtime for three months when we were working at *Esquire* magazine because there was a Hitchcock retrospective going on. That's the great-

est way to learn the arts of screenwriting and construction. Nobody is more didactically useful than Hitchcock. Some people
are great directors from whom you can't learn a thing, like
Fellini. He's a great director, but all you can do is make a fake
Fellini. But you learn from Ford and Hitchcock, especially construction from Hitchcock. When we wrote our first screenplay,
I literally didn't know about the format, how to write certain
things down; we didn't know the technical names for things. We
didn't know what a tight two shot was as opposed to a wide shot;
we didn't know what a medium closeup was and what a closeup
was. There weren't too many screenplays published then, but
one of them was Budd Schulberg's *A Face in the Crowd,* which
Signet published in paperback. I knew the movie very well, so I
read that script, remembering the movie in my mind. "Oh, that's
a medium closeup, that shot!" Now I knew what a medium
closeup was because I compared the script I was reading to the
picture that I'd seen. That was the only homework I did.

The only thing that's happening right now that I really
don't like is that there are no longer genre films. I've worked in
genre films a lot and that was wonderful. What I like to do is
bend those genres; I love genre films twisted and made with a
present-day sensibility. That's a power to use. What there are
now are trend movies, and that's one development that I think
is alarming. They make trend movies of teens getting laid, or
crazy people in the woods massacring people in summer camps,
or people being lifted up into the sky on spaceships, or computer kids. I blame the Hollywood part of the industry because
there are an awful lot of people in power who have no knowledge of the past, no interest in it or sense of the heritage of
movies. What happens in their thinking is "Let's jump on the
bandwagon," and they do that until the bandwagon breaks from
the weight of garbage that's piled on it. Suddenly, the last seven
projects in that trend don't get made. They suddenly turn
around and say, "Teenagers-who-get-laid movies are out."
There are a lot of people who've got those scripts in development who say, "Oh shit, I thought this was going to go on
forever. What's the next trend?" That disturbs me a lot. However, I have done blockbusters like the *Superman* movies and the
Santa Claus movie, which cost fifty million dollars, and it's all up

there on the screen. I love having that kind of budget and that kind of opportunity to work in developing something like that. I don't think everybody should just be making little personal movies. On the other hand, I think there are fewer and fewer "grown-up movies" being made, so every time something comes along like *Prizzi's Honor,* which is so wonderful, everybody I know latches on to it: "Oh, boy, this means we get to do our intelligent movie written for grown-ups." Then you find out it just ain't so. For every one of those movies that gets made, there are forty that don't. Very often they get made only because Redford or Nicholson wants to do them, not because Hollywood wants to. They have this "Let's be nice to Jack and he'll do us a favor next time" attitude.

But there are certain directors who manage to do their work and run counter to whatever the trends are and they get to succeed or fail.

A director I like a lot is Blake Edwards. There have been certain movies he's made that have been enormous commercial successes as well as critical ones. *10* is an extraordinary movie— I think it's a classic, and because of that he got to make *S.O.B.,* which everyone hates except me and my wife. He'll always get to do his work, but I don't know how many guys get that kind of charmed situation. It's shocking that certain directors are not working now, and it's not because they haven't been trying. I don't want to mention names, but there are some directors who haven't made a movie in three or four years. That disturbs me. You look around and see what gets made and you think, "Christ, let's go back to the old days. Take a chance on this guy. Look at what he's done! Let him make his movies." But I'm not complaining personally because it's working out for me.

*G*eraldine *P*age

Actress; acting teacher

Filmography:

1947	*Out of the Night*
1953	*Taxi*
	Hondo
1961	*Summer and Smoke*
1962	*Sweet Birth of Youth*
1963	*Toys in the Attic*
1965	*Dear Heart*
1966	*The Three Sisters* (videotape recording of Actors Studio performance)
1967	*You're a Big Boy Now*
	Monday's Child (videotaped theater)
	The Happiest Millionaire
1969	*What Ever Happened to Aunt Alice?*
	Trilogy ("A Christmas Memory" episode; originally for television in 1966)
1971	*The Beguiled*
1972	*J. W. Coop*
	Pete 'n' Tillie
1973	*Happy as the Grass Was Green/Hazel's People*
1975	*The Day of the Locust*
1976	*Nasty Habits*
1977	*The Rescuers* (voice only)
	The Three Sisters
1978	*Interiors*
1980	*Harry's War*
1981	*Honky Tonk Freeway*
1982	*I'm Dancing as Fast as I Can*
1984	*The Pope of Greenwich Village*

I'd take *Wuthering Heights* to a desert island. I went completely bonkers over it when I was a teenager. I was so bad my parents finally forbade me to see it anymore. I saw it fourteen times. I have no idea why; you'd probably have to get a team of psychiatrists to explore all the ramifications. But I went bonkers: I could recite all the dialogue, hum all the music, describe all the action. I think it's one of the most perfect films. Later, when I was older and more sober, I got such a bang over the technical things in it: the cross-fades, when one image faded out in one corner, the next one came up and balanced it. I miss the square screen. You have to put in a lot on the sides now— wall brackets and things—but with the square screen the focus is really intense; you have your eye on what it's about and you can have a little space around the edges. But now it's diffused.

When I saw *Wuthering Heights* as a teenager, I believed it; I didn't think of it as a movie. I thought of it as an event or a history. But there was nothing else to do in those days, in the Depression; I just went to the movies automatically. I think I came to want to act by being in a play in church and having such a wonderful time, feeling such a huge communication with people. Right away, in that first play, I decided. But that decision was very unrelated to movies because having gone to movies all my life, I thought that in the movies you had to be good looking and I was a wallflower. I thought I didn't look good enough to be in the movies. But Miss Pilgrim, who was the director of the church plays, took us to see plays at the Goodman Theater school, and I knew that the students ushered, so at intermission I went up, examined the ushers and decided, "I look as good as that!" I risked it, and I've been happy about that since, although the business is horrible. You have to be so completely unrealistic that you ignore it. But you can let a lot out when you're acting. I really get a lot off my chest in this play [Sam Shepard's *A Lie of the Mind*].

I would think that today's teenagers might be losing something because of video and television, but who knows? When I was going to the movies all the time, they used to say, "Isn't that sad. She doesn't read. She's not going to have any imagination." Each generation has to make its own little world out of what it's got.

I think a lot of times a director who has acted makes a good actors' director—or should be better—because he should remember the problems. Of course, all us actors love freedom. One of the things I liked about Peter Masterson, who directed *The Trip to Bountiful,* was that he didn't spend a lot of time acting like a "director." He very quietly sat there and watched and listened and would come in and say something very pertinent once in a while. And it was his first film. He was terrific. Under *some* circumstances it does help to have a director give you a line reading. In other words, you come to a puzzle and you can't figure it out. You've tried this and this and you've run out of everything and it still doesn't make sense to you, and any hints that they give you that are general don't help, then a line reading can help. Of course, when you want that, it's very hard to get anyone to give it to you. But, as a general rule, it's not good to have someone give you a line reading before you've had a chance to find out what you can do with it. It's kind of frowned on generally.

You know, there are some scripts you read and can see everything in your mind's eye and some you can't figure out what's going on. But I think a lot of people try to theorize and separate things: Do you do this *or* that *or* something else? But you do all of them and sort of mix and match, because when you start reading it, your imagination immediately starts to connect things you see in it to what you know and then background things start to build in your mind. It took me a long time to have the nerve to wait and not to make too many decisions too early, to find out what might occur when I begin interacting with the other people.

I studied for eight years with Uta Hagen. She is fantastic. I also studied two years with Mira Rostova. She would let you do the whole scene, then make you wait a long time while she thought; and she would always groan as if you had killed her, and then she would say some little succinct thing, right on the target. It was great. In the years I spent with Uta Hagen, I think I almost learned more while I was listening and watching than when I was actually up myself. I learned so much.

The first time I got up in front of a camera in *Out of the Night*, it was horrifying, absolutely horrifying. The next was *Taxi* with Dan Dailey, I had a little, tiny part. Then I did *Hondo* with John Wayne. After *Hondo*, I didn't work in the movies for seven years. Then I did *Summer and Smoke* and *Sweet Bird of Youth*. I was still uncomfortable. By the time I made *Toys in the Attic*, I felt better because Richard Brooks on *Sweet Bird* had let me watch dailies and because by then I had been around it more and was more used to it. I began to start enjoying film work more and getting myself closer to what I wanted to do. The first time I saw myself I thought, "I didn't know that was what I was doing! I didn't know my teeth slanted down like a barracuda! Who is that?" I wanted to kill myself. And they said, "Miss Page, please don't flap your mouth." So I went in front of the mirror and practiced saying "I love you" with an unmoving mouth. And they said, "Don't wrinkle your brow," because on the screen it's fifteen thousand feet tall and it looks like the Grand Canyon. So I really practiced being expressionless, which, comparatively speaking, is what you do in film.

The most fun about making movies is you get paid first, so no matter how rotten everybody says you were, you've got your money. That's the best thing about making movies. The other thing is if you get something right, it's there. You don't have to be aware that it's all evaporated into fading memories.

It was difficult to do the same play every night until I went to Uta Hagen. I did an unbelievable amount of stock, summer and winter, a different show every week, and after the opening night, I'd be so restless. After the third performance, I'd be so bored and looking to start the next thing. Once I started working with Uta, I learned it only starts when you get the audience. It's only the beginning. (But I have been in so few plays that ran long, I may never complain.) She taught me that every night is different because of the different audience. The play I was in the longest was *Absurd Person Singular,* for two years, and it wasn't until the last week when I knew I was leaving that I sort of looked around and saw the play from a different perspective: "Oh my God, where have we all come to? We're all exaggerating things." I've found you have to be so careful when you do something over and over again that it doesn't feel the same, so you do a little more and little more until you realize suddenly you're hamming it up.

In the theater you're together with the audience; you're almost umbilically tied to them. When they breathe, you breathe. It's really as if you're one thing. The crew of a film is like a little audience, as well. I remember when Ruth Gordon and I were filming *Whatever Happened to Aunt Alice?* and we had a big fight scene in the kitchen, the crew gave us a big hand afterward. It was wonderful. We felt like we were right back in the theater.

I have no problem with the teenage movies being made now. Was there ever an era when most of the movies for teenagers were wonderful things that would have satisfied all the adults? We liked our movies, and the kids now like theirs. The problem I see is that every time there is a big long trend of a certain kind of movie, they overdo it. They need to change.

The only thing I've noticed is that it's hard to make a good movie. The average movie is never going to be of superior quality. It's impossible because we're all human and not that many really superbly talented people can get work at the same time. It's always going to be true. One problem is a tendency to talk a lot about films for women, and the heroines have gotten very tough, aggressive, and unappealing. You lose sympathy for them. It's very misleading I think. I've gotten good roles only because I've been so stubborn and turned down so much stuff because I couldn't do anything with the roles they offered. As soon as they find out you can do something, they say, "Oh that's what our movie's about." But they've only abstracted one element out of what I've done.

I think all the roles I've played were great roles, even starting with *Hondo.* The way that was written, it was wonderful. In those days, the fifties, when Senator McCarthy was reigning and it was such a repressive atmosphere, we had a script that had the Indians being real people, well-understood, sympathetic people. When they told me they wanted to put me in a Western with John Wayne, I said, "What! Who, me? What are you doing?" Then I read it and said, "Has he read this?" It was a beautifully written script. And, of course, *Summer and Smoke* and *Sweet Bird* were fabulous. *Toys in the Attic* wasn't bad; Lillian Hellman knew how to put a pen to paper. And I had so much fun in *You're a Big Boy Now*, Francis Coppola's film, such a wonderful character.

Of the recent movies I've seen, I loved *Silverado* so much. I can't understand why people don't. It's so funny, witty. People complain that it's not a real Western, but I say, "Thank God!" Everybody is so wonderful except Jeff Goldblum, which I don't understand because he's always so magnificent in everything. I loved it. I really enjoyed *Runaway Train*, although it was peculiar in spots. It was so weird. And Jon Voight is great. In this movie he really convinced me I wouldn't want to mess with him. He's enormously underrated.

Unfortunately I never saw Marlon Brando do anything that really knocked my socks off, although his reputation is as our greatest actor. I was out doing stock in the Middle West with a gang of people from the Goodman Theater, but we heard all about Marlon in *A Streetcar Named Desire* in New York, and we were all so excited, wanting something wonderful to happen. When Christmas came, I was the only one who could go to New York on the vacation to check it out. So I went and saw *Streetcar*. When I got back, they said, "Tell us, tell us, is he really so great?" And I said, "Forget it; it's nothing." They got so mad; everybody wants something wonderful to happen. They almost lynched me, but I said, "No, forget it; he's a sleepy-eyed, curly-haired little guy who's moaning around the stage." I found out many years later that Marlon was on Christmas vacation and I was watching Ralph Meeker. So I never saw him play the part until I saw him in the movie, and when I saw him in the movie of *Streetcar*, I had already seen Uta Hagen and Anthony Quinn do it on tour in Chicago. When Anthony Quinn cleared the table, it was cleared; so when I saw the movie, it didn't impress me, and by that time, I had played Blanche in stock. When I saw the movie, I thought, "That's not Stanley; Anthony Quinn is Stanley." Plus, I thought Vivian Leigh played Blanche backward, because when I played it in stock, I thought I'd discovered what her problem was: She had this idea that what men wanted was nooky, and to survive you really had to come on like a floozy, because that's what they wanted, otherwise they'd leave you to die somewhere. But the way she was brought up and who she was recoiled against it, so she had this tension of trying to come on and not being able to. But Vivian Leigh, under Mr. Kazan's direction, played it like she really was a floozy trying to pass herself off as a lady.

*A*idan *Q*uinn

Actor

Filmography:

1983	*Reckless*
1985	*An Early Frost* (TV movie)
	Desperately Seeking Susan
1986	*The Mission*

It's such a limited question; I don't even have a favorite film anymore. It used to be *Last Tango in Paris,* but I don't like thinking in those terms—"best," "worst," "best production of the year"—and I wouldn't want to watch *Last Tango* twice in a row anymore. I think it's a film you grow out of, not that it isn't a great film, one of the best I've ever seen. I love the film and I think it's very funny—extremely adolescent, romantic, and some things about it are really full of shit, but the actors transcended that. If you read about what the original script was and what Brando turned it into with Maria Schneider, it was something completely different. Brando brought it to a humorous, dark level about that macho myth.

That brings up something I've been thinking about a lot lately, which is the lack of women in films. There are so few women filmmakers, crew members, women executives, so few women who have the power and the input. But the interesting thing is that now all the models given to us by "feminists" are urban, hip women who have the kids, the career, and we don't see neediness in this image projected by the media. In the case of women, the image is to be tough with no vulnerability. Of course, the same things goes on with men, as well. And the *Rambo* phenomenon—what I don't get is that within the industry it's not kosher to like *Rambo*, but so many of them went to see it. That's what pisses me off. I would not go see that movie because I think that's supporting it. You can get the idea of what the movie's about by seeing a clip.

I do a lot of yoga. I'm just in the embryonic stage with it, but I relate yoga and acting. To me, flexibility is the key to acting and also to maintaining a performance. Even though I'm working four hours a day in the Sam Shepard play *A Lie of the Mind*, I'll spend another two or three trying to get ready to be flexible in that four hours, so that I'm not mechanical or acting out of tension. If the performance doesn't change every night, doesn't have a fluidity, it becomes a dead thing, a repetitive act. The same is true when you do a lot of takes. There always has to be something new, real, free, and totally grounded. Even if their personal life is a mess, there's something appealing, something grounded about the great actors. It could be a confidence or a sense of insecurity that they're honest about. I relate it all to yoga in a certain way, and I haven't even begun to plumb the depths of that connection. Yoga, in a certain way, teaches me to be honest on stage, because you can do really arch stuff in acting, especially in Shepard's play—there's a tendency to go out there. But if it doesn't come from somewhere that's believable or if people don't recognize it as possible in themselves, then it becomes an exercise you're watching in a detached way. The idea of doing a performance is to affect people, to draw them in.

Repeating exactly the same thing over and over is the beginning of death for an actor. But everyone has his own style. There are no rules. There are certain people who can repeat something that in its essence was pure to begin with, and they reproduce that with amazing technical flair, but that also has the genuineness of life behind it. That's wonderful. Certain actors are better at that than others. I prefer to go in different directions, but sometimes I'll do a take exactly the same. I'll try because I know it's right.

I've been inspired by the greats everyone knows, but I've also been inspired by people I've known, by certain chance encounters in the street, a certain watching of a character, a certain performance I saw in the theater. For example, there's this one black guy—I can't even remember his name—I saw do Athol Fugard's *Sizwe Bansi Is Dead* in Chicago, and it's probably the best performance I've ever seen. No one's ever heard of him. I don't even know his name, and I went out and got drunk with him that night. I only met him that once. So I'm inspired just as much by life and people I know and little instances, things that I see, as by the great actors we all know, like Brando. He's the biggest disappointment too. Not because he denigrated acting, which is fine. I think it's a sign of maturity for an actor to want to stop acting, and wanting to get out of the business can be a sign of a sort of spiritual maturity in a certain way, although not necessarily. I'm not saying you can't work until you're ninety and still be balanced and connected. But certain people realize they have a different path and realize that there's an innate kind of silliness to acting sometimes, which Brando was so tuned into. There's also the absurdity of the money one makes and the absurdity of the star-making machinery, which creates a god and leaves maybe a shell of a feeling inside one.

I don't mind that Brando denigrated acting, but then do something else with your life. I get the sense, though I don't know him, that he could have done things on a higher level of acting, away from Hollywood. If he didn't like that, get away from that—do something else. You can't be ruled by the fact that you're a major star and you have to live with it. You don't have to live with it. You can always do something else. He could've done *Hamlet;* he should have done all the great Shakespearean roles—if he wanted to act. He says he doesn't want to act, but I don't believe that after watching his performances. He loved it when he was doing it. But far be it from me to be the one to lecture Marlon Brando.

De Niro is an example of what I'm talking about. He doesn't stop doing what he loves to do. He's got a tremendous amount of courage. He's one of the great actors, I think, of all time. In a certain way the only reason I'm an actor is because it's the only thing I can do. I worked at a lot of other jobs and ended up getting fired or quitting every six months. My best job was a hot tar roofer. I was a janitor and a dishwasher—before I even thought about acting. When I was eighteen, I was living in Ireland and I started seeing these plays for real cheap, and I thought, "What the fuck am I doing with my life?" I'd always wanted to be a writer, but I realized I didn't have the discipline to be a great writer, so I thought, "Maybe I'll try acting." I always liked to goof around. I was a bit of a class clown and I loved literature.

I really like acting in film and theater, but I prefer acting in theater because it's a more complete experience. It's more demanding physically in a certain way—it's uninterrupted, no machines. You have to admit to the presence of machines and the crew in film work and then try to forget about it, but never forget about it to the point where you can't use it as a tool to help rather than hurt you. This is very hard when you're doing something very intimate and just before the take there are forty people talking about some broad they screwed last night or making a joke about the scene. Not all crews are like that, and I don't mean they're malicious, but sometimes you have to close yourself off. There are a lot of ways of dealing with it, but, personally, I usually get to know the crew very well, get friendly. They are part of the whole process.

Acting is always a political thing, I think. The thing I've done that's been the most satisfying has been *An Early Frost* because of the response and what it did for people. Certain people I know who would never ever admit to having any feelings of sympathy toward gays were moved. The director, John Erman, was really good. He had tremendous respect for actors' input and their creating a reality. I mean, television is a horrible medium to work in, in a certain way, because you have no time. We shot a two-hour movie in twenty days, which is insane. You'd never do that with a feature, but if the people are good and the director cares, you can still do good work. Someone who has an overall view, who has guts—that's important—is a good director.

I'd like to work with Jonathan Demme because I like the Talking Heads movie, *Stop Making Sense,* so much and the *Sun City* video—I thought that was great. I'd like to work with Martin Scorsese because he's just the best. I did work with him for a couple of months on *The Last Temptation of Christ*. We were all working on it for months; we'd had all the auditions. I was going to play Christ. It was scrapped because of the Born Again movement's incredible letter-writing campaign, and a very intricate promise of boycotts and pickets of all Gulf and Western and Paramount products. One man who is in control of one of the biggest theater chains was a Born Again, and he called Paramount and told them if they made this film it wouldn't show in any of his theaters. So that meant over a third of all the theaters in the country wouldn't distribute it. No one else would pick it up. Marty's trying to get money for it now in other countries. But I really believe things happen when they're supposed to, and that wasn't supposed to happen then. But it was terrible at the time. Maybe that movie should never be made for Hollywood.

The things that bother me most about the film business now are the poor quality, the shallow investigation into the intricacies of life, and the arrogance of the film industry—not only telling us what we want, but on down the line to the way people are treated. There are still good movies being made, obviously, but everything has become so corporate. The guys who used to head the studios, although they were tycoons and businessmen, seemed to have a real interest in story and character and development. Now we have the president of Coca-Cola or the president of an oil company running the show, and they have no idea. They're hiring their friends, and so on. That may not be the whole thing, but down the line there's an incredible ineptness. If the film industry, the market research people, and the corporate people could do away with creative people, they would. The only reason they still have them is that they can't predict. This year [1985] we had a slew of teenage films that died a disastrous death at the box office, and in a certain way, it's the healthiest thing that could have happened to the film industry—to see all these films that were just like last year's die, to see them all go bad. They are getting lessons from the people who are saying, "This is shit."

It bothers me a little that people may see my films at home on video. I have a VCR and I use and like it, but it shouldn't become a substitute for going out and seeing a movie in the communal, tribal experience of sitting in front of a big screen and watching something—like sitting around a campfire listening to a story. It is really no substitute for that experience. The small screen cannot possibly give you the same experience.

I will continue to do whatever I want: a play, an independent film made in Ireland for no money, a blockbuster. I'm doing a film with the Taviani brothers soon. I don't live within Hollywood's confines. I could live and die without Hollywood. I want to do a studio film if it's a great part, with a good story, and a good director—that's all. And if not, I won't do one. I won't do a film for money, but I won't let them pay me less than I think I deserve, which is what they always try to do, especially if you do another film for little money and take a cut in salary. Then they want you to work for that price for a twenty-million-dollar movie.

*H*arold *R*amis

Writer; actor; director

Filmography:

As actor:

1976–78   *SCTV* (26 episodes)
1981   *Stripes*
1984   *Ghostbusters*

As writer:

1976–78   Head writer, *SCTV* (39 episodes)
1978   *National Lampoon's Animal House* (cowrote with Douglas Kenney and Chris Miller)
1979   *Meatballs* (cowrote with Dan Goldberg, Len Blum, Janice Allen)
1980   *Caddyshack* (cowrote with Douglas Kenney and Brian Doyle-Murray)
1984   *Ghostbusters* (cowrote with Dan Aykroyd)
1985   *Club Paradise* (cowrote with Brian Doyle-Murray)

As director:

1980   *Caddyshack*
1983   *National Lampoon's Vacation*
1985   *Club Paradise*

I wouldn't take a film; I'd take a girl; I'd take music. I've lived on islands, but not alone. I've spent a lot of time on Hydra in the Aegean. It's very small, about 2,500 people—no roads, cobblestones, but it's fashionable in season. It was a real cross section. I love the feeling of microcosm on an island. It's very dramatic; everyone becomes the star of his or her own life —high drama.

But if I had to take a movie, I'd take a Marx Brothers movie. Harpo and I have the same birthday, and my father looks like Groucho. My father loved the Marx Brothers so much that when I grew up I thought they were like gods. Every time a Marx Brothers movie was on TV, the whole family would sit around—this was repeated hundreds of times—and we would laugh. So they were like surrogate father figures for me. My father had four brothers, and I wished they were the Marx Brothers instead of the Ramis brothers. My father is actually quite funny—he has a Groucho sense of humor, a dry wit, and he can't stop himself from commenting on everything. But if he was as funny as Groucho, he wouldn't have had a grocery store for thirty something years.

I loved Harpo. Their movies always cracked me up and I loved the populism in their films. I like the slightly more mature Marx Brothers comedies. The early ones were taken from stage plays, and I always thought they were rough in certain ways, and they had a different energy. There was something more spontaneous in *Duck Soup* and so on, but one like *A Night at the Opera* was slightly more attractive as film, something technical maybe. But I think the opera-wrecking scene is amazing. Almost anything they did is amazing. The Marx Brothers are always in my mind. It's the same with Frank Capra. I could take *It's a Wonderful Life* or *Mr. Smith Goes to Washington*. I'm a real sucker for inspirational populist politics—good people doing the right thing under tough circumstances and succeeding.

I don't write in an exploitive way because I think it's going to be commercial. It's morally the only way I can write these things.

When you grow up in the lower middle class, there's this built-in resentment to society. We discovered in *Animal House* that out of this sort of morass of the sixties, people were tending toward Woody Allen, Neil Simon comedies. John Lahr wrote a great essay on this: He felt these comedies were portraying people trapped in a society that couldn't understand them, that no longer made any sense, where traditional values were eroding constantly, and where they were always victims of it. Lahr felt it was counter-productive and demoralizing to the society to accept the view that we're helpless and neurotic and nothing can be done. When I worked on *Animal House* with Doug Kenney and Chris Miller, our instinct was to return to a Marx Brothers feeling: "Yes, our heroes are outcasts, they're the underdogs, they're déclassé in every sense, and yet they win." They're not mortified by their social position or by the society around them. They have a clear moral mind, even though it's not a conventional morality.

We modeled *Animal House* after every gang we could think of from Archie, Jughead, and Veronica to the Marx Brothers. It was the classic gang structure: Our Gang, the Bowery Boys. We sort of abstracted from there, and there was much about male bonding and how college is all about male bonding. So we put this male gang together—guys we would have liked to have known or based on guys we actually did know in some cases.

The audience response was so tremendous for one reason because people were looking for a way to see themselves as heroic in this kind of society. *Rambo* is another response; but I've made a moral commitment not to see any of these movies dealing out death. I hate to be manipulated just to be excited or titillated by violence. Those teenage movies—a lot of them really exploit everyone's desire to fly. So many of them have people getting on spaceships. We may have contributed to this current trend in movies where each scene is a successful reversal: There's some opposition and there's a clever switch. The lead is never down. It's probably true of many of the films I've worked on, although I watched *Stripes* the other day with a friend who hadn't seen it, and there's some travail in *Stripes*. Bill Murray has an actual sincere confrontation with Warren Oates that works and feels potent as an argument. We went so far as to mention duty, honor, and courage. But when people went to copy *Animal House*, I think they missed the point. They thought the crudity and the grossness was the point, but we went to school when that attitude was the real attitude: We were against all institutions generally. We lived that way, flaunting it. I was in school from 1962 to 1966, and each year was a major watershed. From the time Kennedy was killed, things changed so fast every year I was in school that it was remarkable. When Vietnam came, all that energy was ready to be mobilized. It had already been there in the streets over other issues. Even before civil rights, there was this sort of raunchy activism—prankishness for its own sake. We had a very hard time selling Universal the idea that the heroes of the film could be the slobs. They said, "How could these people be the heroes? They're disgusting!" We said, "That's the point. That's who our heroes were. There was a competition to be the most disgusting."

I would also want to take *The Godfather* and *The Godfather, Part Two* because they're great, they're epic. I like Francis Ford Coppola's epic work; I don't like his later work. Or I would take *1900* or some other big film, really rich with a lot of things going on in it. I thought of *Amarcord* when you asked me this question. It's so sweet, that whole depicting of an entire town with such feeling, making it so personal and keeping the specific types of people. I love Fellini's sensibility. I like Martin Scorsese's work. I think *King of Comedy* is a tremendous movie, and everybody trashed it. Jerry Lewis was playing something that was so unusual but so right for him. People who do comedy or who enjoy any celebrity at all really appreciate much more what it's about. Dan Aykroyd has said to me that he's waiting for a Mark David Chapman to step out of a crowd and plug him one day. You feel that ambivalence in people: They do love and hate you at the same time. My wife just read me a great quote from Jonathan Miller about being a celebrity. He says that normally you know exactly as many people as know you. There's a wonderful symmetry in it; but when you're a celebrity, many more people know you than you know, and there's something unbalanced about that, and they have this terrible ambivalence about you as well.

It's very difficult to get a film made. I helped my wife sell a script to Orion, to Jon Peters, a few years ago, called *Dancing Backwards*. It was about a woman from Long Island who at her mother's funeral finds out she was really adopted and has a sister living in Atlanta. She goes to Atlanta, finds the twin sister, and they couldn't be more different. The sister from Long Island is kind of shy, Jewish, and neurotic; and the sister from Atlanta is just full-blown vain; her husband's wealthy, and she's written and is starring in a community play about a woman's artistic struggle. Jon Peters wanted it to star Goldie Hawn and Gilda Radner. Then they said, "How about Goldie and Barbra?" And it just bogged down in this casting package problem. But now there's a revival of interest because Barbra Streisand and Dolly Parton want to do a film together, and I think the script has been recirculated. But the film is about women and it's very hard to sell scripts about women. Two women writers I know were telling me an idea for a film: Two women living in Los Angeles decide to marry two Russian men in order to get money. I didn't have a lot of time and I was in a shitty mood, so I said, "All right, pretend I'm a studio executive and you just told me that film idea, and I say to you, 'Forget it, no one wants to see films about women.' " Then I said, "Now tell me the same idea, but tell me it's about two Russian men who want to come to the United States—same movie—but if you say it's about the two guys, rather than the two girls, suddenly you can sell it."

IVAN REITMAN

Producer; film director

Filmography:

1978   *National Lampoon's Animal House* (producer)
1979   *Meatballs* (producer)
1981   *Stripes* (producer)
        Heavy Metal (producer)
1984   *Ghostbusters* (producer, director)
1986   *Legal Eagles* (producer, director)

It's tough to choose because I have such a broad range of interests. I do love the Marx Brothers movies a lot, and one of the criteria would be that the film is viewable over and over. I think their films are. They may not be the single best movies, but I can sit down and watch them at any time. They're really funny and they're funny on a lot of levels and in a lot of different ways, and they're still very contemporary. *Citizen Kane* is a great movie, a great movie to watch once or twice. It's comedy that people seem to be able to watch over and over again, because if it's done right, something funny can make you laugh a hundred times. It's not the surprise, necessarily, that makes you laugh. It's the confluence of events on the screen. I understand that my films are being viewed over and over. I think it's because what's funny in them works over and over.

I don't focus on films in a specific way. Certain directors have a wonderful critical eye: They remember a film in all its shots, how it was put together, and they can reconstruct it. But when I watch other people's movies, I don't usually look at them that way. I may if I am really going to analyze them, but I try not to. I try to watch them like a normal member of the audience, so I just get an overall emotional response to them.

I think Bill Murray is the Groucho Marx of today. He is somewhere between Groucho and W. C. Fields—that's why they're still contemporary—and he has the same cynical, ironic attitude on the surface and warm heart on the inside that they have. John Belushi had that kind of power and it was more than just physical power. I would have loved to have directed him. He would have been totally different than you've seen him. I did a show Off-Broadway with him called *The National Lampoon Show,* which also had Bill and Harold Ramis in it, prior to *Saturday Night Live.* The thing about Belushi is he took that stage and he did it verbally. He just commanded it. He spoke and he had this real power that somehow got sloughed away because of what he did in *Animal House,* although that was also great. He could have been an actor of the caliber of a Marlon Brando— he had that combination of physical presence and verbal power. He loved to imitate Marlon Brando because he was actually very similar to him. That's not the reason I mention that actor, but it's that same kind of presence and power that Brando has and that Belushi, in fact, had. It's too bad that most of his films after *Animal House* were so lousy. Danny Aykroyd is also very special. He gets overlooked because he likes to play support a lot, but his importance is very much like Chico's was in the Marx Brothers. You take those guys out and suddenly Groucho looks really bare. I think Aykroyd's a very fine actor and has one of the most imaginative film minds. He's a good actor and he's a very good writer.

Comedy is a really complex emotion—the hardest to evoke and terribly undervalued. It's usually easier to write about heavier stuff because it's generally pretty straightforward, usually a good angle to play as a writer. Comedy is so ethereal. Who knows why we're laughing? People look for simple common denominators, you know, the old slob comedy title, but it's really much more complex than that.

I began at university directing plays and musicals. In fact, I was introduced at the time to the European school of filmmaking. I had never seen a Godard movie or a Truffaut or a Fellini until then. There was a film club that I was interested in joining, but before I did, I actually talked myself into a summer film course with the National Film Board of Canada, which was really a course to teach English teachers how to teach film classes in high school and university. It was not a filmmaking course, but I used my stay to make my first short film. I became the pest in the class and the way they got rid of me was to give me two hundred feet of 16-mm film, a light meter, and a camera, and so I just went off and did something. I play a number of instruments, and I taped some stuff at various speeds and I cut the tape into various pieces and overdubbed it, so I had a soundtrack that was about two and a half minutes long. I decided that I'd try to shoot a movie based on a soundtrack—let the soundtrack be the script. That's the way I started. In the end it was quite comedic and the comedy came out of the rhythms of the soundtrack. I pixelated some stuff—I did stop-motion animation with my camera because it had a one-frame capability. I just took events I saw in the streets, almost like a documentary filmmaker, but it was all in the editing and in the inner motion of the visuals. I was able to cut together a pretty interesting film that I've now lost. I'd like to see it again; it seemed like it was pretty good at the time.

I directed two shorts at university, both of which were successful: *Orientation* was sold to Fox as a short for theaters. It told about the first few days of school and was actually the forerunner of *Animal House*. It cost about eighteen hundred dollars and made about twenty thousand, which was remarkable for a student film. I made another short called *Freak Film,* which we did overnight, and it was quite funny. I directed a movie called *Cannibal Girls* that stars a couple of *SCTV* people, Andrea Martin and Eugene Levy. The problem with that film was that I had no script; we just made it up as we went along, but it was sort of a horror comedy. I sold that to Sam Arkoff at American International and was broke after that. I started working in television for about six months, at which time I started working with Doug Henning on what became *The Magic Show* on Broadway. That sort of crossed me over into producing. I produced about four or five mostly horror or action movies with a small company called Cinepix in Canada.

I chose to go into producing because I didn't think I was a good enough director yet, but, in retrospect, I think I should have continued to direct. I think I would have been further ahead right now. I would have a greater body of directorial work and I guess I'd be more experienced. But I directed about a third of the movies anyway. I had a rule with the directors I worked with, that if they fell behind, I would take a second-unit crew out and shoot it myself. Apparently it's something Roger Corman has done as well. *They Came from Within* was David Cronenberg's first feature and *House by the Lake* was Bill Frust's second, so they would get into trouble because we had impossible schedules. I would have a second cameraman and would sort of steal the second camera and a couple other members of the crew and I would shoot. I ended up shooting most of the action sequences on those films.

The nice thing about producing and directing, especially if you've been successful, is that you're basically your own boss and there's nobody else second-guessing what you're doing. I've heard all the horror stories about what other directors have gone through when there's been a difference of opinion between them and the producer, never mind between them and the studio, which often happens. I've managed to avoid that because I've never worked for anyone else. I'd sort of like to try it, just to be a director for hire, to see what it's like. It's almost happened two times, but for one reason or another I've never taken the movies that were offered. But I do rely heavily on Joe Metrick and Michael Gross, who coproduce the films with me; they were the associate producers on those other films I mentioned and will coproduce the next ones. They do most of the day-to-day work, but in terms of the overall choice of what film to make, how it's marketed, how it's cast, I have the luxury of making up my own mind.

I work very intimately with the screenwriter on a weekly basis and eventually it becomes a daily basis and then hourly, but I influence the stories a great deal. I like to have the writers available. I like to have them around on the shoot. I like to develop the stories a lot, especially in comedies. You can never foresee all the possibilities of a situation until you're actually there. So I'm often redeveloping the scenes. In the editing, once the first cut is made, I'm really good at it.

I totally believe in test screening. Two weeks after we finished shooting, we screened *Ghostbusters* to an audience of five hundred just off the street. They saw a pretty decent cut, about twenty minutes longer than the finished film. But I'm pretty ruthless in the editing room, so I get the stuff out pretty fast. I had a very short schedule on *Ghostbusters*, so I was editing while I shot.

We had two hundred special effects shots in *Ghostbusters*; literally eight of them were ready at the time of the first screening, so we showed that film without any special effects in it. I just got up and explained to the audience that what they were going to see was rough, that it was a work in progress, that at one time it would become a science fiction spectacular, but the spectacular was missing today, and they were going to have to use their imaginations. You see, for me it was important to know that the story worked without all that. I knew if the story was going to be fine at the screening, everything else was going to add to it. And, in fact, the film played pretty much as it plays now. It wasn't as spectacular to watch and people did make accommodations for the missing footage, but the same things that they applauded, they applaud in the finished answer print.

I have almost a computerlike remembrance of what happens at a screening. I will tape it with just a sound cassette player to hear how the audience sounds. I don't have to see the film to remind me; I usually never forget. I can recall any moment in a film and how it played. I just go by the emotion of the room. It's not just by the laughs; it's by the smell of the room; and I remember how I felt while I was being forced to watch it as if it were new—because of the audience in the room. When you see it yourself, you're always guessing. You're reading into it your own very tired thoughts because you've seen that material too many times. When you see it with a cold audience, an audience with no ax to grind one way or the other, it's like you're seeing it for the first time, and so you can be fresh to the movie. That's why I welcome it, and I screened *Ghostbusters* eight or nine times with audiences that were a cross section of the film-going audience. They invariably like the same things from screening to screening. It doesn't matter how young or old they are, unless you have a real specialty item, like a Cheech and Chong movie.

I think everything I do will at least have a comedic undertone. I believe I have the ability to make people respond in a number of different ways. So far, I've basically made them cheer, laugh, and maybe scream. And I think I can make them cry as well and probably will. But I don't want to make a film where they *just* cry. I wouldn't mind making a film where they laugh and cry and cheer all in one. And, in fact, I'm working on one—it's in the script stage.

I went away from that first idea of letting the soundtrack dictate the visuals. I've made pretty verbal comedies. I'm always being accused of making physical comedies, but, in fact, if one looks at the movies I've directed, they were based on the verbal growing out of character. I think I will go back more to letting the music lead. The music is always there in my head; I hear the music when I direct a scene. What I mean by that is I understand the rhythm of the scene—you get a sense of pace from that—and I understand how to tell a story in pictures. I'm not particularly great at that like some other directors, such as Steven Spielberg, who is extraordinary that way. I have focused on character a lot as a way of getting comedy, and I think I'll now start to go the other way again, taking a much stronger visual approach to the film. I've never much worried about it. *Legal Eagles* is an edited type of film, very clean, easy. The camera is usually in the right place and not doing much, because it usually interferes with comedy. *Legal Eagles* is led by the actors' rhythms but cut properly and directed properly so it's a much clearer, more forties approach to filmmaking. In this new film I think I can allow myself a stronger visual interest and still keep what I have. So I supervise every aspect of the film. I used to write the music, but I don't anymore. I've worked with Elmer Bernstein seven times, so we have a real rapport.

Of the people working now, I think Larry Kasdan is really good; I think John Huston is still great, and I love the movies of Billy Wilder. I think Ron Howard is a very good director—I've liked his films. And Coppola is kind of a big puzzle to me because his middle films are so extraordinary, but I didn't quite understand his other films. There's a whole group of his contemporaries who don't seem to be able to continue in the same spectacular manner they started their careers with, and I don't know why that is. That's not historically what happened in other generations. They at least built up to a certain point before they began losing it. Most of those people have extraordinary power —Friedkin, Bogdanovich, Coppola, Cimino. My guess is it's because they attempt to top themselves. One can't overdirect and one can't monkey with a story so that it loses its inherent charm and quality. I made one of the most successful comedies ever, so I have that sense of what you can do that can make 250 million dollars, and I decided not to worry about it. Actually, one of the films I'm developing is the story of two young kids; it will be made for 6 or 7 million dollars instead of 30 million like *Ghostbusters.* There's no way in hell it can do anything more than ten percent of *Ghostbusters,* but it seems like a great story. Maybe it will be very successful. It touches me and that's the reason I want to do it.

Even though there's little government support for young filmmakers here, you have the studios. It's possible for a U.S.C. graduate with a good short film to make a development deal with the right studio, and if he happens to have the right screenplay, he's in production. It's happened a number of times. Often what happens, of course, is he makes the development deal and nothing is heard from the studio for five years until they scrape again. That's the hardest thing—getting that first feature made. I found it wonderful to have grown up in Canada at the time I did. I was fortunate because I came in just at the time of a burgeoning national awareness that included the arts, and there was this desire to create a national Canadian film industry. Having just produced a number of shorts in Canada that were pretty good, I was able to go to the Canadian Film Development Corporation, which was like the government bank to help develop movies. They gave me some money to make my first movie. I have a feeling if I were to have made the shorts in America, I probably would have been like the U.S.C. kid at a film studio, and I probably would have had a different career. I like to believe in the inevitability of talent, but sometimes it takes a very long time and sometimes it happens too fast.

Richard Roud

Program director of the New York Film Festival; writer

Books:

Max Ophüls: An Index
Jean-Luc Godard (Doubleday, 1968, 1970)
Jean-Marie Straub (Viking Press, 1971)
Cinema: A Critical Dictionary, ed., 2 vols. (Viking Press, 1979)
A Passion for Films: Henri Langlois and the Cinémathèque Française (Viking Press, 1983)
A Critical Biography of François Truffaut (work in progress/working title)

Mr. Roud is a regular contributor to *The Manchester Guardian, Sight and Sound, Film Comment,* and other publications; he also contributes to the programming of the New Directors/New Films series, cosponsored by the Film Society of Lincoln Center and the Department of Film of The Museum of Modern Art.

There's a simple answer: I'd take Buñuel's version of *Robinsón Crusoe* because then I'd learn how to build a hut and how to get along. But for sheer pleasure, if I had to have a favorite film, it's probably Renoir's *Rules of the Game*. It's hard to explain why; there are all kinds of reasons. If I had to guess, I'd take *Rules of the Game* and figure out the hut-building part myself. Then again, I could take *Citizen Kane*. *Kane* and *Rules of the Game* were made within a year of each other (1939 and 1940), and both made a great impression. I suppose I also thought of *Citizen Kane* because Orson Welles died yesterday. *Rules of the Game* is a film I've seen over and over again, and every time I see it, I find something new or different. I see connections I hadn't seen before, and *Citizen Kane* is the opposite. It's still the same and never gets boring. I can see it over and over again. I come home sometimes, turn on the televison, and there's *Citizen Kane* and I think I don't want to watch that again, especially not on television, but I sit down to watch a few minutes, then a few minutes more, and I see the whole film again because I couldn't turn it off. It grabs you and doesn't let you go until the end. You want to see just one more scene, then this other scene.

I don't think people have favorite films because they identify with them; it's because something they saw was a different kind of movie than they ever saw before and they thought to themselves, "Oh, so movies don't have to be always like this and this and this. They can do other things, different things." At a press conference someone asked Kurosawa his favorite film. He didn't answer the question directly, but he said the first film that made him decide he wanted to become a filmmaker was Abel Gance's film, not *Napoléon,* but an earlier one about a raiilroad engineer, *La Roue* (*The Wheel*), which used montage in an incredible way, a lot of superimpositions of things. It's very flashy, very fancy, a sort of landmark, I guess. For him it was, "Oh! This is another way of making movies!" That's what turns people on.

In the sixties people were better off than they are now. They had fewer financial problems and they were more willing to go to a movie that made them think, that wasn't pure entertainment. Of course, it's hard to say if times have gotten harder or not, but I think they have in a way. Now people want to be entertained, that's it. Period. And the least effort they have to make, the happier they are. It isn't a universal rule because there are some films like *Terms of Endearment*—whether you liked it or not—that aren't action films or teenage films, and that one did very well. It worked on you and you got mad. A friend of mine called it *Terms of Endurement.* That's what's going

on for the time being anyway. Let's hope things will pick up. I
don't know whether Wim Wenders and Jean-Luc Godard, who
feel cinema is almost over, are being too pessimistic or not.

Technologies like Showscan pull you in, but into what?
They don't seem to manage to tell a story, and on a huge screen
it's rather difficult to. CinemaScope has practically disappeared
because it didn't fit into the television screen properly. You have
to scan or crop, and this is the first film festival [New York Film
Festival, 1985] we ever had without a CinemaScope film. Perhaps having film do things video can't is going to rescue film,
but, on the other hand, how do you do an intimate love scene
with all that space around you? It's not that easy. Someone will
come along probably and be able to do it; then everyone will
say, "Oh, it *can* be done!" A lot of people resisted CinemaScope
because it was only good for snakes and funerals, but people
had the vision to make very good films in CinemaScope. Maybe
Showscan is the answer, I don't know.

We at the New York Film Festival try to show the films that
are not teen films, that are adult films, and keep up people's
interest in those films and let them know there are still possibilities. Many of them do get bought and shown, to small audiences
perhaps. But then in 1984, the best I hoped for *Stranger Than
Paradise* was maybe a couple of weeks' run across the street, and,
amazingly, it seems that a lot of people wanted to see something
that was different. I'm now more optimistic, although, of
course, filmmakers like Wim Wenders have to go around looking for money for each film; therefore they have to endure
more. But I don't think it's that bad. We are in a trough of the
wave, but you can't be up all the time.

It's impossible to pinpoint the criteria for what we accept
for the Festival—originality, quality—what is quality? There are
five of us, and we change one person every year. It isn't that
difficult, you know; there's so much junk around and so little is
good that the films almost select themselves, although naturally
there are a few disagreements about films. It's done several
ways: Films are sent in; we write to people asking them to send
films in to view; the whole selection committee goes to the
Cannes Film Festival because, apart from the competition section, they show a lot of films there in two weeks. You can't see

everything; you take a chance; you split up and each sees one film. We get back together and say, "This one's not bad; it's showing again next Tuesday, try and make it." I spend most of my year going around to film festivals and other places to look for new things.

We've introduced lots of people to American audiences: the first Polanski feature, the first Bertolucci feature. Godard was discovered before we existed, but we kept interest in him up; the same is true of Truffaut. Terry Malick's *Badlands* and Scorsese's *Mean Streets* had their premieres at the New York Film Festival. Bogdanovich's *The Last Picture Show* was first shown at the New York Film Festival. It's a long list: Wim Wenders, Fassbinder, Forman, Passer. The first Fassbinder was shown in 1971, and the first Herzog film, *Signs of Life*.

Who are the young lions? I don't know. Maybe Jim Jarmusch. But let's wait for the second and third films. The history of cinema is full of people who made one good first film. I'm not predicting this, but it has happened.

We make mistakes. There are also films we want and can't get because they have a release date or the producer or distributor decides to go a different route: He wants to have a Christmas opening or something like that. We used to have problems and still do occasionally, especially with Hollywood films. They're afraid that if they show their films in festivals they will get an "art" tinge. I can't understand that because I can't imagine up in Peoria: Ma: "Let's go see this film." Pa: "No, that was in the New York Film Festival; that must be an art film." For the people who know, the film festival label is a turn-on, rather than a turn-off. The others won't know, but some of the studios have this idea. But it changes every now and then.

There are also films we show that we think somehow we're going to save by showing, and don't. For example, that film by Jonathan Demme that had two titles, *Citizens Band* and *Handle with Care*. I really loved it and the critics really loved it, but it just didn't catch on. Everyone who *saw* it loved it; the others didn't want to go see it. What makes people want to go to a movie? That's the thing—what they call in Hollywood the "want to see phenomenon"—nobody knows. At one time they thought sequels were the answer. If you loved *Jaws*, you'd love *Jaws II* more, but it didn't work for *Airport*. The first one was a great success, the second one wasn't, and the third went its way down. The James Bond films all worked their way up. The first one, *Dr. No,* did well and the rest went up more and more, with a slight drop when Sean Connery left, and then they picked up again. There's no way to know. Nobody *has* to go to the movies. You have to buy shoes, you have to eat, you have to wear clothes, but you don't have to go to the movies, especially when you have television at home. And now with VCRs, a lot of people are watching that.

Also, I think movie theaters are not what they used to be. They used to be beautiful places. They may have been a little schlocky, but they were grand. The Roxy, for example, was gorgeous. It was an experience to go there. Lots of times they do restore them, like Keith Memorial in Boston, my favorite, but Sarah Caldwell has taken it over for her opera company, which is fine. I'm glad somebody is using it, but it's not being used for movies. Moviegoing was an event; there was no television and you went to the movies automatically at least once, twice a week. Now you stay home unless there's something really important to go out for; you can get your image fix, so to speak, at home. I think movies will have to go on, though, because television is going to have to go on putting money into movie movies because people don't want to see films made for television. They want to see films that have come out, have been reviewed, been talked about, and then they want to see them for free at home. So I think movies are going to survive because television companies are going to have to make it their business to see that movies survive. Oftentimes the highest ratings are for showings of old movies—not too old—*Gone with the Wind* did awfully well on television and so did *Bridge on the River Kwai* and many more. To keep the supply up they're going to have to continue putting money into films so they can show them on television. Maybe movies can become like Broadway: a small number of theaters only in big towns, and there will be some material for television.

Some people claim there's going to be high-definition television soon—two thousand lines and so forth—but still it won't be the same because going out and staying home are two different things, especially with comedies. It's much more fun with people around you laughing, not just two or three people chuckling; and with old movies it's terrible because they left spaces for the laughter so the audience would hear the next line. So when you watch the Marx Brothers on television, there are gaps because they wanted the audience to hear what was coming. If you're home, even if you're laughing, no matter how hard you're laughing or how loud, it's still not the same as a whole theater, so it's kind of strange.

Alan Rudolph

Screenwriter; film director

Filmography:

mid-1960s	hundreds of short Super-8 films
1968	*Riot* (assistant director)
1969	*The Big Bounce* (assistant director)
	The Great Bank Robbery (assistant director)
	The Arrangement (assistant director)
	Marooned (assistant director)
1970	*The Traveling Executioner* (assistant director)
1972	*Premonition* (assistant director)
1973	*The Long Goodbye* (assistant director)
	Terror Circus/Barn of the Naked Dead (director; uncredited codirector Gerald Cormier)
1974	*California Split* (assistant director; uncredited script work)
1975	*Nashville* (assistant director; uncredited script work)
	Welcome to My Nightmare (cowriter)
1976	*Buffalo Bill and the Indians* (cowriter)
1977	*Welcome to L.A.* (director; writer)
1978	*Remember My Name* (director; writer)
1980	*Roadie* (director; coauthor of story)
1982	*Endangered Species* (director; cowriter)
1983	*Return Engagement* (director)
1984	*Choose Me* (director; writer)
	Songwriter (director)
1986	*Trouble in Mind* (director; writer)

Someone once asked me what kind of book I would take on a desert island and I said the phone book. You can think up a story for every name you come across. There are about fifty films in the top ten for me, films I like to see a lot. I've seen *Citizen Kane* three times, always on television. *Touch of Evil* is a great film. European films in the modern era, such as Bertolucci's films, are exciting. I like Truffaut's films, Fellini's, and Ken Russell's. *La Strada,* by Fellini, was an important film for me. I was a young person, and I remember not being able to read the subtitles fast enough. The same with Bergman; I couldn't keep up with the subtitles and I didn't want to drop my eyes from the screen, and so I just watched and was amazed. Music has influenced me almost more than film because it contributes to your internal mood and that's really where films are made. Probably the most important film I ever saw was also the first film I ever saw—*Gone with the Wind.* I saw it when my parents took me to a theater here called the Carthay Circle. I saw this big, loud, colorful movie and sort of understood a lot of it. It was that simple in a lot of ways—it worked.

I like a lot of the classic Ford films but I don't like all of them. I mean, *The Searchers* didn't change my life, but Hawks' *Red River* and Ford's *Stagecoach*—now there are films that really affected me. I remember seeing Ed Sullivan and *Stagecoach* in one night on TV. *How Green Was My Valley* was another big Ford film—I liked that one a lot.

Invaders from Mars was an amazing film when I was a kid because the hero was a kid. I guess they're remaking it now. I was the same age as the hero when I saw it, about seven or eight. I have no idea whether or not it has any real merit, but the story probably has as much effect on my story sense as anything else. The story is about a kid who wakes up in a farmhouse—it's all done in that real phony Hollywood way that was wonderful. It's dawn; he looks out the window, and a flying saucer lands in the sand dunes behind his house. He goes to wake his parents, he and his father go out, and it's not there. His father falls in the sand, and then he goes back into the house. Suddenly the father's all mean and he's got this little mark behind his neck. Gradually all the people that this kid trusts—the schoolteachers, the policeman, his mother, his girlfriend—change. They have this horrible attitude—mean, cold, bloodless, uncaring—and they all have this little mark on the back of their necks. He can't find anyone to talk to. Watching this movie as a kid, you realize it's all the things you care about in life: your family, friends, teachers. There's this big brain in the desert and they go down there to try to kill it and boom! the picture's over, you think. The kid wakes up and whole thing was a dream. Again, as a young person watching this, you say, "Wow! This is amazing!" Then he looks out the window and the flying saucer lands, and that's the end.

You're really only drawn to what you understand, and so I think filmmakers who have been able to translate their dreams into film are the ones who are really lucky as humans because they have gotten to do something that would have been inside them anyway and might not have gotten out. Films today encompass everything.

I think the film I would take to a desert island would be the dailies from my next film. Even if I were there forever, I would take them; you never get them right. You try to let the film go as fully realized as you know how, but dailies always show so much promise. You might as well have promise for the future. That's fair—that's a film on a desert island, and I get to change it every once in a while. But one good thing about film is you get music with it, and I would definitely want a woman projectionist.

I enjoy all three stages of filmmaking, but because editing breeds the most tangible results, it's the most effective in a way. But nothing replaces shooting. The way I shoot is rather spontaneous, so I get a lot of things and I worry about it later. Writing is the least fun, but in many ways, the most rewarding because you do that first.

Filming has its own hypnotic feel, and because you're dealing with so many people, it's like being a sugar cube on an anthill. The personalities, the interaction, and the dream that the shooting period creates—both when you're working and when you're not—put you in one state of mind. At least I am for five, six, seven, eight weeks during the shoot. That's probably the most special, though not necessarily the most fun. I basically think through a camera, and that's where I seem to get most of my good ideas—there and driving. During the shoot, anything can happen and usually does, because you're working with actors, who, I think, are the most precious part of any film, the part that needs the most protection. In most films, the actors are the most important element because the behavior of the characters always becomes more important than the performance. Acting as a measurable skill is always best when you can't find it, and that usually comes through a behavioral performance for me. Actors are the smartest group of the bunch. Actors are amazing. I've never had any bad experiences with actors outside of small-minded small-town people. I try never to deal with those people, the people who stayed in some small city and affect all the bad habits of actors. I've only run into one or two of these situations. I've worked with Keith Carradine three times and I find him growing as a man and as an actor. He's an absolutely special person, a blessed person. He's becoming more versatile, funnier, and in this new film, *Trouble in Mind,* I saw him do some things I've never seen an actor do before. I like every actor I've ever worked with. They've brought themselves to the role; they've been right there all the time. It's wonderful on a shoot to try and promote and stimulate people who are working at the top of their skill, in every function, every category, every person on the crew. Casting is everything: casting actors, casting crew. When you select properly and see somebody really grow, it's fantastic.

It's like my work with Robert Altman. I had written some things, but they had never jelled. I wasn't doing anything, and I'd been a good assistant director. They needed an assistant, but I said, "I don't do that anymore." This was 1972, and I had missed *M*A*S*H* and I thought Bob was a young Canadian. I saw *McCabe and Mrs. Miller*—one of the great films ever, certainly in the top ten if you keep a list of those things. I saw it and said, "I'll do anything, anything." I became assistant director to him and watched. He goes from A to Z more gracefully than anyone I've ever seen in terms of shooting a film. He really knows how to do it. He is truly centered. I had some slight interest from the outside after *Nashville* and I was anxious to do my own things. Bob sensed that and said, "Listen, I want you to write something for me, and I think I can get a film produced for you if we can do it for less than a million dollars." *Welcome to L.A.* was basically an addition to the budget of *Buffalo Bill.* They got two films for the price of one. Then the studio saw it and dropped it. But Altman was definitely the catalyst for what happened after that. He's truly great, truly a visionary, and one of the boldest and most innovative filmmakers America's produced.

There are so few people doing anything today in America, and yet they think they are. It's because the values involved are all distorted in terms of the marketplace. Anytime anyone has any effect on anything, it's because he's done something commercial that's made a lot of money and therefore he or she gets listened to. There are really only a handful of filmmakers in America who couldn't conform to that if they had to and who have any kind of vision. I'm not a necrofilmiac, but in the last twenty years of American film, I think Altman and Kubrick are the two real visionaries. Woody Allen has his own thing, but it's so exclusive. I think Mike Nichols has a lot of greatness, so does Scorsese. But Kubrick's films have been the most enigmatic, the most influential for me.

It's the vision of these filmmakers and their control that allow you to enter the filmmaker's world for a period of time. Nic Roeg is like that. Phil Kaufman will be one of the great filmmakers this country has produced when he finishes his body of work.

Walter Hill is really good too; he knows what he's doing. Fosse makes films that make you aware you're watching someone's point of view, but it's also a matter of technical skill, which for me has always been rather second nature. I'm a rather low-tech filmmaker—but visuals have always been real easy for me —it's where I live in many ways. What I learned from Altman wasn't taught by him, but you can learn a lot if you're aware. His technique and technical side are rather mysterious because they're all geared for what he does. I understood just about everything he was doing, but when I made my own films, I reverted right back to what seemed to be part of my own point of view. It was very fluid for me to do my own thing, and Bob's technique always seemed to enter my consciousness when I was filming a technical thing like sound or something that was a

gree with Godard. I don't think this is cinema and this isn't.
I think anything that works is great cinema. When the projector
goes on and the screen lights up, that's cinema. Whatever comes
on the screen, that's cinema. Cinema doesn't have to earn its
way on: "Oh, that's interesting but it isn't cinema." I don't buy
that.

One of the things I've found in all films that are great is
hidden meanings, different levels, different layers, and this is
something that's rather important to me—that it's not purely on
the surface. Again, I tend to be a classicist, but I like to keep up
with a lot of pleasures in the modern cinema too, so it's very
difficult for me to zero in on things. I have certain tastes; I have
certain ideological stance. I tend to be somewhat of a romantic
and I believe in the rationality of film. I think narrative is the
key, and narrative has its own ideological implications. Narrative tends to emphasize the individual. I don't reach out for
collective expression very much. I've said before that my deep-
est instincts are Christian rather than Marxist. I believe in individual redemption; I don't believe in revolution that much. So
the kind of stories that interest me are about individuals func-
tioning in a certain way, of course, within a certain context. I'm
also interested in relations between men and women; the sexual,
erotic appeal of film is very great.

The problem with the desert island hypothesis for film—
and it's true for all art—is that if art has any value at all, the
value is how you live within a social context with other people
and how you live in history. The desert island hypothesis is that
you are cut off from history completely—you are isolated from
everything and you have these jewels that gleam in isolation.
And I don't think it works that way. To use a word that's become
clichéd, abused, and ridiculed—art has to be constantly relevant, and art no longer lives when it is no longer part of your
living consciousness and social existence. It no longer has any
purpose. I think on this desert island great films or great books
would just make you sad, remind you what you're cut off from.
I think the idea of a desert island is pleasure and I can think of
much better things to take than films. You know, take a wonderful woman. Then again, I don't know really whether sex is
that interesting apart from the social context. I think if you just

mechanical thing. But my consciousness never seemed to be
affected in the same way as when I was working in direct contact
with him.

Island Alive is a company I was dead center in the forma-
tion of, and *Choose Me* was their first film. We came in for
$750,000, then spent a little more and ended up paying
$900,000. We used Screen Actors Guild actors and Writers
Guild writers, but nonunion crews. We kept some people working and gave them points and so on. But Island Alive was there
to sort of guide that in a way. Now it's got growing pains and is
going through a re-evaluation of what it is and what it's doing.
It's a shame because you can only keep the spirit alive for so
long before someone wants to make it into something it wasn't
designed to be. We wanted an alternative place for creative
filmmaking without the demands or requirements of a major
studio, and that's why Island Alive was formed. And, as a result,
it made a quick and high-quality mark on everyone. *Choose Me*
in some ways led the charge on the notoriety a lot of independent films got last year—of which there were some great ones.
The best films of the year in America were *Blood Simple* and
Stranger Than Paradise. I liked them a lot. But now when you see
something that's successful on some level, everyone wants to
turn it into big business and it will be sad if that's Island Alive's
fate.

What's hard is finding the money. I've had the usual problems, but I'm not afraid to work for low budget. The best ideas
are free and the people who work for reasons other than money
are usually giving their best work. There's a budget where you
should be able to make seventy-five percent of all the movies
you've ever wanted to make, and it's different for every filmmaker. But for me, the way I've put it together, if I could get
three or four million dollars, I'd be happy for a long time. But
investors don't take ads out in the papers. You've got to go find
them. Raising money is a full-time occupation, so I don't do it.
I try to focus in on a project and then if I have to invent a way
to make money, I do that. I've been lucky lately, but then I
haven't made much money. The key thing is to keep on making
real films. To me, money is not a priority.

Andrew Sarris

Writer; film critic

Books:

The Films of Josef von Sternberg (Museum of Modern Art, 1966))
Interviews with Film Directors (Bobbs-Merrill, 1967)
The Film (Bobbs-Merrill, 1968)
The American Cinema: Directors and Directions 1929–1968 (E. P. Dutton, 1969)
Film: 68/69 (co-edited with Hollis Alpert; Simon & Schuster, 1969)
Confessions of a Cultist: 1955–1969 (Simon & Schuster, 1970)
The Primal Screen: Essays on Film and Related Subjects (Simon & Schuster, 1973)
The John Ford Movie Mystery (Indiana University Press, 1976)
Politics and Cinema (Columbia University Press, 1978)
The History of the Cannes Film Festival: 1946–1979 (Chelsea House, 1980)

Mr. Sarris has been the main film critic for *The Village Voice* for about twenty years; his writings on film have appeared in virtually every film journal and magazine worldwide.

I can't answer desert island questions be
a desert island type. I'd rather starve to death tha
I'm not a pioneer; I'm not a very physical person
to be brought to me. I'm not very active; I'm n
thing I believe is that I wouldn't enjoy movies,
they were the only movies I had. Everything I e
it's part of a larger context. I don't think there
that can sum up everything there is in movies.
way about music. There aren't ten pieces of mu
nies that you can say, "Ah, this is all you can say
civilization," as some people do.

The whole question of pleasure is strange. A
give me pleasure, that I enjoy, are not necessari
terms of their aesthetic value. If I had noth
wouldn't enjoy it that much. Their enjoyment is
other things, is dependent on other things. I thi
to do any one thing over and over again. Nobo
at the same thing over and over. I can tell you
things are, but they depend on having a lot of
go along with them. There are certainly people
remarkable work in films. I think *Madame De* (
remarkable film; *La Règle du Jeu* (Jean Renoir)
zoguchi) and a lot of Mizoguchi films; Hitchc
ning with *Vertigo* and about ten or fifteen othe
Keaton films.

Madame De has perfection of form with ps
—it's not what it seems. There are about fiftee
I like, a lot of the British and American or
Hitchcock is the greatest person or artist wh
film. But the two people I like to teach the m
and Buster Keaton. And I think a lot of other
have been great even if there had been no c
Hitchcock and Keaton are great because the
and they expressed themselves in cinema.
larly didn't have a very wide view of the wor
a great soul and he's not a great human be
myself on. But his humor, his formal brillian
huge pleasure. I don't believe in anything
I don't think there is any such thing. Cine

had perfect sex in a vacuum on a desert island for twenty years, you'd get very bored with it. I think if I had my druthers with a magic genie, I would like to get three gourmet meals a day, and that would be more important than anything else. I wouldn't have to see a movie. The thing is I'd have to be surprised, I'd have to have some magical way of new things coming into my life instead of the same things over and over again. I had that experience when I was sick. I had a Walkman and somebody gave me all the background music from all my favorite movies, and I got tired of them after a while. They were things that I loved, but they went on and on—and I wasn't even on a desert island.

So that's not the way I like to talk about art; I like to talk about art, movies, in relation to everything else. You can't cut off the associations, cut off history, the progress of history, new things coming, and—this is particularly true of film—there's always an eternal now to film no matter what the style, the narrative tradition, the trend or anything is. You're always seeing a "nowness" of the way film has evolved. It's always breaking through. You see people getting old and dying on screen, passing by and so forth. And that, I think, is a part of it, and it's a dynamic process. I don't believe in isolating film. I don't make any special claims for film in relation to education and so on. I think all of my best students in film have been people who were good in other areas. The more you know, the more you can take into a film. I don't think film is something you can take out of. I think film is most rewarding when you can pour a lot into it. Film tends to sharpen things, to heighten, illuminate. But is really doesn't invent things, create things, in the realm of ideas.

I was reading some piece written by somebody attacking educationists who think love of learning is the key to education, which is silly. What's important is people learn about real life, and, actually, in terms of what we know of the world, about ninety percent is vicarious. I mean, how many people do you know? People are always saying, "Know human beings." Usually those are people who talk about common sense and experience and all that. They've lived about seventy years, they know about twenty-three people, and they've mastered about fifteen maxims that have never stood up any way, and they think they know everything. They've kept alive—that's something. That's something you learn directly from experience. The rest you learn indirectly. I've learned things from film. I think you need to reach out, find out a great deal, see a great deal, and begin to see relationships between things—that's the most important thing. What little I've done has created the bulk of my knowledge and it's indirect. I would have known much less about Japan had there been no Japanese cinema. I've never been to Japan. So what would be the alternative to my real-life experience? Japan would practically not exist in imagination—it would be one less dimension.

People think it's very easy to study film, but film is very difficult. A film that I've seen perhaps thirty-five times is *Casablanca*. I know and can repeat all the dialogue in the movie. I've seen the movie so many times, I'm bored with it. I think it's a lovely film, but I've seen it too many times. You would think that there was nothing left to surprise me, but last week somebody came up with something that I had never noticed before, and it's not something obscure. He was talking about Curtiz's direction, which is really zippy, and the one scene before Major Strasser arrives at the airport with Claude Rains, Ingrid Bergman, Humphrey Bogart, and Paul Henreid. There's one strange thing that happens at that moment—it's very unusual and it's done for speed, but it runs counter to nature, to reality. What happens is in this movie all four people get out of the same side of the car. Nobody ever notices that; you don't care. They didn't want to waste any time with people walking around the other side of the car because they wanted to get to the climax as quickly as possible. It was expediting the *mise en scène*. But I never noticed that in all the times I saw *Casablanca*.

Many films today are sentimental. They have a jazzy look—like music videos—and look brand new, but underneath they are old and reactionary. I go a little ways with romance, but less with fantasy and magic. But that's my taste, the way I am.

What I think is happening in movies basically is much more fragmentation in audiences. There are separate audiences, less of a meeting ground of the different ages. Currently there's an initial feeling abroad that *Goonies* is not going to be this year's

E.T. because *Goonies* appeals to the real young audience—toddlers—it's not an adult picture. Its biggest audience will be adults taking their little toddlers, but the adults won't like it much. They're not going to like it as much as *Rambo* and *Fletch*. And the trouble with the toddlers is that they don't have the economic power to see the movie twenty times like *E.T.* and *Ghostbusters,* which are aimed at teens. Teens have all the money in America right now; as far as pop art is concerned they have everything—they'll see a movie ten times.

When I was a kid, everyone went to the same movies: Kiddies and grandparents would see the same picture and they could talk about it and communicate. People have stopped going to the movies as a regular habit. Very few people see a lot of movies and therefore you have a few movies making more money than anything ever before and other movies making nothing, so there's a big risk. But making movies is easier now and a lot of interesting movies are being made. The technology has been simplified and demystified and more people know how to take care of the technical aspects. The problem now is not one of production; it's one of distribution and exhibition. It's getting people to see movies. And media advertising—the amount of money spent is so huge, it's overpowering.

But I find the economics of movies completely unreal now. I mean, the amount of money people think they have to spend on a film and what they have to spend on advertising. It's like what's happening with theater right now—fifty dollars for a seat. Eventually that type of thing is going to collapse, and you'll go back, I think. But it is possible to get go-aheads on a certain level because of the many new ways of distributing and eventually reaching an audience. It's a hopeful sign.

The best films I've seen lately were *Lost in America* by Albert Brooks, which was very, very funny, and *Prizzi's Honor,* the John Huston movie, with Nicholson and Turner. There's no shortage of good movies, and there are a lot of talented people around everywhere; the question is what is going to be expressed, what's going to be shown? That's hard to answer. It's hard to tell about careers now anyway. They take too long to set up deals, to set up production, and some big actors can be off the screen for years, and then if they come out in a flop, no one sees them.

The next time you see them, they're old people. People aren't working enough, working quickly enough, and there's no habit audience anymore. It's funny because the criticism of movies has improved tremendously—it's very sophisticated, it's way ahead of its audience.

Now everything is gossip—even the political news is gossip —that's all anybody is interested in. Films are selling different kinds of fantasy today. We're really in a Reagan era where people are in what Tom Wolfe called the "Me Decade." There's not this conscious decency there used to be. Now people pride themselves on their greed, their acquisitiveness, their material success. And audiences want fantasies about winners; I mean complete winners. They don't want noble losers. Even the Frank Capra movies that had happy endings of sorts had a lot of suffering in between. People now won't put up with the suffering. The hero now has to win in every reel. He just can't win in the end, after being tormented all the way through. The audience won't put up with it. Some years ago, John Travolta was about the biggest star after *Saturday Night Fever* and *Grease* made so much money. Then he made *Urban Cowboy*, which wasn't a bad movie, but he was sort of outshone in that by Debra Winger, of course, on the steer, and Scott Glenn, who was much sexier. But there was one scene in it where Travolta gets chewed out by his boss at a blue-collar rig type of job and he takes it; he doesn't say anything like, "Screw you." Audiences won't put up with that. This has always been true to some extent, but it's really worse today, strangely. Arthur Laurents, who wrote *The Way We Were* and was very involved in the shooting, really got to hate Robert Redford during that period. There was a scene in the movie in which Redford and Streisand meet again. He's in naval uniform and he's drunk, so she takes him home and they go to bed together. There was supposed to be a scene the next morning where he says, "Next time it'll be better," but Redford and his writer, who he carries around with him on the set, said, "No, I don't want that scene." Laurents' interpretation was that Redford's fans would be very disappointed because even when he's dead drunk, Bob should perform great. I don't know whether it's true and it's told against Redford, but Redford's right in terms of stardom. If you want to be a star, you have to be on top. The audience doesn't want to suffer through their fantasy. They want pleasure; they want to see their fantasy live, like you want to see your team win. You don't want them to be a loser like you. That's why *Rambo* is making so much money. *Rambo* is just perfect for this time. And now we're going to have another orgy with *Rocky IV* knocking over a Soviet boxer. That's the mood we're in now—we want to win, win, win. The girls in college are going to have everything: They're going to have brilliant careers, make five hundred thousand a year, have three beautiful kids, and there are not going to be any problems. So they have their babies at sixteen, emulating Amy Irving and these other unwed actresses and models, and when the baby starts crying they turn around and there's no one there to take care of it. In other words, there's this con game going on right now; values are being inculcated and these poor slobs are paying the consequences. I don't say it's better in a Marxist country. They have a different privileged class to whom they tell different things. It's not a political solution. Everywhere it's a lucky few exploiting an unlucky many. That's what human history is.

Volker Schlöndorff

Screenwriter; film director

Filmography:

1966   *Young Torless* (also coscripted)
1967   *A Degree of Murder* (also coscripted)
1969   *Michael Kohlhaas* (also coscripted)
1970   *The Sudden Wealth of the Poor People of Kombach* (also produced and coscripted)
       Baal
1972   *A Free Woman* (also coscripted)
1974   *Übernachtung in Tirol*
1975   *Georginas Grunde*
       The Lost Honor of Katharina Blum (codirected with Margarethe von Trotta and coscripted)
1976   *Der Fangschuss*
1977   *Nur zum Spass/Nur zum Spiel*
       Coup de Grâce
1978   *Deutschland im Herbst* (one episode)
1979   *The Tin Drum* (also coscripted)
       Kaleidoskop (also produced)
1981   *Circle of Deceit*
1983   *Krieg und Frieden* (codirected with Heinrich Böll)
       Swann in Love
1985   *Death of a Salesman* (for television)

First of all, I don't think I would take any of my movies. I never like my movies; I always like other movies better.

I'm never pleased when they're done, and that keeps me going because I always think the next one will be the one I like. I'd rather exchange the projector you would supply for a camera and take some raw stock and film very carefully, image by image, frame by frame, which means I have more fun doing movies than watching them.

I came to the movies because as a child I was fascinated by the circus, and then I was told that nowadays the circus doesn't exist, nowadays it's the movies or television. I thought movies are very similar because there's a crowd of people; they travel around together with a camera, and they live in hotels and live the adventures as actors. It was this idea of being on the road together with a troupe of people, and that's what I still enjoy in making a movie—to unite a crew and actors and go somewhere with them, even if it's a studio next door. But most of the time it's somewhere else. We have a common goal: to turn out something at the end. I never managed to do a movie near to where I lived. First of all, because I was always moving around a lot. The few studios in Europe would have been much too expensive for our movies, so we had to go other places to make the movies and film the locations. So a lot of traveling has always been included in it. Now it wouldn't make any difference because the moment you're in the studio or on the set, you create a world of your own where the rules of the normal world don't apply. First of all, you repeat things over and over again, which you can't in normal life. You don't have to comply with any laws or anything. You're your own lawmaker. It's a very liberating and fulfilling activity: You have to have inspiration and ideas as well as be organized; you have to be able to deal with people and, at the same time, be very selfish and try to stick to your own visions. I can't think of anything more complete as a human activity. Maybe a warlord has that, but then he kills people and we don't. The director, of course, is a little like Mr. Barnum. It's a boy's dream. It doesn't always work this way and it's tough and demanding, but that's where the need to work originally came from for me, and that's what I still take pleasure in. There's nothing like the first day when production starts and the trucks are loaded and everybody moves on. You arrive at a hotel and the rooms are given out; and you know now you have to get it all done and you have to get people together. I like that. That all comes out in Christian Blackwood's documentary on the making of *Death of a Salesman*. It was a very intense and difficult work, but what a great time we had just being together practically day and night.

Each film is a new discovery. It's also very much a way to escape from solitude. I admire writers so much because they sit by themselves at a desk and their work is completely solitary. We need that later on to make the movie, but I would always have the feeling that life passes by outside while I sit somewhere writing. I do not have that feeling when I make a movie because life is always there where we set up the camera.

For me it's always the feeling that everything gets more alive when you lose a lot of inhibitions. People do things in front of a camera that they would not do in real life; you ask them to do things that you'd never ask them in real life. I find that you can live out a lot of your fantasies and dreams in filmmaking. I always liked the term "dream factory," not the negative meaning when it was applied to Hollywood, but it is indeed a dream factory. One works a lot from conscious and unconscious dreams, and people who see it in the theater again start to dream, not in an escapist way but in a positive way. It enriches, I think.

There are so many influences one isn't aware of after twenty or more years of filmmaking. I couldn't trace it back. All I can say is that when I saw Kazan's *On the Waterfront* when I was fourteen or fifteen, I thought, "Gee, I would like to do movies like that, as committed and emotionally powerful and with a purpose beyond just telling a story." At that point I didn't even know there used to be German filmmaking. I saw *Waterfront* during the silence, in the fifties. Later on, I discovered the work of Fritz Lang and von Stroheim and Lubitsch and Murnau, and, of course, like a lot of other German filmmakers, I felt this was the true tradition that was lost and we should pick it up somewhere and try to bridge the gap toward those great filmmakers. But whether one or the other really influenced me in my work, I don't really know. I was an assistant director for five or six years in France, mainly with Louis Malle and Jean-Pierre Melville, and several others too, like Resnais on *Last Year at Marienbad.* But these two, Melville and Malle, in very different ways, influenced me. I learned the trade from them just like if you are going to be a carpenter, you learn it from a carpenter. I had rather a father-son relationship with Melville. Louis Malle is more like a brother and a very close friend, but they both had the skills already, and so I learned from them how to deal with people and all the techniques. Those were the years of the *Nouvelle Vague* and there was an incredible activity. I was working in two or three films a year and gained a vast experience there.

In the sixties, everything was moving. A couple of years later, the student movement came and all that was in the air. It was really a moment of almost cultural revolution in Europe, not only in Germany but in countries around as well—in France, etc. So the filmmakers were just part of this general turmoil within society that was questioning itself. There was an honest curiosity about one's identity, not only on the side of the filmmakers but everybody around. Maybe that's why it happened at that moment; I don't know why it didn't happen ten years earlier as it did in literature because literature in Germany happened in the early fifties. I don't know why we had to wait till the early or even mid-sixties. I don't know that, and I don't know either why we are all in New York now.

We still have the means to make our small-size movies, especially in Germany and France, but we don't find the issues or the world there that exciting anymore. It is like a dead museum, everything is so pacified in an awkward way. The problems aren't really solved; they're just silenced. So we look for the energy you get in New York and the Third World. I know this is true of Herzog, and Wenders has a project that will take him around the world. I would always give preference to a movie that takes place somewhere in the Mideast or Africa or Central America or Asia, but I do know that the audience does not follow us to those places. There's a real resentment against movies with issues, be they social or political, in any way. I think it is not lack of curiosity but a profound resignation within the audience, who feel they can't change those things anyhow. As long as we all believed we could change it, there was an interest for it, but once you realize, right or wrong, there isn't much hope for change, then you become pessimistic and would rather not know about it. Within the so-called art-house circle you have the feeling there's been a change in people's interest. I don't know what they want to see now. Nobody has figured out how to know what people want; you have to follow your own curiosity.

I can't be a terrible optimist on certain issues: I think there will always be changes up and down. The theaters are in danger of being eaten up entirely by television and cassettes. On the other hand, people will always want to go out; they don't always want to stay home, so there have to be places to go. I hope maybe another sort of theater will appear and I still keep a little hope of that despite the development of a technology that is against all humanity. The more you have video and cassettes and cable programs, instead of getting a wider and wider plurality of products, you get more and more of the same everywhere. It's a pseudo choice. You don't really have a choice because all the products are done the same way. They're all done in mass production for mass distribution and the same goes for the book market, for instance, and that, of course, is very saddening. But you have to stay optimistic. If it turns out you were wrong, at least you did something. Even though people are financing movies with video presales, those movies are never seen by anybody. The distribution goes more and more to this sort of supermarket principle. It's like television, where they have the "Movie of the Week." I think with the advertising campaigns you have the "Movie of the Week" in the theaters as well. The video market is just following that, so it will end up that everybody will see the same movie the same week and the week after that they'll all go to see another "special" movie. This is all very saddening and I think the film community should react against it everywhere. This is a policy that is set by the maker companies and by the exhibitors, and policies are things that can be changed by a free will. If the studios now only produce for the teenage generation and each tries to outdo the other in the run for the teenies, at the same time they chase everyone from the theaters and they're just not coming back. So it works against their own capitalistic interest. But in the short run, they think, "Well, we can make the money and let others do the serious movies. We'll work for the teenies." But that's very shortsighted thinking. Just to tell the people about this

might not be enough. I don't know; I'm not going to do a political program here, but we in Europe by economic necessity try
to do a lot against it with laws, regulations, and quotas. But that
is a boring way to do it.

Most films, like plays, are written and come from the tradition of being played in front of an audience; and for an audience, a writer writes certain punch lines or creates certain
situations where he knows he will get a certain response. Every
one of us who is sitting in that audience participates in this.
That gives the real life to the movie, and you can never get that
from a cassette that you view at home all by yourself. For the
moment it's sad to see that only movies like *Rambo* or *Invasion
U.S.A.* really have this participation of the audience, which is
perfectly all right because the audience is longing for these films
where they can scream and yell and laugh and in some way
partake in it. To see such a movie on a cassette is probably very
boring because half the fun or more is to be in the audience.
That is where filmmaking should continue the tradition of
vaudeville, the circus, burlesque, and things like that—try to
create that sort of interaction with the audience. Through the
permanent pressure of the media and this stream of situations
that come to you over television, you get so cynical toward images that you're almost blind and you get emotionally blind as
well. You don't partake anymore in the movies you see. One is
erasing the other, and from morning until night you grow up
with television six or eight hours a day. I don't think there's
anything left in us.

Things like Showscan bring out sensations, not emotions. I
think the dark of the theater and the length of the movie without interruptions are very important to build up emotions and
to get involved, but we are less and less used to it. I see all the
negative aspects of the situation, but I prefer to stay optimistic.

Since I have a foot in the door of this country, I am trying
to go on a little bit. I don't know whether I would settle down
here. I plan to go back in a few years and go on doing European
movies. But at the moment, I am so curious about this country
that I want to make one or two things here. I am working on
scripts with different writers and actors and we will see what
comes out of it. At the moment I have the possibility of working

with major studios if they accept the sort of projects I propose. I don't care where the money comes from. I worked on the scripts, but I hardly ever wrote an original screenplay; I always have adapted from novels and I always worked with the writer for the sake of the dialogue, and that I can do here as well. For someone who is looking in from the outside, I know there are difficulties. But it's just another point of view. I felt with *Death of a Salesman* that I had all the advantages: They knew the play; they had done it before and all that, so I had material to work from.

I directed *Salesman* almost through coincidence. There was a meeting with Dustin Hoffman first, and I just told them my ideas of doing the play without applying for the job at all, because I thought an American could do that better. But Arthur Miller said the play is so venerated—an institution—that it might be more interesting to have someone from the outside doing it. He'd be less inhibited and maybe bring a freshness to it and even have it discovered anew for the actors through this director's reactions. That's how it happened.

It was a very privileged way of penetrating the American civilization that, after all, is the world civilization because it goes everywhere. That's why everybody is attracted to come here. There's no way to resist the American way of life anywhere anymore. You feel you'd rather have it firsthand if you have to have it at all, which apparently is the case.

For better or worse, American cinema dominates, and it's not only the enormous power of the major companies in the market. It is also that people all over the world watch television when they don't go to the cinema. So whether we live in France, Italy, Jamaica or anywhere else, we are all a little schizophrenic because while being Bavarians, at the same time, we watch *Dynasty* and *Dallas,* and so on, as if it was next door. This permanent brainwash conditions you to look again for the American way of life when you go to the movies. What you buy when you buy a ticket to an American movie is not a ticket to a show but to a way of life, which you are also imitating by wearing jeans and drinking Coke and eating burgers.

*B*udd *S*chulberg

Novelist; screenwriter

Filmography:

1937   *A Star Is Born* (additional dialogue only)
1938   *Little Orphan Annie*
1939   *Winter Carnival*
1941   *Weekend for Three* (story only)
1943   *City Without Men*
1954   *On the Waterfront*
1956   *The Harder They Fall* (novel basis only)
1957   *A Face in the Crowd*
1958   *Wind Across the Everglades*

I think of *Citizen Kane* right off the top of my head. Aside from the fact that the story's about power in America, and success and failure have always interested me, I've looked at it again and again in terms of its narrative power and technique. It was a kind of breakthrough on the part of the screenwriter, Herman Mankiewicz, who never gets enough credit based on what I consider the misleading auteur theory. It seems as if Orson Welles, inadvertently or advertently, sucks up all the credit because of critics like Andrew Sarris who always attribute everything to the director when it's not always so. The screenwriter William Goldman mentions in his book that when a movie is bad, they almost always list the writing credit; it's good or great, they almost never mention the writer. It's always some mysterious, spontaneous work. He cites many examples of things of his that bombed and he was named by the critics, but for the ones which did well, he's never mentioned. *Citizen Kane* is an outstanding example of a work that was brilliantly shot by Gregg Toland, who was some kind of genius, and it was ingeniously laid out by Herman Mankiewicz. So, more than enjoy, I like to study that picture.

The use of various narrators in *Kane* as a springboard for flashbacks that finally form a composite or collage treatment may have been done before, but, frankly, I don't remember seeing anything like it before. It had more of the feeling of a novel than a film, yet it was not literary; it stayed pictorial.

I also like *Grapes of Wrath* a lot because it was so truly an expression of the effects of the Depression thirties, what they were really about. It succeeded in taking a very long, detailed book and maintaining the Steinbeck flavor. Once again, I lean toward the screenwriter because while John Ford did a marvelous job, Nunnally Johnson made a substantial contribution, as did Dudley Nichols' screenplay for another film that I like, *The Informer*. I also like *Viva Zapata!* While it may at times be historically inaccurate, it caught the poetic mystique of the peasant-leader figure that Zapata was—it caught the mystery of that. Again, Elia Kazan, who was always one of the most receptive directors to writers, brought to the screen the feeling that Steinbeck had had in the original work.

The difficulty in adapting a source novel to film is always that one has to discard so many pages and details without distorting the basic work. It's a very difficult job for that reason. On another Steinbeck novel Kazan did, *East of Eden*, they decided that it was impossible to do the whole book. They would just take one section of the book and do that, otherwise it would have been too unwieldy. Stanley Kubrick is also good at adaptation, and *Paths of Glory* is another of my favorites. I wish he'd retained interest in that kind of content. Those are the films that still interest me. Now they're out of style with all the sort of grown-up kiddie movies that are so much in vogue. No, I will not take *Rambo* to this island. It is maddening to see that kind of success with this kind of message—outdoing John Wayne. Either Stallone is reflecting the man on the street, or he's following the example of De Mille who used to cynically exploit the tastes of the people: If they liked sex combined with religion, that's what he gave them.

I might also want to take *The Treasure of the Sierra Madre.* I just looked at that the other day. God, the performances are wonderful. There again, I love the Traven book. I remember when John Huston was still a kid and we were talking about Traven—we both had a Traven attraction—and we were talking about the book even then, when he was in his early twenties, before he even started directing. They adapted the book really well, plus the performances. It was a marvelous, steady, straight job. I just looked at it a few days ago and was enthralled again. It's a marvelous picture.

I might take one of my own films. I would take *On the Waterfront* if I were someone else, but, frankly, I'm sick of looking at it. I don't feel like looking at it again. I might take *A Face in the Crowd* except that I've also looked at it on and off. Andy Griffith was great in that, but he has never done that kind of work again. I'll never forget the last moments of it because he had been pushed to his limits and beyond and he realized it. He said to Kazan and me right after the last shot, "You S.O.B.s, you're never going to do this to me again." He thought he'd been pushed so far. He just didn't want to go where that took him; it was really too hard, and thereafter he has stayed mostly with what he was comfortable with. He didn't want to explore those boundaries. It was not merely adventuresome; it was emotionally frightening really.

I was on the set for all the shooting of that and of *On the Waterfront.* Kazan and I were together almost all the time. He also worked very hard with actors; he certainly was a great actor's director, and he was also a writer's director. He was trying to dramatize the theme and your characters. He was really involved with that, not just showing off and getting good performances but involved in what we were saying. In fact, we felt we were saying it together. He didn't do what directors sometimes do today, which is let the actors just go with the basic idea. He would develop talent at the Actors Studio, and work with the script when making a movie. In trying to loosen Eva Marie Saint in *On the Waterfront,* Marlon Brando did some improvisation with her on the side. He was very helpful with her because it was her first film and she was rather tense in the beginning. Although it was basically all down there on the page, I would say that in *On the Waterfront,* Brando did create something that was not in a sense anything anyone could write, while still pretty much sticking to the script and the dialogue. He was our best. It's some special aura, some sense of unpredictability. You don't know exactly what he's going to do and that makes it more like life. He's the best actor we've produced. It's just a shame that he doesn't stay with it. He always has had a derogatory attitude toward acting; he has tended to express that throughout his career. Some actors can get by and even become stars just on the sheer magnetism of their personalities, but I think the best of them are, in a way, no matter how magnetic, interpreters, whether it's Brando or Olivier. It's something beyond magnetism, some kind of understanding of what they're doing.

One film the idea of which I always loved, but that didn't work out exactly as we wanted because of trouble with the director, Nick Ray, was a film called *Wind Across the Everglades* with Christopher Plummer and Burl Ives. It was on a subject that always fascinated me—about the Audubon agents at the turn of the century, trying to save wild birds like the egret from the hunters. The rage at that time was to have feathers on hats, and they were slaughtering birds by the tens of thousands and selling their feathers. Nick and I had been friends, but once we got on the set, we didn't get along because I was used to working with Kazan and Ray didn't want to work that way at all. He wanted to be master on the set. I couldn't get near him and I felt we were losing our picture. He was off the wall at that time. We realized this the first day when he got back from Europe, but it was too late to get out of it. I finally finished the picture myself. It was a mess. There are things in the film that are extremely interesting, but it's just flawed and imperfect.

I never really wanted to direct a film—that was the only time I stepped in, about halfway through, out of necessity. Frankly, I was interested in getting back to books. To do the film, prepare and cut it, I needed a year and a half, and it was time I begrudged. I thought of directing only during that time in the Everglades; I didn't think I could ever be a great director, but I realized I could do it. I thought about it and then rejected it.

I feel it is more difficult now to get a screenplay produced. The business is so fragmented that it depends on whom you know and how to get your work to them. Instead of having five or six studios to focus on, you have to know where all these different parts are. In the older days, people stayed for years, sometimes all their lives in the same studio job. Now they seem to be playing musical chairs every two or three years. Usually at the time they go, no matter what the merits of their projects, they get shelved with them. It is discouraging to a lot of people.

There have always been screenplays with merit that haven't been done, however, even in the so-called golden time. And sometimes the better they are, the more trouble they have being done—too original or too controversial. Every writer I'm sure will tell you the same story, that their favorite script never got done. I know I have some favorites that never did.

Susan Seidelman

Film director

Filmography:

1982   *Smithereens*
1985   *Desperately Seeking Susan*

It's funny, there's no one film I would choose, but there are certain filmmakers' works that I would want to take. I probably would want to take some Preson Sturges comedies, like *Sullivan's Travels* or *Miracle of Morgan's Creek,* just because I think it would be nice to have some humor on a desert island, and his is the kind of humor you can watch over and over. It's not just silly comedy; it's satire that works on a lot of levels. I think Preston Sturges is good company. I don't know whether he wrote his own scripts. I know Billy Wilder, whom I also like, cowrites with I. A. L. Diamond.

There are certain movies that I can watch over and over again and never get tired of, like the early Fellini movies: *The Nights of Cabiria* and *La Strada,* because I would love to be on a desert island with Giulietta Masina. I love her; she'd probably be good company on a desert island, and her face is so wonderfully animated that you'd never get bored watching it. There are certain actors and actresses whose faces you never get bored watching, and I think Giulietta Masina's face, while not conventionally pretty by any means, is one of those. It's so alive. To me, she has something like what Chaplin had—a female version—and what she does with her face always surprises you.

I like certain things with a sense of humor. Fellini's early films certainly weren't comedies, but Masina has a charming quality to her that's really likable in some way, although more serious than Preston Sturges. But there's also a likable quality to his movies. With *Smithereens,* some people didn't see some of the comedy that was there. Susan Berman reminded me of Olive Oyl with those long, skinny legs and the high-top sneakers, and her face reminds me of Giulietta Masina's. She has a real animated kind of clown's face—pretty, but a clown's face. There were some serious points in the film, as well, about the way she looked at life and what happened to her, but I tried to balance out the seriousness with a certain ironic tone, in that the character was slightly larger than life in some ways. It's like pushed realism. I like the sense of life on the streets. One of the things I liked about *Cabiria* was that little shack right off the highway in the middle of nothing. Maybe people live like that, but it's not exactly realism, like the guy living in the van under the West Side Highway in *Smithereens.* In reality, his tires would have been ripped off in ten seconds flat.

I don't think all movies have to be fun, but you can make a point without making it so deadly serious. Movies should work on lots of levels. You can say something about character, but you can also give people an adventure or make them laugh. In the beginning of the New Wave in France, they had something that I hope I don't lose, a tossed-off quality to that kind of filmmaking that I really liked. They took themselves seriously, but, at the same time, the films had little in-jokes in them, little throwaway stuff, and it was alive. Maybe because of the amount of money it takes now to make a film, it ends up like a big dead fish.

I think ninety percent of effective acting on film is in the casting. You can't deny the person. Who you are comes out on the screen except if you're Meryl Streep, who can be billions of different people. She's a good actress, like Glenn Close is probably a good actress, but it's the kind of acting I'm not interested in. So you pick the right people for the parts, and what interests you about the person comes through in the film. I don't like "acting." I mean, I don't like actors who "act," who seem like they're acting. I find this method style of acting really boring or uninteresting for what I want to do in my movies. Madonna is a good example of what I prefer. I think she's wonderful on the screen, but I think she's saying, reading the lines. She's acting, but she has what I wanted the character of Susan to have, so all she has to be is natural in front of the camera, say these lines and do these things and incorporate what I thought was interesting about her into the character. Rosanna Arquette was very good too, but she's more of an actress. I think the character she plays is somewhat different from who she is, but that goofy, vulnerable quality is part of Rosanna.

So many of the actors I like are the old actors like Judy Holliday and Betty Hutton, who knocked me out. I just saw *Miracle of Morgan's Creek*. Hutton was wonderful. In this one she gets knocked up; she doesn't know who the father is. It's great. It was made during the Hays period, when censorship was imposed. But it's essentially a racy story: She goes out one night with a group of soldiers and they all get drunk, and the next thing you know she's got a beer-bottle wedding ring and the soldiers have left. Cut. It's about three months later and she's in a doctor's office being told that she's pregnant, and she doesn't know who the father is. Actually, she's married so it's not about an unmarried pregnancy. She did get married, but she was so drunk she doesn't remember it. That was the concession to morality. What she does is try to convince the schlumpy guy next door who's in love with her to marry her, and then she feels bad because the guy's so sweet and she can't go along with it. It goes on and on, but it's really an amazing story for the times. It's really hard to think of actors I like as much now. There are good actors like Sean Penn, who Madonna married, and maybe Debra Winger is a good actor, but their style doesn't appeal to me in the same way. I also like Sissy Spacek to some extent and I like Shelley Duvall. I like Cher—she's good in *Mask,* and she's got a little bit of that quality, that mystique, that makes her more interesting. I also like Ellen Barkin, who hasn't done that much yet. I think she's a very good actress. She's got a sort of off-beat face. It's funny because she was like the runner-up for the Madonna part and I went for Madonna, although Barkin now looks a lot like Madonna to me. She's pretty, in an untypical way. But I never liked those actresses like Jill Clayburgh.

The script for *Desperately Seeking Susan* had been around for a while, and the original was a bit different from the way it appears in the movie. The changes just evolved over time and some were made to adapt the script to the casting and locations. I think the producers had sent it around to different studios and no one could see it, could get a handle on it and what it was. And then the producer saw *Smithereens* and liked my work, sent me a script, and I liked the theme of it instantly. I liked the title too, besides the fact that it has my name in it. At one time there was talk, which I instantly dismissed and the producers never liked either, of calling it *The Personals, Classified*—one of the one-word titles. Not only was the idea sort of romantic— desperately seeking—but the s's in it—desperately seeking Susan—just works, alliteration. So they gave it to me. Originally, it was developed at another studio but the writer and I didn't like the script that evolved from that studio. The film has certain messages, a comedy part to it, also a jeopardy part to it, and also a social satire part—contrasting these two life-styles and kind of satirizing them. It's hard to balance them so that one doesn't overwhelm the other, and I think that in this earlier draft from the studio the jeopardy subplot was getting too big. We were making too big a deal of the danger and it just threw off the balance. It's hokey anyway, so you have to keep it real light, put it in there with a wink. You can't take all that too seriously. When we tried to take the danger too seriously, everything was falling apart. So Warner Brothers put it into turnaround, and I thought after that the movie wasn't going to get made. So I was pleased when six months after that, the producers heard from Orion saying that they wanted to make the movie, going back to the original script, revising it, but trying to keep it in the right balance. When Orion gave the go-ahead to do the movie, they gave it on the basis of the script, me as the director, and Rosanna Arquette as the star. That was the package.

I was looking for somebody who would have this kind of edgy street quality for the second lead. I just had a feeling about Madonna. The story is about a woman who becomes obsessed or infatuated with another woman and then takes over her life and style. There was something about Madonna that seemed she was the kind of girl who could pull that off. She's more like Mae West than Marilyn Monroe. Marilyn Monroe exuded vulnerability, and Madonna isn't vulnerable. It's weird because in some way what the script is about—Roberta kind of taking over Susan's persona—is what millions of little girls do with Madonna, but this movie was done before that whole Madonna craze. I knew about her because I have musician friends who are part of the New York music scene and they knew her, and also I have a friend who was involved in some movies and Madonna auditioned for parts in those movies that she didn't get. But also the timing was good because I think if Madonna had been famous—luckily she wasn't when I cast her—there would have been more pressure to make it a Madonna vehicle, and that would have been bad. She got famous just at the time the film had already been shot, so they couldn't alter the script.

I would like to do a road movie, but a different kind of road movie. I'm interested in American pop culture, like Americana, some element of kitschy pop culture. I would like to do a movie that would have those elements in it. Most road movies sort of glorify the West, the mountains and all that. I prefer things such as in Florida, where they do all those things like watch alligator fights. I have an idea for a script that I've been working on with somebody. It's a road movie with a woman, an ex-con. She's broken out of jail and is on the run. I have a real attraction to feisty women who have a vulnerable side to them but have some guts.

I didn't see the Wim Wenders film I was in, *Chambre 666*, and I felt embarrassed about that. I felt rather manipulated. It wasn't really his fault; it's just that I felt silly. I don't think I'm a pretentious person and I don't like artistic pretensions, and I remember there was something that made me feel weird. I was told to go to this hotel room—it was arranged between my people and Wim's, and I didn't know what it was about, just something to do with film. I was given this card that said something like "What do you think the future of cinema is?"—one of those questions, the future of cinema, the sort of philosophical question that's hard to answer. I looked at the card and I could think about it for about five minutes. I was told to go into a room, sit in this chair; someone turned on the camera and then walked out of the room, and I was to answer the question. But I couldn't help but be aware that there were two guys standing in the bathroom, waiting to turn the camera off after I had finished. You were aware that there were certain props put in the room. I was thinking, "What should I do? Should I be creative and play with the TV set behind me? Should I look out the window pensively?" I couldn't pretend I didn't know I was being filmed and that there were all these options, so I felt a bit awkward. What are you supposed to say in three minutes in a hotel room about the future of cinema?

Without making a moral judgment, I find something bizarre and fascinating about the success of *Rambo*. You can't ignore the fact that *Rambo* is making 100 million dollars. What does that say about the time we live in? Another thing I find interesting is *Beverly Hills Cop*. It's made 200 million dollars, and what's so weird about that is that it's a very ordinary movie. Why this particular one? Somehow that caught people at a special time, or there's some element that film has that makes it bigger than its parts. Maybe part of the appeal of that movie is that Eddie Murphy does have this Everyman quality, and that it sets this Everyman in a beat-up Chevy in the opulence of Beverly Hills. In times like now, where we're more materialistic, people who don't have those things enjoy watching him get back at the rich guys. The same thing is true with Stallone.

It seems like right now there's no real alternative or underground cinema as there has been in other times, although the success of *Stranger Than Paradise* and *Blood Simple* show there's some sort of alternative cinema. But it isn't a movement in the same way as the German alternative cinema of the seventies.

*M*artin *S*heen

Actor; director

Filmography:

1967   *The Incident*
1968   *The Subject Was Roses*
1970   *Catch-22*
1971   *No Drums, No Bugles*
         When the Line Goes Through (unreleased)
1972   *The Forests Are Nearly All Gone Now* (unreleased)
         Pickup on 101
         Rage
1973   *Badlands*
1975   *The Legend of Earl Durand*
1977   *The Cassandra Crossing*
         The Little Girl Who Lives Down the Lane
1978   *Sweet Hostage*
1979   *Apocalypse Now*
         Eagle's Wing
         The Final Countdown
1980   *Man, Woman and Child*
         Loophole
1982   *Gandhi*
         That Championship Season
1983   *The Dead Zone*
         In the King of Prussia
1984   *Firestarter*
1986   *Chain Reaction*

Movies for television:

1971   *Mongo's Back in Town*
         Goodbye Raggedy Ann
         Then Came Bronson
1972   *Welcome Home, Johnny Bristol*
         Pursuit
1973   *Message to My Daughter*
         Catholics
         That Certain Summer
         Letters for Three Lovers
1974   *The Story of Pretty Boy Floyd*
         The California Kid
         The Execution of Private Slovik
1976   *The Last Survivors*
1979   *Blind Ambition*
1980   *The Missiles of October*
         In the Custody of Strangers
1982   *Choices of the Heart*
1983   *Kennedy*
1984   *The Guardian*
         The Atlanta Child Murders

I think my obvious choice is *Citizen Kane* because it's so innovative and broke so much new ground, making so many other things possible. First of all, it's difficult to think about taking a film on a desert island because you have to take a projectionist; then I wouldn't really be alone, would I?

Most of the time I do a role based on what the paycheck is about. I don't try to pretend that's not the case. There have been those films, like *Badlands, Apocalypse Now, In the King of Prussia* with Emile de Antonio, and a few others here and there, mostly in television, that I did because I could not *not* do them consciencewise. But with all due respect for the people I've

188 ■ 　　　　　　　　　　　　　　　　　Movies for a Desert Isle

worked for and the projects as a whole, most of them were for
paychecks. I wouldn't have done them for nothing. It just happened to be that some of them were socially relevant and some
of them were not. The only film I ever did in my life that I
looked at afterward and realized that I should not try to improve on was *Badlands*. That was the only truly satisfying experience in television and films because it was a time in my life
when I was right for playing the part, and it was mainly Terence
Malick whose brilliant script attracted me so. In fact, it was the
only time when I turned down a script because I felt I was
wrong—I thought I would spoil it for him, and I cared too
much for it. It was written for a nineteen-year-old boy, and
when I read it, I realized what a powerful piece it was and I was
too old. I was thirty-two at the time and I thought I would give
another dimension to it that it didn't require. I told Terry and
he said, "I know that and I'm thinking that if I go with you, I
would make the character a bit older," which, in fact, he did.
But my original reaction was, "My God, this is such a powerful
piece. He's such an extraordinary man," and I was so dearly
fond of him even after only knowing him for a few weeks that I
didn't want to spoil it for him. It's an extraordinary work.

Certainly Malick did create a wonderful atmosphere on the
set, but there was such an excitement with him. He never quite
did things in the normal way—and of course I don't mean that
in a derogatory fashion. What I mean is he invented ways of
working that were unique and he created an atmosphere that
allowed some things to happen that were very unusual. He
would set up a scene, we would rehearse it, and he would stage
it, and then we would get what he was driving at. We would play
it and he would be satisfied. And then he would say, "Now do
one for yourselves. Let's see what would happen here." He
would give us this great freedom within the framework of how
he had structured it, and very often wonderful things would
happen, and he ended up using a lot of those takes as well.
There was great freedom but also you always had this feeling of
a firm hand guiding the entire effort; in cinematography, in the
script, in production, in sound, music, and editing. In every
aspect of filmmaking there was this firm intelligence omnipres-
ent. Nothing was happening by accident: It was all shaped to-

ward a singular kind of idea, but all of us had a hand in it and we all felt responsible for it.

Of course we all have worked with people who've made us uncomfortable and it always shows in the work. I've worked with some unpleasant people and been surprised at how good the results were. I don't know whether that's technique or not, but I don't so much remember films as I do the times, the locations, places, the people. They are very precious memories I have because you become like a little family for a very intense period of time, and you always carry that energy and memories of those times. The project isn't always the most important part. It's the personal experience.

I've been inspired by several actors. Cagney had a powerful influence on me; his energy and extraordinary individual talent I found very enticing and encouraging. It really inspired me greatly. The first actor of my adult life who had a powerful influence on me was George C. Scott, whom I later became close friends with and worked with several times and whose friendship I cherish. He probably influenced my life as an adult more than any single individual. As a teenager, of course, it was James Dean. He influenced everybody whether they were actors or not. He just crossed every line, every nationality, age barrier, color—everything. He transcended it all, so he had an influence on my whole generation, not just actors, but, of course, as an actor he had a profound influence on me personally.

I spent ten years in New York doing theater and I had the good fortune to spend two of those first years with Julian Beck and Judith Malina of The Living Theater. I was fresh out of Ohio; I didn't even know what a vegetarian was—I was very unsophisticated. That theater became a university for me. It was a political theater, of course, and I was politicized there by the Becks, by their theater, by their ideas. I did Brecht and Shakespeare and the Greeks and experimental stuff and, of course, I was in *The Connection* as a replacement for a while. I toured the first European tour when The Living Theater was invited to represent the United States in the Théâtre d'Nation in Paris in 1961, and the Becks made a grand tour of Europe along with that presentation in Paris. The Becks had a profound influence on me. That was a theater of ideas, a political theater. There were meetings going on in that theater to ban the bomb, Women's Strike for Peace, and Merce Cunningham's studio was on the top floor, where he did dance concerts on "dark nights." It was also a theater for musicians, and The Paperbag Players with Judy Bond played there as well, so you had children's theater. I couldn't have wanted a more well-rounded education than what The Living Theater provided for me. Mind you, I didn't know it at the time. It was a lot of work. They were the most extraordinary theater people. No one even came close to them in intent or talent or ideas until Joe Papp of The Public Theater, The New York Shakespeare Festival, and I was fortunate enough to spend a season with them as well. Joe and I became very close. I did several shows there that I had the time of my life doing. We did experimental plays and a rock 'n' roll version of *Hamlet* as a happening for Joe. I don't know how I would have developed if I hadn't had that in my background, and most of the good actors who came out of New York worked in similiar kinds of circumstances, in groups and so forth.

You could develop as a person, not just as an actor but as a human being. It was an education as well as a training ground; naturally film acting is quite different. As George C. Scott once said, he thought of film acting as posing, which is not a bad interpretation. It's a totally different medium and it's a different art form. It's a new art form—probably the newest one—and yet it's a community effort too. It takes a whole community and has to have an audience just like dance, music, and drama. So it's a combination of those three. It's a performing art, but it's done kind of privately. It's not done in a public fashion because you can edit. I quite frankly have to confess that I don't know that much about film. My background is, of course, theater. When I started getting into film—starting in television in New York doing the local series like *The Defenders, Naked City*, and *Route 66* that came through occasionally and soap operas and specials—the majority of the work was still in theater. So I really didn't know anything about film acting, frankly, until I got to *Badlands* in 1972.

I couldn't stop shaking in front of the camera until I was thirty-two years old and Terence Malick told me how to stop. My heart would pound, my body would shake, and I'd have to

cover it all up in the character and find ways of dealing with my
nervousness. Terence just said, "Relax," and taught me that the
camera can photograph your thoughts. If your thinking is clear
and you're thinking in line with the character, it somehow comes
out. He is also a visual director. If you could say something
without speaking, you did so, because people don't say they
"heard" a good movie. He has a terrific visual sense. It was like
going to school all over again. Until I worked with Terry, I
thought I'd like to try my hand at directing someday. When I
worked with him, I realized I knew nothing. It was a totally
different skill and I didn't think I'd ever attempt it, and, of
course, I'm doing it now for the first time.

The only time the cameras, lights, and so on are distracting
is when as an actor you're going into yourself to reveal some
private moment through the character, and then you trust the
community, the crew, to support you and help you achieve what
you're driving at. They're very supportive generally. They go
out of their way to make sure there's quiet when it's necessary,
and all their energy is poured in your direction to help you,
knowing full well that you are the only one the audience sees
and you are a reflection of the whole community that's trying to
make a film.

My generation has supplied some extraordinarily talented
players: Robert De Niro, Al Pacino, Jack Nicholson—film players by and large—but truly great actors. I think of the generosity these men possess, De Niro in particular in *Raging Bull.* I saw
that movie alone in Paris about four or five years ago, long after
the hullabaloo had died down and he'd won the acclaim and
awards and everything. I went into a theater on a Saturday
afternoon and I was stunned the whole weekend. I could not
recover from the punch of that film. I wondered why I was so
impressed with him, and it occurred to me several days later
that what he had done was so extraordinary that it made me
proud to be an actor, to be in the same profession. Here was
this handsome young movie star who could have played any
role—romantic, comic, whatever direction he wanted to go—
and he chose to play this rough, almost less-than-human character who was not very likable. By doing so he was telling us,
"You see how important it is to be charitable, to be kind, to have

a sense of humor, to love? You see how important it is to be humane and compassionate, because otherwise you end up like me, banging your head against a cell wall, alone." He chose to show in one essence the very worst part of himself, hence reflecting the very worst part of ourselves, in order to teach us that there is a better self. He taught me that extraordinary lesson by subjecting himself to the darkness. And Scorsese is a wonderful director.

We have to accept that dark part of ourselves; it will never change until we accept it. It made me particularly proud to be an actor. I'm taking that one example because it's so striking that an actor can have that influence. It's a responsibility. The more talent you have, the more painful the responsibility is and you have to continually challenge, to go into the areas you don't want to go into. Very often we are challenged to accept the cup as offered, not altered, and that's the most difficult thing. I see De Niro doing that, Al doing that, Jack doing that; I see George C. Scott doing that so repeatedly—exposing a part of themselves that is very painful but very necessary in order for us to see that part of ourselves that we will never expose. Acting is really doing publicly what everyone else does privately. And it's not an accident. Those choices are made to look accidental but it's never an accident; it is a choice, and a whole community stood around and supported the energy, supported the work. It's hard to believe there was a set of sixty or seventy people standing around, photographing those very private, very powerful moments, but that's the real craft, that's the acting, that's the courage, that's as much talent as it takes.

It's fun to explore varying degrees of your own character. One of the most rewarding aspects of being an actor is looking at some work that you've done before and saying, "Well, that's quite all right. I'm not that same person. I've grown since then. I wouldn't do it the same way." It's a very good thing to have, a marker, as it were, a yardstick to measure your own personal growth. It's limited in one sense, though, to that craft.

I love the theater, mind you, but I don't have that energy anymore, and I don't have that dedication, God forgive me I love the theater, but I don't have that discipline. I'd be afraid I wouldn't show up some night. But Joe Papp has gotten me interested now in doing *The Normal Heart* in London and I'm going to a limited run at the Court Theatre next February [1987].

We're just getting ready to do our first production here, and I'm going to be directing. My company, Sheen-Greenblatt, finally got its first deal—a CBS Afterschool Special—about teenage pregnancy. I don't know a thing about camera and all that, frankly; I'm just bringing together some good friends who are supportive and want to work with me. I think I will be good with the players, and for a film it's a very talky piece.

I think the main thing will be to create an atmosphere where the very best can happen, where exploration is possible. I don't think you can ask for much more than that. As a director, I'm just going to try to create an atmosphere, particularly for the players, that will allow them to relax and relate to each other and to themselves, to the very best part of themselves, to show me a part here and there of their heart, soul, and spirit. And if the camera's in the right position, it'll photograph it. I'll just be the director and they're the musicians. The composition is already written. I've just got to be able to orchestrate it a little bit and give them support and energy. We just really have to trust each other. Filmmaking is a community effort; it takes a whole bunch of people to make a movie, and then a movie has a life of its own. It's going to be the story I read; now I have to make it visual. I have to photograph the story, and the girl has to tell her story, so all I have to do really is allow them the freedom to tell me the story or tell it to the camera.

Penelope Spheeris

Screenwriter; film director; producer

Filmography:

1981 *Decline of Western Civilization*
1983 *Real Life* (produced only)
      The Boys Next Door
1984 *Suburbia*
1986 *Hollywood Vice Squad*

In 1973 Ms. Spheeris formed her own company, Rock 'n' Reel, which specialized in films for the music industry. She also produced Albert Brooks' *Saturday Night Live* film segments.

I'd take *Road Warrior*. I don't like *Mad Max* or *Thunderdome,* the new one, at all—it's too fluffy, not as tough as *Road Warrior.* It's like *Flash Dance,* and I don't think *Mad Max* made any sense. It was a student film, all disjointed. It was very primitive, but not primitive in a charming way, primitive like we're learning how to make a film here. I don't mean to be looking down at George Miller—look at what the guy's done. I think he's a genius because of *Road Warrior* and also because of his piece on *Twilight Zone*—the airplane sequence In *Road Warrior* I like the fact that right when they have this beautiful love interest pop up—this blond woman—you say, "Oh great, here is where we slide back into everyday ordinary Hollywood moviemaking and the hero is going to fall in love with the lovely young thing." The moment you think that's going to happen, they kill her. It's tough and doesn't compromise—that's why I like it, and also it's just absolutely history-making. The way they shot the chase sequence in the end—the man made history there as far as I'm concerned because it was so relentless. I don't think we had seen a chase like that up until then. The famous car chases from *Bullitt* or *The French Connection*—you could sleep through them next to that one.

I also enjoy doing films with a lot of action in them and I like to think that there are some tough characters in my films, but tough characters with heart, which is the personality of a lot of people in *Road Warrior.* You never forget the human element. I even like being sentimental if it's tough enough on the other side. That's what made the films in the forties and fifties so effective.

I get my inspiration from the news. I watch a lot of television news. I don't really read much news, but I watch TV news —I can't stop. To me it's the ultimate source of entertainment. I don't mean to be too weird by saying that, because it's so depressing. I really mean it's the ultimate source of education. They do get pretty sensational sometimes.

When you asked me what film I would take on a desert island, I almost said I would take the Frederick Wiseman collection. I have an enormous amount of respect for him. He can take a subject and make people who are sympathetic to that subject love the film, and, at the same time, people who are against the subject like the film. That's true art. The guys in the army loved *Boot Camp,* and the war protestors loved it. The best one was *Titicut Follies,* about a Boston mental hospital. He's different from documentarians like the Maysles brothers who take a stand—"This is what we think." The great thing about Wiseman is he says, "Objectively this is the way it appears on both sides. You, the viewer, choose. How do you feel?" If you want to get philosophical about it, it's impossible to be purely objective, but you might as well try for it. I like that better than subjective filmmaking. I try to be objective. For example in *Suburbia* I try to say, "This is the situation. There are the kids on one side and there are the vigilante rednecks on the other side, and they both have their reasons for doing things." What happens is that people are so narrow-minded they never stop to look at other people's reasons for doing things.

Another of my idols, John Cassavetes, works very loosely, very much in the style of improvising. I'm pretty much of a Nazi about having a scripted piece that we have to shoot. I don't think I'm well versed enough to improvise yet. *Hollywood Vice Squad* is my fourth film. Maybe by the time I've done twenty films I'll find that I'll work in that loose style. I have a little problem this time because I'm dealing with the Hollywood Vice Squad. It's written by the captain of the Hollywood Vice Squad, so it's real pro-cop and a little bit slanted toward the good guys. I'm doing some changes.

I've written nine screenplays, and I've only been able to get one produced, *Suburbia*, but I've figured out how to make it in Hollywood: You just go into meetings with people and tell them you want to do whatever they want to do, you want to do it really well, and you can't wait to do whatever they want to do. They love it. Over the last ten years I've written that many screenplays, but the usual reaction I get is "No." I wrote one film called *Boy Child* that is about a woman who has an abortion, but the fetus doesn't die and it's raised in a research hospital. When it's seven years old, it comes back to find its mother. I have problems with people saying, "Absolutely incredible. That would never happen. We can't even begin. . . ." Right. It would never happen like the *Wizard of Oz* would never happen. That's part of the deal. I'm not doing a news broadcast. Hey, guys, it's the movies, okay? You say the word "abortion" and they freak out.

My first film, *Decline of Western Civilization*, was a documentary. I met some businessmen over in the Valley who wanted to do a porno movie, so I told them that a punk rock movie would be the next best thing to a porno movie, and why didn't we do that? I'm glad I documented that period of time because if I hadn't done that film, there would be very little now to prove that it ever happened.

I'd like to do some heavy metal rock videos, and I have been asked to do films I've not written. *Hollywood Vice Squad* was not mine, and I'm doing that, and I was asked to do *Boys Next*

Door, which I did for New World. Roger Corman is one of the geniuses of our time. He shouldn't be producing; he should be directing. They love him in Europe. He has this sort of innate, instinctive feel for audience-exciting stuff—what makes exploitation films—and I think that's great. I don't worry about the audience being exploited. You know what you're going to get when you go to such a movie. You're not expecting a Cimino film or a Bertolucci film; you're going to see a film that Roger Corman directed and you know that you're going to get a lot of action and a lot of sexy violence and all of those things that make good movies. I like films with sex and violence in them. I also like heart, but the thing is they don't usually get combined. You don't usually have a lot of feeling and sex and violence put all together.

Harry Dean Stanton

Actor

Filmography:

1957	*Revolt at Fort Laramie*
	Tomahawk Trail
1958	*The Proud Rebel*
1959	*Pork Chop Hill*
1960	*The Adventures of Huckleberry Finn*
	A Dog's Best Friend
1962	*Hero's Island*
	How the West Was Won
1983	*The Man from the Diner's Club*
1967	*Rebel Rousers*
	Ride in the Whirlwind
	Hostage
	A Time for Killing
	Cool Hand Luke
1968	*Day of the Evil Gun*
	The Mini-Skirt Mob
1970	*Kelly's Heroes*
1971	*Two-Lane Blacktop*
	What's the Matter with Helen?
	Cisco Pike
1973	*Dillinger*
	Pat Garrett and Billy the Kid
1974	*Face to the Wind*
	Where the Lilies Bloom
	The Godfather, Part II
	Zandy's Bride
	Cockfighter
	Rancho De Luxe

1975	*Win, Place or Steal/Three for the Money*
	92 in the Shade
	Rafferty and the Gold Dust Twins
	Farewell, My Lovely
1976	*The Missouri Breaks*
1978	*Straight Time*
1979	*Flatbed Annie and Sweetiepie* (TV movie)
	Renaldo and Clara
	Alien
	The Rose
1980	*The Black Marble*
	Wise Blood
	The Oldest Living Graduate (TV movie)
	Death Watch
	Uforia
	Private Benjamin
1981	*Escape from New York*
1982	*One from the Heart*
	Young Doctors in Love
1983	*I Want to Live*
	Christine
1984	*Red Dawn*
	Repo Man
	Paris, Texas
1985	*One Magic Christmas*
	Fool for Love
1986	*Pretty in Pink*
	Shelley Duvall's *Faerie Tale Theatre*

My favorite film to date that I've done is *Paris, Texas*. With all due respect to the others, it's my first real film role because it was a character who finally had some dimension and wasn't a "heavy." It was just a matter of good material and that's the whole ball game right there—the material. If the script—

the concept, the dialogue, and the structure—is not there, and it doesn't have the depth and an innate power to it, then it's bullshit. Sam Shepard happens to be one of the best writers anywhere.

Rancho De Luxe is another one I like. It was exciting working with Tom McGuane. He also wrote Missouri Breaks, which I did with Marlon Brando and Jack Nicholson. Brando is a phenomenon and always has been. He is awesome. I have to humbly step aside for Marlon. Oddly enough, I don't get tired of seeing Repo Man—I happen to be in that film also, but it's not an ego trip. It has so many levels to it. There's so much going on there that a lot of people have picked up on and still are. That film's going to be playing for years. It's a phenomenon, too. I see something new in it every time I see it. That's the test of a good film—that it's constantly alive, and seems to have a life of its own. You can see it a dozen times and still see different things in it. It's magic.

I'm still constantly amazed at the tendency to reduce characters to black and white, good guys and bad guys. It seems to be built into the culture, the society, to push people into categories. It's like the herd instinct or something: You're getting out of line if you're different. For years—it was my own fault; you can't be pushed into anything unless you let them push you —I typecast myself. They didn't do it; I took the parts. It wasn't just the fact that they were "heavies," or "bad guys"—I hate those terms, they really make me want to throw up; or "character actor"—that really pisses me off; and "leading man," this jealously guarded area, the "leading man"; or "getting the girl." Nobody even talks about it much; it's not even discussed. It's too touchy a subject or too personal. In other words, you have to ask youself, "Am I confident enough in myself—my sexuality, my looks, my face, my body, my persona, my charisma, my whatever I am—to go on screen or on stage and get a girl and make love to this girl, go to bed with her, be intimate with her, and get this girl in the end." Nobody ever talks about that. It's too personal and many actors aren't facing that in themselves.

I admire a lot of actors besides Brando. I admire Nastassja Kinski and Kim Basinger because they have such a thing going for them. It's not just that they're good-looking. Another girl

can have physical looks just like they do but still not have that
something else in there too. There's an inner life, an attitude,
that's, again, magical. I've seen a lot of exotic-looking, beautiful
girls who didn't quite have that presence. The same with some
good-looking leading-man types. They throw these guys in
there who look great but they are fucking boring. And there are
very few actors, either good-looking or not, who really do a
good love scene. I'd love to do a *real* love story. The reality is
missing. I'd love to have an audience see two people on the
screen who look like they're really in love with each other and
devoted and loyal, and really have that love thing going—which
is indefinable—instead of the tension they usually show. You
never really believe that they're turned on sexually by each
other too often. You hardly see that. To me that's a challenge
to do that, before I get to be ninety.

Talent in actors is something else you can't explain or verbalize. Now we're again in the area of magic. I was fortunate to
be born with a musical ear, number one, and I think it's all tied
together. If you've got a good ear and you can sing, keep on a
beat, then it suggests also that your timing is good.

Martin Sheen is one of my favorite actors and his interviews
have had a big influence on me—the way he expresses himself
concerning his work and connecting with people. When I'm
acting in a film with the crew around, the director standing
around, everyone watching, and if somebody's talking or the
first assistant director is looking at his watch, I'll bring that up
real quick. The point is concentration in that situation on
stage also, I guess, but mostly I'm talking about a film where
you're doing a take. In this context, I have to mention the fact
of how we're taught to concentrate. I think Alan Watts explained it beautifully. If you concentrate, first you have to
frown, and that's our concept of concentration. It's totally unrealistic. Real concentration is not trying to block out. Again,
if you're playing a character like Jake LaMotta, which is a
negative-type character in a lot of ways, you go with it instead
of fighting it. The same thing with concentrating when you're
doing a take—you don't try to block out all the people; you try
to include all of them. In some takes I've actually played to
members of the crew, looked off camera at them. They get more

uptight than I do: "What's he doing?" But basically I just don't try to block it out.

Elia Kazan is one of the biggest actor's directors. I've always wanted to work with him or any director who gives you a lot of freedom and trusts your instincts and your input as far as the scenes go, even your cinematographic ideas. I've suggested some a couple of times. Once I suggested a freeze frame for the ending of a film I did with Billy Graham. Other times I've seen what it should look like on screen; I've had a visual picture almost to the point where I assumed it would be shot that way.

Now I'm in a position to work with directors where I can have that kind of freedom in whatever area you talk about: in the scene, the structure, dialogue, the character's or other characters' parts. I try to see the whole thing. I've thought about directing many times and Francis Ford Coppola let me direct a scene in *One from the Heart.* I think it was the scene with Fred Forrest and Teri Garr in the restaurant. I didn't exactly take over the directing, but I love Francis for doing that. He's very benevolent in many ways, and a lot of people may not be aware of that. He thinks big. I guess if I wanted to direct I could. Even now I guess I'm in a position to direct, but one of the things that hold me back is that it takes so long—at least several months to two years—to start a film, beginning with the script. That can go on even longer; in some films I've worked on for five years. As an actor I can do twelve films in five years. I'm looking hungrily, however, for something that's really righteous for me to do, that satisfies all the requirements.

As far as films being made now, they are almost total crap, not total, but a raft of grotesqueness and sickness—violence and heads and blood and women victims and rapes and carnage. It's really sick; I mean sick with capital letters. I'm just hoping it's a cycle and I wish it would end. I question their motives. In other words, are Spielberg and Stallone really considering whether their point of view is going to benefit the community? If so, then great. The artist is totally responsible. If you're just working for yourself, you should be taken out and shot. If you're just trying to be a famous movie star, make a lot of money, and buy a lot of stuff, you're really off on the wrong foot—totally—and it's bad karma.

B_{ob} S_{tein}

Head of Criterion, makers and distributors of frame-access LV-CAV video discs

Collection:

Kane (Citizen Kane)
Kong (King Kong)

Works in Progress:

Frame-access video discs of following
Salt of the Earth

32 great Janus Collection foreign films, including
Grand Illusion, The Rules of the Game, Wild Strawberries,
The Seventh Seal, La Strada, Rashomon, Seven Samurai,
Shoot the Piano Player, M, Richard III.

I would take either *2001* or *Breaking with Old Ideas,* a film made in China in 1975, right at the height of the struggle between Mao and Teng Hsiao-P'ing. It takes place in an agricultural school that is run in the old way, with the teachers having autocratic rule from the top and the students sitting there sleeping in their classes, not doing anything. A woman comes and turns things in the school upside down. The students change the orientation of the teachers. It's a film that is very difficult for most Westerners because it is pedantic; the style isn't what we're used to. On the other hand, the reason I love it

203

is that it sums up in a visual style the aspirations of the Chinese at that point, and also, for most of us, the aspirations of where humanity might go, better than anything I've ever seen. I love *2001* because it also has to do with where humanity is going, but in a different way, not so much in the social structure of humanity—it doesn't deal with that at all—but going to the stars. The movie encompasses what's first seen of prehistoric man—where we've been and where we're going—and, in that sense, I find it exciting. It's the only movie that comes close to having dinosaurs and spaceships in it, and it's probably watchable a lot of different times, although it's a very lonely film, which makes me wonder why I would take it. That's the problem taking it to a desert island. *A Hard Day's Night* would probably be the third choice. I just love it. It has more spirit and vitality than most other films, and it's got music. You could dance to it. I also think *A Hard Day's Night* is really an inventive film visually and it would be a lot of fun to play with.

My favorite major studio release of all time is *Burn!*, which is a message film. It recounts the story of the generic colonial island in the Caribbean, and it's a time when the colonialists are giving way to the neocolonialists. Brando poses as a friend of the people on the island; he's going to right the wrongs of the colonialists, and basically he ends up being like the very colonialists he thought he was going to replace, and literally smashing a rebellion on the island. Up until that point in the film, it's a standard, liberal film. What makes the film absolutely brilliant for me—and I'm sure it's the reason it never got widely promoted or shown—is that at the very end of the film one of the people whom he has crushed comes up and stabs Brando in the belly. It's visually shocking and that kind of content was unheard of in studio releases. It's the only film that I've seen from a major studio that I don't have political problems with. It really stands as a thoroughly anticapitalist, anticolonialist film.

The other film that keeps coming to mind is one of my absolute favorites, *Nothing But a Man*, directed by Robert Young. It's the only film I ever saw made by a white man that seemed to reflect a certain amount of reality about what it was like to be in the South. It dealt very interestingly with the conflict between the aspiring middle-class black people and the working class. I love it on a lot of different levels. It was also the most real love story I've ever seen between two people, in the sense that in no way was it all lovey-dovey. On the other hand, there was a basic respect that they had for each other that was quite gorgeous to watch and hear. The other thing that gave that film its deep substance was that it didn't have the usual liberal's approach to the content. I don't remember the exact story, but what I remember is when they were fighting, they didn't make the usual "let's shake hands and get along" resolutions you often see in the movies. They fought hard and it was quite clear there was going to be a long struggle and it was going to go way past the time of the movie itself. Ivan Dixon's part was just a guy who was going to do what was right, fight for justice. For that period of time in the sixties, it was a very moving film. *Salt of the Earth*, by Paul Jarrico and Herbert Biberman, is similar, but what *Nothing But a Man* has that *Salt of the Earth* doesn't is that it actually gets you into the characters.

Salt of the Earth is a true story, a miners' strike that took place in New Mexico. The owners of the mine took a very strong line against the miners and viciously collected lots of scabs and, more importantly, vigilante types to combat the miners. When the miners were, in effect, losing, the women came to the fore, but they were really fighting a two-pronged battle. They were fighting a battle against the bosses and also fighting with their own husbands to be permitted to take an active role in society and play a strong role. This is threatening to men in general, but it's particularly threatening to men from that background, where women have always played such a subservient role. All the good guys win: The men sort of have their consciousness raised; the women actually do play a pivotal role in winning the strike; and it was probably the most frequently shown film during the late sixties.

My laser disc company is named Criterion, and our goal has always been to be the Random House of tomorrow. We acquired the rights to about one hundred films for presentation on disc, really to use as an engine to build a distribution network to stores. We have been getting ready for the time two or three years from now when the market will arrive and we can actually start to do original programming. We've decided to do films that we liked rather than films that are famous, like *Salt of the Earth*.

One of the features of this system is that you have two soundtracks that are pretty discrete so that they can each play something different. On the *King Kong* disc we used one soundtrack for the movie and the other soundtrack for the commentary. Ron Haber, who does the commentary, tells stories about the movie. With this system you can freeze the frame and it will stay like that indefinitely. I am able to advance one frame at a time—forward or backward; I can go in slow motion that is continuous and I can vary it; I can go in fast motion. With any kind of consumer tape player you can't freeze an image as well —rock steady—and you can't let it sit on the head too long or it wears out. With a disc like this that runs on a player that costs three hundred and fifty dollars, you can do that. That picture will literally sit there for a year. The television tube will burn out, but the disc won't degrade an iota. Also, you can't get this kind of slow motion—this smooth motion—anywhere else. Nothing is as instantaneous as this system. When you switch modes on a tape player, you can go backward and forward in large chunks; I can go through a half program in about fifteen seconds. And it's effortless. The disc is actually changing the way we watch movies. We're starting to watch movies the way we read books, where you read a paragraph three times to really get it or you go back a number of pages to find something. We never did that with tape, but we do that all the time with the disc because it's so easy. There are a lot of films that are really dense. It turns out that the more dense a film is, the better it's regarded historically.

Most studio releases are now being put on discs, but the big difference is that nothing is being put on in a way that you can freeze the frame and have that smooth slow motion—except *Citizen Kane, King Kong, Raiders, Empire Strikes Back,* and *Star Wars,* because it requires twice as much space to do that. It's more expensive that way because you have to press twice as many discs, so the studios don't generally bother. *Kane* and *Kong* are not available in stores, but *Raiders, Empire,* and *Star Wars* are under the title of "Special Collector's Edition."

In the opening scene of the disc version of *Citizen Kane* as you see an animal cage, you can read "Bengal tiger," and there's no previous edition of the film where you could read that. We restored the film; nobody has been able to see that film in this way for about thirty years. The sign "No trespassing" has never been visible on commercial tapes of the film. If you play that same opening scene in fast forward, there's a light in the upper right corner of the Kane mansion. It stays there for eight transformations and brings your attention quite well into that window that thematically becomes quite important. One customer called us up when he got the disc saying "Did you see this?" People are seeing things nobody had ever seen before. It was built into the film so carefully and yet it was lost to most people who saw it. You wouldn't see these things in real time—even in the original print thirty years ago—unless you were looking for them. With the fast forward and the high quality of the restored film on laser disc, you see everything. But one needed to compress it to understand it. I find this film to be just gorgeous in slow motion. Everybody on the set is moving all the time. It was the first film all these people made together, and there seems to have been something magical going on on the set. I'm quite convinced that one of the reasons the film is as powerful as it is is because of its level of visual complexity. I'm dying to do an exhibit at AFI or somewhere where we have the film running in slow motion, fast motion, and in real time right next to each other, because it has meaning on all those levels. One can appreciate these things more through this medium and this makes the film more powerful. That's what I mean when I say becoming an active viewer; it's the kind of thing where when you're watching a film and you notice something happening in the window, it's not hard to stop and go back and look at it. It's the kind of thing you wouldn't do otherwise. It's not going to take the place of passive movie watching—people read passively too —it's more of a multilayered experience than a passive one.

Another thing we do at the end of everything we do is run the film in four and a half minutes. The reason we do this is complicated. Its origin is that I was sitting in the laboratory preparing *Kane* to send off to the pressing plant and they were running it on the tape machine at twenty-five times normal speed. I was enjoying watching it mainly because I find the film very complicated in terms of its linear structure—it's not linear but a very convoluted chronology. You could grasp the structure of the film pretty easily through this. The interesting thing is that nothing divided our audience as much as this four-and-a-half-minute version. People who are younger or forward-thinking really loved this, and people over sixty tended to hate it. Aside from the second soundtrack and the four-and-a-half-minute version, the other thing we did was to put in what we call a visual essay. The essay consists of four hundred still frames that are text and photos about the making of the film. Also, inserted in the essay are several motion-picture sequences from the film, illustrating points made in the essay, and some parts from the shooting script. In one case, we actually included the original trailer for the film, which was quite remarkable. The essay is done by Robert L. Carringer.

The first part of the essay is all about who is responsible for the film, Welles or Mankiewicz. He proves it's Welles by showing the first script Mankiewicz wrote and the seventh script that Welles reworked. You can see that what Welles added to Mankiewicz's script are the the very things that we know to have been the genius of the film. For example, a thing like the breakfast-table montage was absolutely something that Welles added. It does say in this essay, however, that Gregg Toland, the cinematographer, basically taught Welles everything he knew about filmmaking.

What these discs are meant to do in the grand design of technology is to be hooked up to a computer and combine the computer's power of finding things with the disc's capability of holding things as a storage medium. For example, I can put on one disc several copies of the *Encyclopaedia Britannica,* including pictures and text. The problem, of course, is getting at that information, which is why you need the computer. One way to think of it is as being similar to a floppy disc. These discs are basically storage media. That's what first excited me about this medium.

Right now it's not available for commercial purposes, but the disc hooked up with computers is being used a lot in training programs. I can get whatever frame I want by random access; I press in the numbers. If it's motion-picture footage, obviously you won't have that many critical frame numbers; you're going to have the beginnings of sequences. If you have one picture per frame, since you have fifty-four thousand key important numbers, you have to have a computer hooked up to it. For example, I could choose my camera angle at will if the scene is filmed by two or more camera angles, and it would play the right ten frames of one camera angle, skip the next twenty frames of the other camera angle, and then play the next ten frames of the first camera angle—but it makes those skips seamlessly. In other words, it's as if you are the director choosing what angles you want to look at. It's fabulous to be able to do this because it's the first time you've ever been able to completely control the image. As consumers of passive television, we've never been able to do that before. But it's impossible to explain to a person what's so neat about it. It's so experiential that words don't work.

An example of what you can do with laser discs is the Vancouver disc, an experiment made in Vancouver. It's composed of photographs of everything from historical photographs in museums to posters, someone's scrapbook, and neon signs. Those were put on a disc along with fifteen minutes of time-lapse photography, similar in a way to *Koyaanisqatsi*. What the director of the Vancouver disc did that was really brilliant was to put a soundtrack over each of the still images, so when they play at thirty frames per second, there's still sound. What happens to it because of that is that it becomes browsable without a computer. You can actually enjoy watching it in real time and therefore can browse it. At the time the disc was made, the Canadian version of the Super Bowl was being played and they had to preempt a taped kiddie show and put it on in the morning instead of the afternoon. In the middle of the kiddie show, they cut to a picture from the disc of the dome before it was inflated and told the children there'd been a disaster, that the dome had collapsed and they didn't know what they were going to do. For the next half hour they kept cutting into the show with all these phony reports, with people posing as the engineer of the stadium, etc., saying, "We're working as hard as we can; we haven't gotten it up yet; we don't know what we're going to do; we'll keep you informed." Finally, an engineer gets on camera and says, "We figured out one thing we can try and we worked it out with the phone company. If all you kids call up and blow then we can get the thing up." So, one, two, three, all the kids call and they tell them, "Keep blowing, blow harder, harder!" And they showed the time-lapse photography that was on the disc of the stadium being raised.

matches. But we have to make changes. The same way priests changed and don't perform the services with their backs toward the believers, we have to make some alterations. We have to do something nobody else can, something that cannot be seen on television, something that cannot be read in literature. In other words, we should try to invent film again, something that even in the rain people will leave their homes to see. But right now, there are very few who are really successful. I think Bergman has been successful, apart from his talents, because he is brave and honest as no one else around. Fellini has been successful because his fantasy is so rich that no one else has fantasy like that; and Kurosawa has been successful because he is as wise as our grandfather. The rest—we are trying.

The problem I see is the relation between the moving image and the audience. I watch television at home in slippers, with my waist unbuttoned, chatting with my friends, and I go to the kitchen for coffee. I'm watching television as if I'm watching the fire in the fireplace because it's good or pleasant to watch, like my aunt and uncle talking next door. It doesn't matter what they say; it's just human sounds. That's how television has become. But if they want me to pay attention because something important has to be said, I go to the theater; I get dressed up; I leave my house. I want to go there and I feel I am not only influenced by what I see on screen but also by the way the people around me act. That's a great difference. It's as different as reading a play from watching it on a stage.

I think there are great possibilities in the future with video. One is that the great big movie can be seen and stored in your home, so the producers can be thinking of films that can be sold not only today but twenty years from now. For instance, porno and action films get boring very soon. Fad goes out of fashion, but *Citizen Kane* will always remain *Citizen Kane*. And two, you can write video novels that you can watch for half an hour if that's all the time you have, and that's it. In the same way, I read *War and Peace:* I can read it for a year; maybe once a week I read thirty or forty pages, and I want it to last forever.

I don't want to create any illusions; I only know that people cannot even learn from their own lives, but I hope that if one sees honest films about foreign countries, other types of people, and during the screening one can somehow identify with the people on the screen, then it probably might help to forget prejudice against certain people. Then if one hears the news on television or radio, on would know that the people being discussed on the news are those same people, live the same way, or feel the same way. Just imagine going to war against a certain country and while we start the war we show films to the people of the inhabitants of the enemy country who are likable to us, people whose problems, troubles, sufferings are like ours. We wouldn't be able to fight against them. That's why when the politicians are looking for enemies, they want to convince us, the everyday people, how terrible our enemies are. That's why during World War II in Germany, it was forbidden to show American, British, and French films—so that people wouldn't feel those people were like they were. They wanted the German people to believe they would be fighting against devils.

So film does have possibilities to show our faces, our troubles, to others and also to have people wipe out their prejudices or bad initial feelings—their stereotyping. That's a great possibility. In order to express this possibility there has to be pure honesty and no artificial feelings. When a child gets an injection against an illness, he or she gets the vaccination of the true bacteria, except it's in much smaller amounts because the human organism can only fight against a true, real bacteria. So true human feelings can only be fought against or raised or awakened by true human feelings. That's why the audience likes the actor who can express real human charisma, and not only pretend he is so and so. Big stage actors on the screen are not very much liked by the movie audience because they feel they do not see a human being, but rather an actor who is playing the character. Humphrey Bogart was not playing; he was just there, the same way you are or I am, and we knew that he was our man. The same way that in literature the relationship between the words and in painting the relationship between colors and shadows is the most important, in film the human face is very important because the audience identifies with it and the relationship between human faces. That's why I think that almost the whole film is already determined at the moment of casting.

Natasha Rostov in *War and Peace* is described by Tolstoy through pages and pages and pages. I imagine her by his description; I imagine her wearing the face of those women I know. If you asked ten different people about Natasha Rostov, you'd probably get ten different descriptions. She is described by Tolstoy's words, but if they went out to the street and were asked to choose one Natasha Rostov among all the women there, all ten of them would be different because everybody has a different image and different experiences. On film the actress playing Natasha Rostov identifies with the long list of descriptions that Tolstoy gave us. As the audience, in the first image we'll get a big bunch of information, and everybody absorbs as much of that information as their own experience allows.

Of the new directors, I like Wim Wenders very much. The day before yesterday I was teaching a class at film school. I showed *The State of Things* and my students talked very well of it. The film is about a filmmaker, so I had them watch it together with Fellini's *8½*, which is a work of genius. Amazingly, the students preferred Wenders' film to Fellini's. They said that in Fellini's film, the hero is always interested only in himself and the whole film is only interested in this man's inner world. But Wenders goes out of it—he also sees the world around. I know it is not that simple, but I told my students, "Yes, yes, you're right." It was a real lesson.

A_lain T_anner

Screenwriter; film director

Filmography:

1957	*Nice Time* (codirected with Claude Goretta)
1958	*Living with Danger*, a series of six films produced for the B.B.C. (coproduced, cowrote)
1961	*Ramuz, Passage d'un Poète*
1962	*L'École*
1964	*Les Apprentis*
1964–	*Aujourd'hui* (a series of film portraits for Swiss
1970	television)
1966	*Une Villa à Chandigarh*
1968	*Docteur B., Médecin de la Campagne*
1969	*Charles Mort ou Vif*
1971	*La Salamandre*
1973	*Le Retour d'Afrique*
1974	*The Middle of the World*
1976	*Jonah Who Will Be 25 in the Year 2000*
1977	*Temps Mort*
1978	*Messidor*
1981	*Light Years Away*
1983	*In the White City*
1985	*No Man's Land*

I don't have a film, one film, I would take. I think it's a poor question actually because it doesn't work like that. Films are not like books. Someone who is religious would tell you they'd take the Bible and that would keep him or her busy for the rest of their life on that island. No, I wouldn't take a film on a desert island. There are films that remain—I don't know for how long—there have been films made fifty years ago and they're still there. You can still watch them and enjoy them, but films are something made out of contemporary things and it's not too bad if they die off a few years later because they belonged to that period. They're made of the stuff we live at the moment. Even the film's material deteriorates through the years and can burn or disappear. With books, it's different; we still have the Bible, even books from a little before. But it's not that really, because if you take a book on a desert island, it's something of a lifetime, something you've had before and you think it will keep you going for the rest of your life. You may have another fifty years on this island. What can you do with fifty years of projecting the same film? After two years, you'd hate it—maybe before that—not that you'd really hate it, but you'd think it was irrelevant. And I wouldn't take a novel, a story, because a story becomes irrelevant unless it's Dostoyevsky or Tolstoy. So I wouldn't take a film apart from this notebook and I'd throw it into the sea when the script was finished.

Eternal books can exist; eternal films cannot exist, which doesn't mean that film is less profound. It can be very profound and it is at its best an extraordinary art and a way to penetrate reality. Films give me the possibility to cut through and try to understand reality by repatterning it. That's why I always make a film about the present. I'm completely incapable of even imagining shooting a film in costume or even one set in the fifties or in the future—science fiction. For me film's just a tool to try to make something possible in the present. That's why for me it's not eternal.

Two years ago I was invited to the Locarno Film Festival. I had carte blanche—they give that every year to writers and directors—and I was to pick out six films, not my six best, but films that were important in relation to my own activity, films that at a certain stage of my work had some kind of influence or by people who had an influence on me. So I will tell you what I chose. They are not *my* six best and they are not the six best ever on earth.

There was a film by Ozu, whom I admire very much, his best-known film then, *Tokyo Story*. Ozu's not a god; I don't have gods like that, but he's a very great filmmaker. It's the story of two old people who travel from the provinces to Tokyo to visit their children, who are established in the capital. I have seen it many times. I discovered it when I was working at the film archive in London in 1955 or 1956. It's Japanese and therefore of a different culture, so it's not a direct influence on me, but it had some influence somewhere, hidden. There was also a film by Jancsó, *Red Psalm*, that I wanted to check because I liked it when I first saw it in 1972. But it didn't really stay with me through the years. It's a typical Jancsó film with, I think, ten takes through the whole film. Technically it was something I was very much interested in, not only technically but aesthetically I was very much impressed with that sort of thing—to make a whole film in ten ten-minute takes. I was very fascinated. There was a short, a forty-five-minute film by Lindsay Anderson, and it was a very personal thing. The film was marvelous, *Every Day Except Christmas*. It's about the night market in London, when people bring their vegetables, fruits, and so on and people come to buy at five in the morning for shops and restaurants. The market was Covent Garden, but now it's been put somewhere out of town. It's a marvelous documentary film, poetic, and the people were fascinated by it. It was also a personal choice for me because I made my first short at the same time. We were shooting at night in Picadilly Circus, which is a few hundred yards away, and sometimes the two groups crossed at three in the morning. But it's a fantastic film that has an incredible sense of nostalgia. It was thirty years ago, more or less, and it looks like the nineteenth century. All the characters, all the workers, in this market belong to the period of Dickens. Their faces, their caps, the way they dress—everything—belongs completely to the past. It's incredible.

There was also an American film I liked by Monte Hellman, *Two-Lane Blacktop*, which I admire very much. I like road movies; I like the sense of loss you have on the road on long trips, and this I feel was the best road movie. It's completely free of message, of any kind of interference of ideas; it's just there, beautifully made.

I chose an underground film, *Dynamo*, made by an American who lives in London, Steven Dwoskin. He's made a lot of underground films and is probably the best underground filmmaker in the world. It's a two-hour film on striptease acts in a shabby little strip joint in London. It has a repetitive kind of music; it's a kind of film based on fascination, not on the body of the strippers. It's not a sexual or sensual thing about striptease or the strippers. It's about total despair and it's incredibly fascinating. It's underground because it's too repetitive to be commercial.

The last film was a Bresson—I wanted to have *Four Nights of a Dreamer*, which is a very little-known film of his. It was a commercial disaster when it was released, even in France. Bresson is well-known today, and his films in Paris have one hundred thousand spectators, but this one had three thousand. It was completely ignored. I loved it and saw it many times, but unfortunately I couldn't find a print, so I took *Pickpocket* instead —which is probably the greatest film ever. Why I say that would take a very long time to explain. It's the closest thing to perfection in the way it's shot and cut. A mixture of something very cold and aesthetically controlled and something that becomes very emotional is really the best thing you can achieve in film: to have complete control over form and in the end have the emotion come out of that and not out of the story and what happens to the characters. It's incredible to achieve that. His use of sound and his cutting are incredible. The cutting is fast, violent, tense, and wild. It's one of the very few films that when you are watching it you are totally convinced there was not one frame less or more to leave in or cut out. The spectator doesn't think of that, of course, but it's there and it works.

So that makes six. Maybe I'd take those six, and I'd watch them once a year.

What is a film script? It's security, insurance, nothing else. A well-structured script is what people are willing to invest money in. And then when it goes to the filming stage, if the director has this security, he is just a foreman on a building site who gives orders according to what he reads in the script.

From this little notebook I will have to write fifty pages of a so-called script, not a shooting script with camera angles and technical indications, just a story line because I need to give it to the people who pay for the film. I write the dialogue; sometimes I put it in the script, sometimes I don't and leave it for the last minute, the night before—maybe even for the last second and put it on a piece of paper and give it to the actors. In *The White City,* I had three pages and lost them, and for the first three weeks I shot without one line of anything. After three weeks I asked my partner, the coproducer, whether he could find those three pages somewhere—and he did—just to check if I was making the same story. It's not a question of dialogue, not having a script; it's a question of changing the whole attitude toward filmmaking because a script is something literary, and literature is perhaps the thing that has the least to do with film. Film is closer to music and painting and architecture. First they adapt a book, then there's a second literary thing that you have in your hands—the script—and then you have a film. I think somehow this is completely wrong. This is very difficult, especially for me; some people may be better at it.

To have no script is to put yourself in danger. And by danger, I mean that you have to try to find the vibration of the material at the last moment. The material is the actors, decor, clouds, wind, temperature, mood at the moment, and also putting yourself in the conditions, in the production conditions, and being able to say, "No, I won't shoot. I'm sort of blank. You look stupid. The clouds are terrible. The cameraman is drunk, or he didn't have a good night's sleep, so we won't do it." *In the White City* was a reparation in this sense: The story was made for that—one actor who is a great actor, capable of being alone without words and being shot like that and giving something. Few can do that. We shot in sequence, in chronological order, day by day, so we didn't have to do scene sixty-four here, scene twelve B there. There was nothing like that because there was no script, but, of course, it's very tricky because one has to have security too and not everybody is capable of invention at the last moment.

But the cameraman isn't going to put his camera on his shoulder and traipse around actors who improvise; it's not that at all. Once the choice is made, it's just as precise and strict as if we had a big shooting script. Camera movement, lighting, words in the mouths of actors—everything—it's completely nonimprovised. So there's a two-stage sort of thing. *In The White City* is my best film, but it's like a mayonnaise—all films are but especially films that are made like that—it could take or not. Of course, you have to put yourself in the right conditions—the unit, the people you work with—all this I knew was right.

In a studio you can do what you like because you just make a drawing and they do it. You can remove walls and more or less do what you like within that space. But outside, when you scout for locations, when you see a place it may be nine in the morning and sunny, and you say, "Okay, that's exactly the place we want. Put the camera there and the light comes out of that window." But when you shoot it could be four in the afternoon and the sun will be coming from the other side, so it changes everything. That's why when you don't work in studios, there's no point to having a shooting script. You have to adapt and feel every new situation, but what you must have is a precise aesthetic view on how you're going to have to shoot the film. If you have this in mind, you can always adapt it to the situation. If you don't then you are in a mess.

When I shoot I know how it's going to be edited since I'm my own editor. I know I have long shots and I know the importance of a cut: The longer a shot is, if you don't cut it within the scene, if you have the sort of shot made of one scene, one take, the importance of editing gets larger and larger. Contrary to what some people think—that my films are not edited because they don't have a lot of fast cuts—the longer a shot is, the more precise the cut must be. The cut is the thing and the cut should be seen and felt instead of unseen and unfelt. I will tell you a little anecdote from *In the White City* that is so revealing. We were in this hotel room. It was part of the decor for the film, but still it had real windows overlooking the river—big windows with big red curtains that were quite heavy. When it was windy, the curtains went up and out of the window. It was amazing—something you can't put into a script because it's only when you see it that you realize it's fabulous. It's not in my bedroom in Geneva that I can write that about the port of Lisbon. We did a minute and a half of that, which is very long in film time. When we arrived at the editing stage, we had this marvelous shot and I found the right place to use it. By itself it's meaningless, of course, but in relation to the shot before and the shot after, it can mean something. We made the join and the cutter working with me said, "What do you want to leave? I mean, one minute and a half!" I said, "I know, try ten seconds." We watched that and we knew it wouldn't work; the curtain shot was much too long or much too short. There was no reason to use it as a cutaway because there was no cutaway to have in that case. So I told my cutter to put in one minute instead of ten seconds. We watched it and then it became the real relation between the shots, but it was too short. I told him to put the whole thing, one and a half minutes, but it was too long. So the truth was in between. We tried one minute, twenty seconds and it was right plus a few seconds. The five seconds too much will make the difference by adding something too heavy. Five seconds is not all that long in a lifetime but there was just the thing that was a bit too long that I wanted to get—the feeling of too much. It's a question of the duration of images in the film and a kind of purely musical rhythm. As Godard says, filming is making music out of painting. It's a good definition of film. I think film can bear repeated watching because of that, but not too much.

A few months back they had *White City* on television, which is such a reduction of everything and a different kind of watching things. It's the only one of my films that I sat through, fascinated. I hadn't seen it for quite some time, even on television. I could watch it because its impact depends more on fascination than on the storytelling and the ideas brought to the movie. It was everything we would have refused fifteen years ago. Then the word "fascination" was a dirty word, but fascination and manipulation are not the same thing. But people are not hypnotized by sound and picture cut together; they're just fascinated because they invest their emotion into characters and stories—identification.

If I were in a situation where I absolutely needed money, I could get jobs. I've been asked one hundred times to do things for television, but I've turned down those offers because I've been able to survive with films. It's a completely different thing, even though there are cameras and actors, because there's nothing at stake; there's no challenge. Good or bad, it will be shown, and nobody will care; there won't be any feedback. It's like the w.c.; you pull the chain and out it goes. It's exactly the same thing. Nobody cares. It's not that I want anybody to care about my films, but the big difference when you make films through the years is that you have a kind of feedback and you know in various countries what people do with them, good or bad, so you have the impression that you're not just working for nothing.

But half the budget for my last film, *No Man's Land,* was from video presales. Actually, if we were dependent purely on the film market, it just wouldn't have been made, so I can't really complain. I mean, I hate television, but it gives me half of the budget. Every country in Europe has state television, and there are lots of people working for television with a sense of guilt because they wanted to work in films or have a life in film, so they offer an open door to put their money to good use and to make something different that they are completely incapable of producing themselves. They don't have the people to do that, so they give money outside to pay for those kinds of things. They are all in a very unstable position. They just feed on cinema because video or television is incapable of producing anything. But in the long run I don't think it will work because the kind of energy and creativity you need to make films can only happen when you know you will have a screen and a theater. Once you know it's only to be sold in supermarkets in a little box, you won't find those energies anymore. In contrast to the geometry of the distance and the cold image of television, in film, the warm photographic picture projected there in the dark is a ritual; there's still some magic there, although less and less. There's still that idea of myth, double, mirror; that kind of relation still exists in cinema. Even with a bad film it exists. It's lost on television.

Douglas Trumbull

Film director; special effects creator; artist; screenwriter; producer

Filmography:

1964   *The Moon and Beyond* (a short created for the World's Fair)
1968   *2001: A Space Odyssey* (one of four special effects supervisors)
1969   *The Andromeda Strain* (special effects)
1970   *Silent Running* (writer; director)
1977   *Close Encounters of the Third Kind* (special photographic effects supervisor)
1979   *Star Trek: The Motion Picture* (special photographic effects supervisor)
1982   *Blade Runner* (special effects supervisor; designer of futuristic city)
1983   *Brainstorm* (director; producer)

Mr. Trumbull is also cochairman of Showscan Film Corporation, producers of a revolutionary 70-mm high-speed, high-resolution film process.

I don't think that there's a film I would take under those circumstances because I think films are a contemporary, social, commercial, entertainment event that's very transitory even though there may be films you could legitimately say were great works of art. Because of the fundamental narrative style of movies, in that they have a plot and certain dramatic machinations, or even because of photographic attributes or beautiful scenery or great performances or whatever the attributes of film are, I don't think most films wear very well with multiple screenings. That's not to say anything derogatory about film. But how many times do you want to read the same book? A great piece of art you can experience a number of times, but you don't want to hear it over and over, any more than you want to hear a joke over and over. A joke is funny the first time, but it's not so funny ten times out.

So one of my philosophies is to try to move in the direction I started in because I had this unusual experience of working with Stanley Kubrick in *2001*. That was my first movie. He knew he was trying to do something unusual, and he was looking for people who had expertise in particular areas. I had just happened to have made some space films for NASA; I knew how to paint stars on black paper and spaceships and, you know, I was in the right place at the right time. I was twenty-three years old, but I was doing a specialized thing that he needed. So I went to the "Stanley Kubrick School of Film" for two and a half years in England. It was a fantastic opportunity. I felt Stanley was consciously trying to create a very experiential piece of art work. I don't think he ever talked about it as an art work, but he felt that it was going to be a very nonverbal, experiential, subjective experience for the audience. The things that people tended to say on screen were not of great importance. The important thing was the experience of actually being transported into the future and then being transported into another dimension, and having these subjective experiences. I was thrilled at the opportunity to have done that, intrigued with that kind of filmmaking; and I tried from my artistic sensibilities to make a piece of film that I would see as art that could be experienceable more often. So I have always been interested in experiential film and creating events that are subjective experiences for the audiences, that are not entirely or heavily dependent on plot per se, because it's plot that makes it viewable only a limited number of times. I've always felt that film is a very powerful medium, but it could be more powerful, so I've been spending a lot of energy on this Showscan development, which I think is a fundamental development in the history of film.

Showscan is really a new look at how movies can be made. In reviewing the history of motion pictures and how they were developed—Edison's work and the Lumière brothers—you have to understand that in those first days of the deployment of motion pictures it was a very empirical art form that really grew out of stage illusions. Before the existence of motion pictures, there were stage illusion shows of magic lanterns and re-creations of the last days of Pompeii or the burning of London. Things were re-created with special effects as an experience in the theater, in a completely darkened theater. There were magic shows where all kinds of illusions with weird tricks and ghosts and apparitions were created for the delight of the audience as an experience. When the notion of creating motion with movies was created by the first inventors—and even then it came out of that stage illusion—they secondarily realized they could tell a story. The first films were not necessarily story films. They were more like stage performances committed to film. Then all the conventions started to develop about how to do a closeup, and how to do all the conventions we know to be moviemaking. But the crude technology of the time was a strip of plastic film with sprocket holes on the sides and the piece of rather crude mechanical machinery to click that film through the camera, and then process the film, and then click it through a projector (of course, the first cameras were hand-cranked and the projectors were hand-cranked; speed control was very crude). Those were the conventions that established the motion picture industry, and since that time it hasn't evolved very substantially. We have acetate film instead of nitrate film; we have color film instead of black and white; we have stereo sound instead of mono; we have sound instead of silence; we have wide screen instead of narrow screen; but fundamentally there hasn't been any real development of anything substantially different from that medium.

For many years people have talked about the hypothetical future—what it would be like when we have 3D, holographic movies-in-the-round kind of idea, a totally experiential, life-like event. The truth of that is the technology to do it is way, way off in the future, if ever, and even if something like that existed right now, if I could give you a 3D holographic camera and a 3D holographic theater, it would take generations for the creative talents on earth to be able to figure out what to do with it and work out all the conventions of dealing with it: how to work in a real-time situation and all the things that would be attributes of a real-life experience. So you wouldn't suddenly see worldwide exploitation of any new medium like that, even if it was technically solved, because the creative community has to know what to do.

In my research I asked what we would do that would still fall into the realm of conventions we all understand creatively in terms of cinematic construction, photographic techniques, building of sets, creating special effects, going on locations, but that would dramatically enhance the experience and make it more powerful, more involving, more emotional. I did a lot of experiments with every process known to man throughout the history of film. I experimented with 3D, wide screen, Vista-Vision, Super Panavision, and anamorphic lenses—sort of studied the history of film from the very beginning to the present day. I found that there really wasn't anything among all the processes that had ever been developed that I thought was substantially different. There were different shapes and sizes but nothing fundamental. That was when I decided that maybe the frame rate was something that needed to be reevaluated—the numbers of frames per second. You see, you're taking a series of still photographs and projecting them in rapid succession. They learned in the early days that if you had enough of them and the screen was small enough, your mind could assemble those still photographs into an illusion of motion. That's what movies are. As you increase the size of the screen, the motion from one still frame to the next becomes a very sizable amount of motion, and on a very big screen from one frame to the next can be several feet of displacement. You get to a point of diminishing returns, where on a very big screen it can be very objectionable to see these still photographs scrambled across the screen, and it doesn't work.

But I also found out something that was quite different from that technical problem and I found it out from thinking about television and how it works. I was trying to figure out why people like television so much, why television is such a powerful medium, and why people will watch endless hours of the most obnoxious material and still remain transfixed. I read a couple of books, and one of them was by a man called Jerry Mander, *Four Arguments for the Elimination of Television.* In one of the sections of the book he talks about the technology of television, how it works, and how the image is created on the screen by a rapidly flying spot of electron beams that's exciting phosphorus on the screen. The image is really assembled in your head; it never really exists on the screen. What's happening on the screen is just a rapidly moving scan. He proposed that the way a television tube is excited into light is like a visual narcotic, that there's something about that rapid, very intense, stimulating, fast-moving sixty-field-per-second video process that the brain finds very appealing and very soporific, and people tend automatically to go into an alpha or beta state when they're watching television. I do think in very broad terms that television is a visual narcotic, that there's something that's like a sedative about it that you crave. If you walk into a room that has a television set on, you can spot the television in your peripheral vision very, very rapidly because of the kind of color saturation and brightness and flicker rate of the television that's different from the rest of the real world, which is not flickering and not made out of electron beams and phosphorus. So I said, "Well, could you do film with any of those qualities? Could you make film with that kind of attractive intensity to it?" I started studying it and I found out that because of the twenty-four-frames-per-second rate that the world has adopted for film, there are, for instance, limits on the size of the screen and limits on the brightness of the screen as well. You cannot make the screen very bright because if you go beyond a certain level, which is about sixteen footlamberts (which is a measurement of light illumination of a surface), the picture will flicker. The movies used to be called the "flickers" in the early days because they did flicker, but the Lumière brothers invented a way of showing you each frame of film twice to confuse your persistence of vision so that it didn't apparently flicker as long as it wasn't too bright. That also became adopted as a convention. So most people are not aware that when they see a movie they see each frame twice. If an object is moving across the screen, it's in one position twice, then it's in another position twice, so it's actually stopping and starting hundreds of times a minute, which on a big screen is very alarming. It creates stroboscopic, blurry kinds of nonreal things. It's that double flickering that keeps movies from seeming to be real.

I found out that if you went to higher frame rates, you could brighten up the screen because it wouldn't flicker. If you go to anywhere over fifty frames per second, it will no longer flicker. And if you increased the frame rate, you could make the screen much larger, move objects very rapidly, and it wouldn't blur, it wouldn't strobe, it wouldn't be objectionable, and you could create much more dynamic motion.

When I started discovering some of these things, I did a series of tests. We found out clinically that as you increase the frame rate up to the zone of about sixty frames per second, you can drastically increase human beings' sense of physiological stimulation and involvement in the movie. Now when we actually do it in 70 mm on a big screen with very bright illumination, very powerful sound, interesting special effects, and actors performing dramatic situations with conflict, drama, suspense, anxiety—all the kinds of things you can do cinematically—we find we have a very, very powerful development on our hands. It's very interesting to me to see how powerful it is even on the closeup of a girl's face where there is nothing happening—just a closeup of somebody's face—but it's very erotic, very intense. I just did it to show what would happen when we have a very tender love scene between Robert De Niro and Meryl Streep. It's going to be very, very intense.

We standardized at sixty frames per second with each frame shown only once on a very large screen with very powerful sound, very bright illumination, extremely clear lenses, and a lot of attention to detail throughout the whole process so the quality that arrives in the theaters is as high as it can possibly be. Technically, it's the Rolls-Royce of processes.

All I'm saying is that I seem to be moving around with people on earth who are spending a lot of energy and time in trying to upgrade things. My personal feeling is that movies are rapidly becoming obsolete as an art form, and it has something to do with the fact that people are generally overstimulated in daily life. We are surrounded by neon signs and honking horns in a very rapidly changing society. We are surrounded by television commercials and shows. Television commercials are among the most intense mediums on earth. More dollars are spent per second on television commercials—special effects, fast cuts, very tightly compressed information—than on television shows. So we're surrounded by sophisticated media, and I think it's creating a kind of psychological burnout on the part of the audiences. You can see when you go to this summer's movies or last summer's movies that they're going to extraordinary lengths to try to stimulate the audience, and they're not getting any reaction at all. It's interesting to note the bumper sticker mentality of movies and how they are succeeding: You realize the kind of stimulation the audience seems to be submitted to.

The home video industry has caused the exhibition industry to slowly self-destruct in terms of quality to the point where the difference between seeing a movie in a multiplex and seeing a movie on television is very small. Now with cassettes being available to rent for a dollar or less, it's just major disaster.

I'm going in the exact opposite direction by being able to provide a form of entertainment that is so spectacular that is won't ever happen on television. The difference will be so well-known and so discernible that the audience will identify the product and say, "Yes, let's go out." And people do want to go out to a movie. That hasn't lessened at all, and with people living in condominiums and cramped spaces and society becoming more and more compressed, the need to go out to a public entertainment or a restaurant becomes greater and greater. So, we think Showscan will be very successful.

This is one kind of movie that would be appropriate on a desert island because you could look at it hundreds of times. We've all seen these Showscan movies I don't know how many times and the impact never wears off, and you see something new every time. You realize this if you think how many times you're prepared to listen to the latest Michael Jackson hit —you can listen to a good record without its enjoyable sensations wearing off. This kind of film is like a record, it's experiential. It's like something really happening to you right then and there. It's more like a real experience.

Many directors who will take this process will tend to do what they've done in the past, and it would certainly be better, more exciting, and much higher quality if you see a space film, or a horror film, or a musical film. It will be fantastic; but what I want to do is start studying the actual concept, try coming up with a new set of rules because it's a new medium. It's just the same as the rules for a feature film being different from those of a "Movie of the Week" in the way you shoot and the way you cut. I'm an explorer and I want to go out and say, "Here's what you can do." That's what *New Magic* is about. [A short film made in Showscan by Trumbull that illustrates its attributes.] I say, "I can make something happen in the theater in real time and you will be convinced that it's a real live event." That's a sort of conceptual integration of drama, moviemaking, technology, and an understanding of the process.

If you look at the fifty top box office hits of all time—strictly businesswise because that's what the list is about, who made the most money—and if you quantified that list according to which films were wide screen, stereo sound, with some kind of special effects or special processes, statistically about seventy-five percent of them are in that genre: action, adventure, what you would call an event film. In that category would fall the *Superman* series, the James Bond series, the *Star Wars* trilogy, the Indiana Jones series, *E.T.*, *Close Encounters*, *Gone with the Wind*, *The Sound of Music*. Those are the kinds of movies that really utilize the wide screen, the giant size, and the powerful sound system with the subwoofers, and the stereo sound to create an event that people are prepared to schlep to the theater to see. The remaining twenty-five percent are films like *On Golden Pond* or *Tootsie* or a lot of films about which you could say, "It's the latest Dustin Hoffman movie or it's the latest such and such movie." But those are movies that don't depend on stereo sound or wide screen. They depend on other factors that have to do with dramatic performance, aesthetic, artistic qualities of directorial style, cinematic approaches, and a lot of very valuable things. But they don't necessarily depend upon the giant screen–stereo sound event.

My feeling is that as the technologies evolve, we're going to go through another phase over the next ten years. When high-definition television comes on screen, the quality of television in your home will be superior to a 35 mm print in a theater, and I think there will be a sudden shifting of gears worldwide. It's already happening in foreign markets because of cassette sales. The multiplex cinema is going to go by the boards. It will be dead, utterly dead, because you're going to be able to get that kind of stuff at home, inexpensively, conveniently on disc, on tape, on cable, by direct-broadcast satellite. There will be a lot of ways to get it with extremely high quality and stereo sound in your home. That doesn't mean there aren't going to be spectacular-event houses, and I think we're going to have a resurgence of the cinema palace kind of concept for that other seventy-five percent of the movies.

Spielberg is going to keep making them; Lucas is going to keep making them; Coppola is going to keep making them. Everybody is still going to be making those spectacular event entertainments, mega-bucks movies, but they will be on bigger screens with more powerful sound, and I hope more and more of them will be made in Showscan. The little movies will go directly on television. Those little movies don't generally cost as much as special-event movies because they don't have the layers of special effects and production costs. And the studios by their nature can't wait to get rid of their distribution and exhibition costs—they hate print costs; they hate the maintenance of prints; they hate the fact that print life is very short now. Most films are not good for more than about three hundred screening before they become horrendously scratched and broken. This will mean that by broadcasting a movie direct via satellite or through pay-per-view cable on a special night of the week, they'll be able to recoup their entire investment and make a huge profit, never having made a print of the movie. They take a negative of it and put it through a Rank Cintel Flying Spot Scanner that transfers films to video. People are not aware that the conversion of twenty-four frames per second to sixty fields happens billions of times daily. It's the nature of television, and so putting a movie on television is done constantly, and all the equipment exists to do it. The high-definition image is not going to be scratched; it's going to be in focus, and it's going to be properly tuned, as well as very convenient and inexpensive. So I almost can guarantee you that two thousand 35-mm prints spattered all over the world is just not going to happen anymore. I also think that this idea that there will be a lot of electronic theaters—large screen, laser-video theaters—is probably not going to happen either. It'll probably be a little blip that will come and go in a couple of years because it won't be able to provide anything different from what you could get at home. Whatever happens in a theater for five or six bucks has got to be definitively different from what happens on television for free or for ten cents. So there's a huge future for spectacular entertainments. One thing about Showscan is that it delivers so much information that there's no electronic medium now available or presently anticipated that will be able to do it for many, many years to come, if ever.

Movies are great; they are great. I mean it; it's a great medium that's survived against all kinds of difficulties: charlatans, poor quality, sticky floors, smelly theaters. It's survived against all odds because it's great. So I say let's go for it, but let's spruce it up a little bit because electronic technology is going crazy, video technology is going crazy, computer technology is going crazy, the audio industry is going crazy—Sony Walkman compact discs in your car. Most people have better sound in their Sony Walkman than in any theater on earth. The sound you get in a theater is not much better than a 78-rpm record if you actually analyze the frequency response. It's pretty lousy. So we think there's a big future in it, but one of the ways is to abandon old conventions. It's the old conventions that have stifled growth. Just get rid of however you thought it should be, forget about standardization, forget about compatibility, just junk all that stuff and let's start with something fresh and new that really works right.

John Waters

Writer; screenwriter; film director; producer

Filmography:

1969	*Mondo Trasho*
1970	*Multiple Maniacs*
1970	*The Diane Linkletter Story*
1972	*Pink Flamingos*
1974	*Female Trouble*
1977	*Desperate Living*
1981	*Polyester*

The one film I would take to a desert island probably wouldn't be my favorite film, but I would take *Berlin Alexanderplatz*, only because it's the longest movie. If I had to watch it over and over, I wouldn't learn every little trick of it—it would take longer to get sick of it, even if I hated it. So, from a practical viewpoint, that's the one I would take. I generally don't like to watch movies more than once. There are very few films I like to see over and over. I guess the ones I hold closest to me are the ones I remember seeing when I was a kid, such as *The Wizard of Oz*, but I've already seen it a million times. And I don't want to say that *Faster, Pussycat, Kill, Kill*, directed by Russ Meyer, and *The Wizard of Oz* are my favorite movies because that's what I always say.

I think I'd take a movie with me that I'd never seen because that way it would be a surprise; it would be the only way I would have the thrill of seeing another movie, especially if it was one by Fassbinder. I haven't seen all his movies. He's my favorite director, then William Castle and Russ Meyer. I like Fassbinder's attitude and his sense of melodrama. My favorite movie of his is *In a Year of 13 Moons,* so I guess that's the one I'd pick of Fassbinder's. I laugh a lot in Fassbinder movies and people give me dirty looks, but I think he had a great sense of humor. I like his characters—they are like people I know; they are people I can identify with. I like how his films look. I like the lighting in Fassbinder films. He made the right kind of movies in my book. I would much rather watch a Fassbinder movie a couple of times than any others. There are so few movies I could watch over and over without them getting on my nerves. It's like seeing the same magic trick twice. The only movie I've seen maybe thirty-five times is *The Wizard of Oz,* and I fast forward it to Margaret Hamilton's part. When she died, I took it out and watched her part. She has been my all-time favorite screen villain because it is the best villain part there ever was. It's the best. She scared children for forty years. I wish she was my friend. I know a lot of girls who are witches, but none are that good.

After I read the Fassbinder biography, I didn't like him too much; talk about shocking! But I've always said anyone who can make four and five movies a year deserves to be a monster. Of course, someone has to give you money that often. Certainly the government helped him out a lot. That doesn't happen here. The government tries to stop you. That's a very large difference. It tried to stop me with censorship. All my life I've had problems with that. Certainly if I was raising money for a film the government isn't somebody I'd call. I'm not the type who can get grants. But in Germany you can. Also, I think Fassbinder was driven to the point of insanity, whiich is why he made his movies so quickly. His group was like the Manson family. Any director who idolizes Douglas Sirk, though, is okay in my book, and he did. I also love Douglas Sirk. It was really great to see Fassbinder and Sirk together because Sirk was sort of his mentor, and it was touching to see Fassbinder and all his stars with Douglas Sirk and his wife. He was one person, maybe the only person, Fassbinder didn't insult.

I like Russ Meyer because he makes industrials about

breasts. He influenced me a lot, not that I want to make movies like his, but I like his mean, aggressive sort of monstrous women. Normally, men play those roles. I use that too.

But I don't know if I was on a desert island whether the main thing I would want to do would be to watch a movie, no matter what it was, over and over, and to read a book over and over would also be deadly. But if I was on a desert island by myself, then it would be a porno movie, but Russ Meyer wouldn't be the director I'd pick because Russ doesn't make porno. He makes sexual comedies. I'd take some of the obscure Russ Meyer movies, like *Mud Honey,* which is one I like very much, and *Good Morning and Goodbye* because it has the nastiest dialogue. I'd probably miss hearing someone bitch if I was on a desert island. That one has a lot of good bitching in it. Look, I wouldn't want to go to a desert island for one day, much less for the rest of my life. I'm not really close to nature, so I would probably kill myself the first day.

As far as what's going on in movies now, maybe I'm getting too picky, but I like fewer and fewer movies every year. I still go all the time, but it's harder to find one I really like. I see all the foreign films. My favorite last film was *L'Argent,* the Robert Bresson movie. It was just unbelievably good. I loved *First Name: Carmen,* the Godard movie. I like a lot of foreign films, usually the real arty ones or the real trashy ones, not much in between, because I like extremes of everything in life. My interest is extremes. I like either one way or the other in people's behavior, in dress, in everything.

I certainly wouldn't take one of my own films on a desert island. I can't even look at my films. My God, I can recite everything in my movies. When I'm on these lecture tours I can't escape them because they're in some strange city for one night. I come out and give this speech before the movie and have to answer questions afterwards. The only time I can stand watching them is when they're in a foreign country and they've been dubbed, because that amazes me. I don't mind watching them in foreign countries, at least the first time, because I see if the reaction is the same and what jokes they don't get because the humor is too American. But seeing it dubbed is hilarious. The only things I see when I watch my films now are the things I hate, so I try not to watch them. I don't even own any of them on video. I have no desire to do anything with them anymore, to make them better. They're just done with. I still like them; I live from them, so I'm certainly glad they're there. But as far as sitting down and watching them, I already know when the laughs are going to come. It's like noise to my ears.

If I could take a movie I hadn't already made, one would be with three generations of women: The grandmother would be Lana Turner; the daughter would be Joey Heatherton; and the granddaughter would be Pia Zadora. They'd all be in love with Matt Dillon and Benjie would be their dog. That would be my dream cast. Or I would also love to do a movie with Liberace and Pia Zadora as a killer couple on the run. Pia, I think, is the great talent of the eighties. She was picked by *Penthouse* as one of the ten sexiest women. I'm laughing because you should always laugh about show business—that's the point. The whole thing is a wonderful joke, and Pia Zadora has had the last laugh: She has three homes and an airplane. She's laughing all the way to the bank, and the bank is already full.

I certainly wouldn't want *Brink of Life* by Bergman on a desert island, although I really like Bergman. I don't like anything with Sylvester Stallone or Barbra Streisand. Their egos are too big; they take themselves too seriously. I think if you're going to be on a desert island what you're going to need is laughs, something you can actually put on and do the dialogue with, become one of the characters and really get into it.

I love Hollywood and New York, but they are the only places that aren't really America. If you're always there, you would lose track of what the American taste is, which is pretty bad, but bad taste is universal. Every country has bad taste, even France. When I was in Paris, I had a retrospective at the Cinémathèque Française. I went to the opening and I saw this crowd across the street at a movie theater. I didn't know what it was, so I asked someone and he translated the title: *They Lick from Behind*. I thought, "See, that even tops anything I could come up with." I was upstaged.

Wim Wenders

Screenwriter; film director; producer

Filmography:

1970   *Summer in the City*
1972   *The Goalie's Anxiety at the Penalty Kick*
1973   *The Scarlet Letter*
1974   *Alice in the Cities*
       Aus der Familie der Panzerrechsen, die Insel
1975   *Wrong Move*
1976   *Kings of the Road*
1977   *The American Friend*
1981   *Lightning Over Water*
1982   *Hammett*
       The State of Things
1984   *Paris, Texas*
       Chambre 666
1985   *Tokyo-Ga*

It depends on what day I'd have to leave for this island. I have films that I would take if I was in a good mood, and if I wanted anything to do with movies on this island, which could just as well be the reason why I would go to this island—not to have any films with me—in that case, I'd take *Salt of the Earth*. But if I was still thirsting for films, I'd take *Only Angels Have Wings*. They are two of my favorite films; I wouldn't take any others. They have something in common, and that is you see them and you know what you're in touch with. *Salt of the Earth*—you see that movie and you come out and you're in touch with people and you know what they're looking for, and maybe you know what movies are for. With *Only Angels Have Wings* you come out and you feel better. They're both extremely honest movies.

Technique matters very much insofar as it's a translation of the vision, and I don't think anybody who doesn't have technique that translates into style can really have a precise vision. People who make great movies mostly have great visions. Technique is very accessible, but to translate technique into style you can have all the technique in the world and not have one single valid image. I think by technique one means film language, not just the means. The language doesn't seem to be that accessible and they don't seem to be teaching it either. At least the necessity for it can be taught.

Maybe I know that when I see *Salt of the Earth* I feel pretty comfortable because I see when they made the film they didn't pose the question to themselves about affecting the audience. I feel respected as one of the audience because I feel this was not a film made for me, in order to evoke this and that. It was made for other reasons, out of a necessity, and to do something good because they felt right about what they were doing. So I can feel it too. I feel respected as an audience. When I make a movie, I do think about a few people, maybe sometimes who I know and maybe only vaguely know. I've met somebody and they tell me why my movie was important to them. One person somewhere in Alaska or Australia tells of one moment—why it was important for them to have seen this or that movie. Suddenly, one moment you're shooting and you think of this person and you know the responsibility, and this person becomes the audience.

It seems that if you're more interested in how you're trying to say something than in what you're saying, then you probably make the same film over and over again. I'm a formalist so to speak: I very much believe in a certain form of shots, in a certain framing, and I believe in certain ideas, but, on the other hand, I believe that from the first day of shooting, whatever you have to tell will ultimately dictate the form of the film. If you considered *The American Friend* all by itself from the beginning, it was clearly going to be very complex and have different points of view, and it was going to be filmed in a way that relied on montage because of the complexity of the story. It's full of intrigue; there are three people, and a weird background that peeks in every now and then. *Kings of the Road* was two people with simple dialogue, not even a story but a very simple direction of line—an itinerary more than a story—so it was obvious there was no need to cut very much. But I didn't know that before. You have to feel it.

In *Chambre 666*, the question I asked of the filmmakers in Cannes whom I filmed was very specific, but only very few of the people there really answered specifically. The question was not about the future of *cinema*, but about the future of the *cinematographic language*. A lot of people take that for the same meaning. I think the language of cinema that has been developed very much by the American cinema, certainly much more than any other cinema, is down the drain anyway. Of course, every now and then we still see a film like a dinosaur, like Kurosawa's *Ran* the other day. It's a dinosaur. Kurosawa still believes in, still aggressively shows this cinematographic language. But these are exceptions: Basically cinema as a language has been swept away by electronic language, and I don't really feel any regrets because it's just a fact. I think maybe there are another ten years where there will be a chance to work in that old, anachronistic language of cinema with cameras and projectors and all that. Then it's going to be electronic. Maybe some reminiscences of that language will still exist in the electronic images, but, basically, the electronic storytelling is starting; you already see it on television and also in movie houses, especially in American movies. The electronic storytelling will make some references every now and then to the language of the movies, but basically it has to and is about to find its own language, and maybe something even more exciting will happen.

Language has to do with attitudes, with finding a form through an element like sound, which is important, but, on the other hand, you have to be able to turn the sound off and still understand the images. That's really the opposite of the electronic image that relies so much more on sound. Movies still have that look of photography, so you understand just by seeing, like painting; you just see. That's what's being lost, the idea that seeing is understanding.

I guess financing films through video presales and having more viewers through the television audience are the condition and you can't change that. I say that's okay—take the money and run. Make the movie and those who'll appreciate it will certainly insist on seeing it on the screen. I even think one has to be grateful that these possibilities exist for financing because otherwise there wouldn't be much left to do in independent movies. So I'm glad there's a video market, and a lot of people don't really care that much whether they see it on the screen or at home. I see a lot of movies on the television screen too and feel quite satisfied.

People whose work I like who are working now are in New York: Scorsese, Jim Jarmusch. There must be more but those are two I very much like and admire.

In *Chambre 666* I think maybe Steven Spielberg understood the question better than some of the others. He gave a very honest, straightforward answer that went to the core of American filmmaking, and a lot of people seem to think that he's talking about money. I think he's talking about movies, but with the right angle from his point of view. I was curious and very confused about the question I asked, and it was at a time when I was rather pessimistic, so I thought maybe it isn't only me, maybe there is a conscientiousness about this so-called last leg of the cinema of this period that we might witness, that might be the end of cinema. So I just was curious, and it turned out that there wasn't that much of a conscientiousness and maybe I was overconscientious. Anyway, I threw myself into another movie that turned out to make me believe entirely in the possibilities of cinema today, *Paris, Texas*.

I'm working on a movie now called *Till the End of the World*, a science fiction movie that I'm going to shoot in fifteen countries. It's at the screenplay, preparation, and financing stages.

Krzysztof Zanussi

Screenwriter; film director

Filmography:

1966	*Death of a Provincial*
1967	*Face to Face*
1969	*The Structure of Crystals*
1970	*Family Life*
1971	*Behind the Wall*
1973	*Illumination*
1974	*The Catamount Killing*
1975	*Quarterly Balance/A Woman's Decision*
1977	*Camouflage*
1978	*The Spiral*
1980	*The Constant Factor*
1981	*Contract*
1982	*Imperative*
	The Unapproachable
1983	*Vaticano Capitale*
	Bluebeard
1984	*A Year of the Quiet Sun*
1985	*Paradigma*

I'm trying to think whether I would ever like to see movies on a desert island. I'm a very practical person and I'm trying to think about it in realistic terms. In fact, I have a VCR at home and I own very few cassettes, so even not being on a desert island, I have to make choices because cassettes are very expensive. But it would be like choosing cassettes, a music cassette or a record. I should take something least evident, least transparent, otherwise there is a risk of learning it by heart. So it definitely has to be something very complex, of a very rich, complicated structure to be sure you would like to see it again and again. When I think of what kind of films, maybe it would be something by Fellini, maybe *Satyricon* or *La Strada;* but there is a big difference because, although I admire *La Strada,* after I've seen it ten times, it may simply vanish, while *Satyricon* is a very surprising film and maybe it would last longer. Maybe I would take a film by Bergman, and if so, it would be *The Seventh Seal,* which is such a revelation. Or maybe it would be Dreyer's *Gertrud.* I think these films won't get old very soon. I would be hesitant to take Elia Kazan's *East of Eden,* which I admire, because I'm afraid if I saw it many times in a row it would lose the magic, and I'm afraid of losing magic, so he's not the right one. I wonder whether I would consider something of Tarkovsky, *Mirror* or maybe *Nostalgia.* They have many layers, so I wouldn't feel the risk that they would vanish soon. It wouldn't be *Citizen Kane* because I've seen it so many times. It is an appropriate movie, but I've almost had it on a desert island. It was part of my studies—I've seen it dozens of times, so I've had it already. Perhaps it would be something by Kurosawa because his magic is very sensual like a musical score. It appeals again and again. If so, it might be *Ran.* I've seen it recently and liked it a lot. But if not, it could be *Rashomon* or *Seven Samurai.* But I wonder whether I wouldn't like to have Renoir on a desert island—*The Rules of the Game* or *Grand Illusion.* Here again, I'm afraid the poetics of Renoir may be inappropriate on a desert island. My intuition tells me that this kind of writing, this kind of novel, doesn't need to be read so many times.

Any object of art that develops in time is conceived for one reading or viewing, and you feel a sort of flow. It is some sign of imperfection if you need to see it many times in order to get some understanding. Of course, there's a factor of the spectator evolving. I remember listening to Stravinsky thirty years ago, and I was very confused, and now I think I read his music very easily. It became understandable to me, but it wasn't thirty years ago. However, the language he's using, which I'm very much familiar with, would be disqualified, would be eliminated from this island. I would favor something I'm not all that familiar with.

There are some films by Rohmer that I've missed, and whenever a film is signed by Rohmer, I'm ready to see it, but I don't think there would be great surprises. There would just be great pleasure. I like Rohmer very much. I've missed one or two of Bergman's films, but considering how prolific he is, I've seen almost all of his work. I've missed more films from the thirties and forties, but they don't appeal to me very much.

Of course, your everyday life has an enormous impact on your film viewing, but I understand that in going to a desert island, I would carry with me all my memories and I know my memories right now. I know some other films would be of no use because they are films that are a lot like *Children of Paradise*. There's a certain soft romanticism there that vanishes particularly easily. I would say most emotional art vanishes, so I would probably tend toward more intellectual films because I know they resist better. It doesn't mean they are any better; they're just different and they're resistant. Again, less emotional literature remains alive longer, and films that have a very strong impact on the first viewing often leave us disappointed later. They don't re-create the same feelings again.

In the late fifties, Ingmar Bergman was the first to prove, to institutionalize the function of the author-filmmaker. Without his example, I wouldn't have felt comfortable with my aspiration of making my own personal films. But of the films I remember from my childhood that had enormous impact on me, most of them I know are not all that good, and I don't want to see them again. My memories are good; I remember they were mostly French films like *La Chartreuse de Parme* from Stendhal, directed by Christian-Jaque, and his *Fanfan la Tulipe* with Gérard Philipe. I think those two have aged. And I remember many films by René Clair, somebody who has been forgotten. I always try to stand for his memory. One of the few things the *Nouvelle Vague* should be reproached for was destroying their great predecessor. They created a new celebrity: I've never understood why they chose Hitchcock, why they tried to prove that he was so big, and they destroyed old masters—they destroyed René Clair, who maybe personally wasn't pleasant to them, but he was a great author. But now considering from the purely sociological point of view what René Clair did, I think it is a tremendous loss that they have destroyed his reputation and position, because he tried very successfully to make intelligent films for a fairly wide audience, and the *Nouvelle Vague* made intelligent films for a fairly narrow audience. That's what made French cinema so weak, and now we are in total crisis because there is no public anymore. The public goes for the cheapest and dimmest films. René Clair was able to make his "Faust," *La Beauté du Diable*, which was a beautiful, witty film, and his *Les Belles de Nuit*, which is, again, a lovely film and a very popular one at the same time. He managed to do it. It was a sort of intelligent, witty, boulevard cinema, and I regret it vanished. He was one of the masters of my early youth, and comparing him with commercial cinema of his time, he was far ahead of it. He was far more intelligent; he was brilliant. I'm sorry his memory has been destroyed. In some countries like the Soviet Union he's remembered as a great master and nobody there paid any attention to the *Nouvelle Vague* theories, even if their films—some of them—were esteemed. I'm not all that alone when I question "Why Hitchcock?"

It's not the lowest common denominator but the most childish denominator that has brought people to the cinema in the last four or five years, and this Spielbergian cinema appeals to children. I think there is something dangerous in a society when its emotions become infantile and stop at this level of development. There's nothing wrong with Spielberg; there's something wrong with society. *Rambo* is less frightening to me because it's primitive, but at least it is clearer. Some of the elements of *Star Wars* are rather praising aggression and have rather negative feelings, but *E.T.* does not. I guess this is a period of confusion and some illusions are vanishing. There was a long period of more than a decade of exultation with social problems, with political problems, and they were trying to exhibit them as ultimate problems of humanity. Now we're discovering that there are other aspects of our existence that are equally important and interesting. I hope this confusion, this regression to childhood, is temporary. I hope cassettes will be of some use. I think the same people who are renting cassettes used to read books. They may be selecting some better films. In the long run we may discover that some films that have been neglected these days will be highly praised later.

It does matter, however, whether a film is viewed on cassette or in a theater; because on cassette, for example, all the flaws of *Amadeus* will be apparent, but all of its beauty will vanish. Its appeal will be half. The greatest appeal of *Amadeus* is in its music and in its rhythmic movement. These are the elements that cassettes usually reduce, while some simplicity in the acting will be more noticeable. I've seen some trailers on television and noticed how poor they look in comparison to the Dolby stereo view of those same scenes in the cinema. But, on the other hand, I expect very little. If I have a chance to talk via cassette, it's still a good thing. I can't complain because I haven't been promised that I would ever be permitted to speak loudly before that audience. Whatever I am offered I will accept if it gives me a chance to continue.

Frank Zappa

Musician; songwriter; recording artist; performing artist; founder of
several record companies (Bizarre, Discreet, Zappa, Barking Pumpkin);
writer; screenwriter; film director; producer; social critic; lecturer

Filmography:

1971   *200 Motels* (writer; director; soundtrack; producer)
1975   *Baby Snakes* (writer; director; soundtrack; producer)

Work in progress:
Uncle Meat

Mr. Zappa's body of work includes thirty-nine album
releases, over two hundred vocal songs, ninety-one
instrumental works, thirty-two compositions for
orchestra and choral groups, four ballets, two video
specials, a book (*Christmas in New Jersey*), and the
preparation of two Broadway shows, *The Works* and
Thing-Fish.

I've never seen a film that could hold my interest for
repeated viewings. There are pieces of music that I can listen to
over and over again, sure. That's art. Film can be art, but if
you're asking me if there's a film in existence that I can think of
in the same way as, say *The Rite of Spring* by Stravinsky, that I
could stand to listen to over and over again, I can't think of any,
which is not to denigrate anybody's efforts in the medium. It's

just my personal taste. If I had to be entertained, I'd probably stick with *The Rite of Spring.* You get to use more of your own imagination when you listen to a piece of music. Movies tend to spell it out for you.

I made three films: *200 Motels, Baby Snakes,* and another one called *Uncle Meat,* which is not finished. The basic idea behind *200 Motels* was putting music and images together in a surrealistic way, but because of the budget of the film it wasn't possible to do the project the way it was supposed to have been done. There are a number of firsts in that film: It's the first feature-length major motion picture to be shot in video, so there were all the union problems that we had to work out between the people on the film side and the people on the video side. A stupid example would be when we were shooting at Pinewood Studios in England. The cameramen's union was there saying, "Okay, we need a focus puller on every one of these video cameras." So that left us with five guys who were hanging around eating sandwiches all the time. The picture was shot in seven eight-hour days, fifty-six hours, and they pulled the plug at the end of the last hour. At that point, only one-third of the actual script had been shot. There were one hundred and ten hours of video edit, after which the edited video master was transfered to 35-mm Technicolor, and then three months of film editing and laying in sound effects and dubbing and all that stuff. The total budget was $679,000. That was in 1971. We shot it on video tape because for one thing, the special effects—the optical effects—that were involved in the film didn't exist in any other kind of medium at that time. If you were paying for dissolves by the foot, the optical bill alone for that one film would have been out toward Venus. So I thought video was the right medium in which to do it. The other thing that was un- usual about *200 Motels* was that there was a symphony orchestra of some one hundred and twenty players and they were actually playing. They were really recording the soundtrack instead of doing it in playback as is usually done. It could have worked better if the attitude of the participants had been a little better. The Royal Philharmonic Orchestra was something less than co- operative. As a matter of fact, on the last day of shooting, some of these nice old gentlemen in the orchestra purposely destroyed the rented tuxedos they were wearing—like mongoloid vandalism. Finally, the way the film was cut together had more to do with the way you would organize a piece of music than the way you would organize a motion picture: where to cut in terms of rhythms, where you would go to from one scene to another, the types of pictorial modulations that would be included.

The film did have a story, but as I said, at the end of the more than fifty hours, we had only done one-third of the script, so I had to make up another, completely different story in the editing room. The biggest mistake that was made during the whole filming was that it was all shot in video tape—at that time it was two-inch video. I guess the cost of each reel was three or four hundred dollars for a ninety-minute reel. The producer of the film decided that since he was an independent working through United Artists, he would make United Artists happy by showing them he was a real tight-fisted, frugal, prudent producer, hoping to grease the chute for future activities. He had all of the master tapes erased and sold for stock. I don't think he's done another film with United Artists since then, but if he just could've looked down the road ten years, do you have any idea of what the outtakes of *200 Motels* would be worth? I just did it because I had my own idea about what I wanted to do and tried to do, but there just wasn't enough money at the time to do it in the right way. I'm not that enthralled with *200 Motels* as a finished product. I made the best of it. *Baby Snakes* is a little more successful in terms of what it sets out to do versus what it achieves, but that's also another low-budget film. I probably have $800,000 of my own money in that one.

Music videos could be an interesting medium, but the problem with music videos is the pictorial vocabulary that is allowed in broadcasting is so narrow that you get the same images over and over again. You could sum it up with "the door, the dove, the legs, the leather." It's the same little components over and over again. On the other hand, if you listen to what the lyrics say, it's still "the girl, the car, the love, the heartbreak," so I guess it goes together. There are people who make interesting videos, but I think for the most part they're in Europe. The only really amusing one that I've seen was a few years ago by Tom Tom Club called *Genius in Love*, with really nice animations, and there have been some other pieces done by a place called Motion Picker's Studio, who do really really interesting clay animation. Picker did the thing of Mayor Koch singing "I Love New York," and Jimmy Carter singing "Georgia." Those are the ones I've enjoyed—I just happen to like animation. There's some animation in *200 Motels* and some clay animation in *Baby Snakes,* and I have quite a bit of it in the unfinished film done by a guy named Bruce Bickford.

I wrote and directed a music video in 1980 because at the time we had a contract with CBS and they wanted a music video to show overseas. I did a song called "You Are What You Is"— the title song from the album we had out. They hired a guy who looked like Ronald Reagan and gave him the electric chair, among other things. It did not get played a lot, especially in the United States.

I think *Miami Vice* is the missing link between detective pulp fiction and MTV videos: MTV videos plus the real sound effects of the gun. MTV is super violent, but you don't hear the violent sound effects. *Miami Vice* gives you the whole enchilada. The current trend today for composers in the business is that if you're a recording artist and you do rock 'n' roll, you get a call and somebody will offer you a license to use one of your songs on the soundtrack of the album. It doesn't necessarily mean that it fits in the movie, but they cram it in there so that when the film goes into release, they can put out a greatest hits album. They know they'll sell x number of copies of that based on the different artists who contributed, and the fee paid to the artist is not that exorbitant. The artist benefits because his song is connected to the movie, so he gets some kind of trickle-down effect from the motion picture advertising. But the net loss is to the viewer, who's been deprived of seeing a real movie with a real score about a real something, and all he's gotten is freeze-dried, mass-market doo-doo.

I did two soundtracks for films other than my own: a cowboy movie directed by Tim Sullivan called *Run Home Slow* and another movie called *The World's Greatest Sinner,* directed by Tim Carey. They were low-budget cheapies. In the case of *Run Home Slow,* I looked at the screenplay first, and in the case of *The World's Greatest Sinner,* I worked only with the print. These things were both done in the early sixties, before I even had a rock 'n' roll band, and if you think *200 Motels* was low-budget, these things were micro. In the case of *The World's Greatest Sinner,* the guy who produced it didn't like one piece of music I'd written, so he took an album of the London Philharmonic doing *The Planets* by Gustav Holst, had it transferred to 35 mm, didn't even get a license, and stuck it in the movie in the place where he wanted it. He didn't give any credit in the film, so I've got my name on it as the composer on the picture. I got this big shock when I went to the premiere and suddenly there was "Mars, the Bringer of War, da-da-da-da" coming out in this one scene.

It's hard to describe the process of writing a soundtrack for a movie, but I'd say if I had to do one today, I'd do it in a completely different way because there's better equipment to do it with. I would do it on a computer. The computer actually plays the music; you link that up with a video tape, and you can play right along with it and edit it.

I did enjoy *Eraserhead,* I must say that. I like the texture of the sound in *Eraserhead,* not necessarily that it was music, but just the idea of the sound blended into strange things that you hear that create a mood for the scene. I don't think there's enough conscious thought put into the psycho-acoustic factor, where you make people experience things in a different way just by changing the quality of what the sound is through equalization or by using something else in the background that creates an attitude and a different kind of setting. Sound can be used as effectively as lighting to tell a story, but usually the film budgets don't have enough money to do it right.

Some of my other favorite films are *Killer Shrews*—I don't even remember who did it. It's one of those fifties black and white science fiction movies. Another stinger is the *Brainiac,* a Mexican science fiction movie with a really cheap mask, a rubber mask with a big rubber tongue sticking out—sheer cheese—and rubber mittens on the guy's hands that don't quite match up to the cuffs under his coat. That's the kind of film I can enjoy because it just makes me laugh. It's so inept, so overstated.

Music will make your life beautiful because you can participate in it, but film, I think, is much more in the realm of entertainment. In terms of the amount of time of participation, the way music is in the United States, it's a virtual wallpaper to the life-style of the people who consume it. The ones who are really into it are listening to it hours and hours a day whether they listen consciously or just for background. If they can choose to hear the things they like, it tends to make their lives more beautiful. With a film, you have to make a conscious decision to see a certain thing and you may or may not be enthralled with it. You've been hooked into the theater by the advertising. There are a lot of people who go to the movies and pay a lot of money for ninety minutes or so of entertainment, walk out, and say, "I was gypped." It's a rare occasion when they go and say, "I've been uplifted."

Conclusion

Although I didn't always include them, responses to the desert island question ranged from "Oh bloody hell!" to "I'd never really thought of that before!" to "Orson and I were just talking about that the other day!" Some knew what film they wanted immediately; others never did get around to making a choice. Of course, the real content of this book is less about what film one would take to a desert island that it is about where the responses to that question take us.

It was the seemingly incidental bits and pieces of information that glimmered during the course of a discussion of reasons for taking or not taking this or that movie that proved to be the real treasures gleaned from this book: Emile de Antonio's final conclusion: Any film is too trivial!"; Robert Altman's view of his work as "telling myself the truth about something." Harold Becker, whose *The Onion Field* stands as one of the most disturbing films in recent years, talks about why movies tend to reduce characters to two-dimensional heroes and villains. We read about the "overnight" success story of Tom Benedek, whose screenplay for the 1985 mega-hit *Cocoon* was his first optioned work to come to the screen after ten years and as many scripts. Ethan and Joel Coen's witty take on *Bring Me the Head of Alfredo Garcia* evokes an image of the two brothers sitting in chairs tilted against the back wall of an N.Y.U. Film School classroom, playing with the question and suggesting that, finally, show business is a good joke. Roger Corman, the progenitor of some of the most illustrious film careers and a genius in his own right, offers advice to the fledgling filmmaker, and Wes Craven, one of those talents, the writer/director of the masterly

253

bad dream *Nightmare on Elm Street,* relates an anecdote about a special effect rendered at the last minute by putting oatmeal on some staircase steps—a graphic demonstration of how the constraints of low-budget filmmaking can become a means of creating art. Griffin Dunne, the star and producer of *After Hours,* talks about balancing his two very successful careers of producing and acting, and vividly describes his experience working with the brilliant perfectionist Martin Scorsese. Marianne Faithfull evokes the swinging London of the psychedelic sixties as she describes seeing Jean Cocteau's *The Blood of a Poet* in the company of Keith Richard, Paul McCartney, Terry Southern, and other luminaries of the period. Henry Jaglom offers an eloquent testimonial to the "perfect dream of romantic love" that he finds so lacking in modern life and so beautifully fulfilled in the films of Fred Astaire and Ginger Rogers. The newest filmmaker to keep the flame of hope burning in the breasts of independents, Jim Jarmusch, writer-director of the 1984 hit *Stranger Than Paradise,* discusses his unique shooting style and why he always casts first and writes after. Lewis MacAdams, poet and performing artist turned film writer-director, tells why he moved south, away from the aesthetic confines of San Francisco into the belly of the beast, Los Angeles, and describes the alternative film and video scene thriving there. James Monaco, the connoisseur film buff, whose landmark book *How to Read a Film* has been a bible to young filmmakers for close to ten years, offers his unique movie-rating system, with categories ranging from "Masterpiece" to "Comedy: Good for Your Health." Paul Morrissey, the brilliant and underrated maker of such classics as *Trash, Flesh,* and his latest, *Mixed Blood,* discusses Edison, Shakespeare, Olivier, and Warhol. Robert Mugge, creator of unique musical portraits on film, astutely dissects the emotional versus the intellectual reasons for taking a film to this island. David Newman, cowriter of *Bonnie and Clyde* and the *Superman* movies, laments the displacement of genre movies by the current practice of making "trend" movies. Harold Ramis, the writer of *Animal House* (which may indirectly be partially responsible for at least one trend) and actor-cowriter of *Ghostbusters,* another mega-hit, recalls the Marx Brothers as his surrogate father figures. And Ivan Reitman, the brilliant producer-director of *Ghostbusters,* compares Bill Murray to Groucho, Dan Aykroyd to Zeppo, and analyzes the career of John Belushi, who he feels could have achieved the stature of Marlon Brando. Richard Roud, director of the New York Film Festival and author of many books, offers an overview of filmmaking, past and present, and tells of the inner workings of the festival. Andrew Sarris, perhaps our finest critic and the American champion of the French auteur theory, discourses on the social and personal contexts of movies, displaying a sense of proportion rarely demonstrated by those in his profession. Volker Schlöndorff, whose most recent credit is the much-praised television production of Arthur Miller's *Death of a Salesman,* talks about filmmaking as a re-creation of the circus he dreamed of joining as a youth. Martin Sheen clarifies the role of the actor vis-à-vis the filmmaking community and the audience, showing us why it is, after all, a noble profession. Penelope Spheeris, a unique filmmaker, whose movies have stretched our notions of what film can and should do, gives her somewhat tongue-in-cheek formula for success in Hollywood. Susan Seidelman, who has certainly achieved that success with last year's hit, *Desperately Seeking Susan,* offers an illuminating analysis of the difference between actors who "act" and those with real personalities.

Interactive video viewing, "predicted" by François Truffaut in *Fahrenheit 451,* has become a reality through the laser disc. Bob Stein, president of a laser disc company, Criterion, describes the experience that includes, among other features, the ability to choose your own camera angles. The laser disc represents one attempt to capture the audience. At the other end of the spectrum, Douglas Trumbull, the special effects wizard of such films as *2001* and director of his own successful features, has developed a spectacular experience for the theater-going audience, Showscan, which he hopes will seduce people away from the television back into the theater.

Alain Tanner, a brilliant, eccentric Swiss filmmaker, treats us to a detailed account of finding the *right* cut, describing a logic of editing that comes from within. Michael Apted, another "eccentric," equally adept at musical films, documentary, and dramatic fiction, talks about his versatility as a means towards personal and professional growth and notes the birth of the character of J. R., when Larry Hagman played a rock 'n' roll manager in his film, *Stardust*. Social critic, musician, writer, and filmmaker Frank Zappa explains the emergence of *Miami Vice* as the "missing link" between MTV videos and pulp detective fiction. John Waters, a genial, witty filmmaker and writer who has raised low taste to high art, treats us to a tour of his wondrous head via his imaginary movies, starring such real greats as Lana Turner, Joey Heatherton, Pia Zadora, Liberace, and Benji. Budd Schulberg, author of such classics as *On the Waterfront* and *A Face in the Crowd*, talks about our greatest actor, Marlon Brando, and working with one of our finest actor's directors, Elia Kazan, recalling an energy sadly missing in today's film world. This world of deal-making is possibly best described from the perspective of a lawyer, Stanley Kallman, the sole East Coast attorney for the Cannon Film Group, Inc., the company that produced almost twice as many films as any other studio in 1985. Aidan Quinn, the young actor who shot like a meteor into the public awareness during the same year, offers insight into his work process that he equates to his practice of yoga. Harry Dean Stanton, who has enjoyed similar success this past year after putting in long years as a supporting "character" actor, discusses the stigma of that label and what it should really take to be the one to "get the girl in the end." Geraldine Page, long recognized as one of the, if not *the,* premier actresses of our time, demonstrates a brilliance, humor, and total lack of pretension that make it impossible to single out any one item of her interview as being of special interest. She covers topics such as her teenage "love affair" with *Wuthering Heights,* her first view of herself on the big screen, and an anecdote relating how she once mistook Ralph Meeker for Marlon Brando.

These seemingly random pieces of commentary come together into a completed puzzle, describing where film has been, where it is now, and leave us with a larger question than what movie would you take to a desert island; that is, what is the value of film and where is film going? Meanwhile, back in the present, despite differences of opinion on which is the best film, who is the best actor, whether the growth of the home-video industry is a boon or a curse on film, almost everyone seemed to be in agreement that the business appears as dry and infertile right now as a desert island. Though the possibility was not raised, not a few of the contributors to this book would be pleased at the thought of creating an especially hellish desert island for some of the Coca-Cola executives now making the decisions concerning what films get made and, therefore, what films we see: Strapped to a chair, eyes propped open à la *Clockwork Orange,* they would be forced to watch their worst potboiler over and over and over, till the end of time.

Appendix

The following, listed by director, are the films chosen by the contributors to this book as the ones they would take on a solitary sojourn on a desert island. The list is as varied as one could expect from a group of people that covers the spectrum from the "emperor" of the film world, Akira Kurosawa, many of whose films were named as favorites by his peers, to rock 'n' roll rebel, social critic, and occasional filmmaker Frank Zappa.

When I began this book, I had an image in mind of many little islands floating isolated in some nameless sea, each populated by a single filmophile sitting before a sheet-draped palm, watching Orson Welles' *Citizen Kane* over and over. However, the winners by a nose, if there are any winners, are the Marx Brothers. (Oddly enough, however, their films do not appear below because no one could remember a particular favorite title.) It seems many of the contributors here share James Monaco's sentiment as he quotes Stephen Sondheim: "Tragedy tomorrow, comedy tonight!"

WOODY ALLEN: *Play It Again, Sam,* 1972; *Stardust Memories,* 1981
ROBERT ALTMAN: *McCabe and Mrs. Miller,* 1971
LINDSAY ANDERSON: *Every Day Except Christmas,* 1957
MICHELANGELO ANTONIONI: *L'Avventura,* 1960
GEORGE STEVENS: *Swing Time,* 1936 (starring Fred Astaire and Ginger Rogers)
INGMAR BERGMAN: *Wild Strawberries,* 1957; *The Seventh Seal,* 1957; *Winter Light,* 1963; *Persona,* 1966; *Cries and Whispers,* 1972; *Fanny and Alexander,* 1984
BERNARDO BERTOLUCCI: *Last Tango in Paris,* 1972
ROBERT BRESSON: *Pickpocket,* 1959; *Four Nights of a Dreamer,* 1971; *L'Argent,* 1982

LUIS BUÑUEL: *The Exterminating Angel*, 1962; *Belle du Jour*, 1967

FRANK CAPRA: *Mr. Smith Goes to Washington*, 1939; *It's a Wonderful Life*, 1947

CHARLIE CHAPLIN: *City Lights*, 1931; *Modern Times*, 1936

RENÉ CLAIR: *Le Beauté du Diable*, 1950; *Le Belles de Nuit*, 1952

JEAN COCTEAU: *The Blood of a Poet*, 1932; *Beauty and the Beast*, 1946

FRANCIS FORD COPPOLA: *The Godfather I*, 1972; *The Godfather II*, 1974; *Apocalypse Now*, 1980

ALEX COX: *Repo Man*, 1984

GEORGE CUKOR: *Gone with the Wind*, 1939

MICHAEL CURTIZ: *Casablanca*, 1943

CARL DREYER: *Gertrud*, 1964

STEPHEN DWOSKIN: *Dynamo*, 1971

BOB DYLAN: *Renaldo and Clara*, 1972

BLAKE EDWARDS: *10*, 1979

SERGEI EISENSTEIN: *Battleship Potemkin*, 1925

JEAN EUSTACHE: *The Mother and the Whore*, 1973

RAINER WERNER FASSBINDER: *Chinese Roulette*, 1976; *In a Year of Thirteen Moons; Berlin Alexanderplatz*, 1979

FEDERICO FELLINI: *La Strada*, 1954; *The Nights of Cabiria*, 1957; *La Dolce Vita*, 1960; *8½*, 1963; *Fellini Satyricon*, 1969; *Amarcord*, 1973

VICTOR FLEMING: *The Wizard of Oz; Gone with the Wind*, 1939

JOHN FORD: *The Grapes of Wrath*, 1940: *How Green Was My Valley*, 1941: *The Man Who Shot Liberty Valance*, 1962

BOB FOSSE: *All That Jazz*, 1979

SAM FULLER: *Pickup on South Street*, 1953

ABEL GANCE: *La Roue*, 1923

JEAN-LUC GODARD: *Breathless*, 1960; *Pierrot le Fou*, 1965; *Two or Three Things I Know About Her*, 1967; *Numéro Deux*, 1975; *First Name: Carmen*, 1984

D. W. GRIFFITH: *The Birth of a Nation*, 1915

HOWARD HAWKS: *Only Angels Have Wings*, 1939; *Rio Bravo*, 1959

MONTE HELLMAN: *Two-Lane Blacktop*, 1971

ALFRED HITCHCOCK: *Shadow of a Doubt*, 1943; *Notorious*, 1946; *Strangers on a Train*, 1951; *Rear Window*, 1954; *Vertigo*, 1958; *Psycho*, 1960; *The Birds*, 1963

JOHN HUSTON: *The Treasure of the Sierra Madre*, 1948

MIKLOS JANCSÓ: *Red Psalm,* 1972

CHUCK JONES: *What's Opera, Doc?,* 1948

ELIA KAZAN: *Viva Zapata!,* 1952; *On the Waterfront,* 1954; *East of Eden,* 1955; *A Face in the Crowd,* 1957; *Splendor in the Grass,* 1961

STANLEY KUBRICK: *The Killing,* 1956; *Paths of Glory,* 1957; *Dr. Strangelove,* 1964; *2001: A Space Odyssey,* 1968; *Barry Lyndon,* 1975

AKIRA KUROSAWA: *Rashomon,* 1951; *Seven Samurai,* 1954; *High and Low,* 1963; *Red Beard,* 1965; *Ran,* 1985

FRITZ LANG: *Metropolis,* 1927

DAVID LEAN: *Brief Encounter,* 1946

RICHARD LESTER: *A Funny Thing Happened on the Way to the Forum,* 1966

ERNST LUBITSCH: *Heaven Can Wait,* 1943

DAVID LYNCH: *Eraserhead,* 1975

RUSS MEYER: *Faster Pussycat! Kill! Kill!,* 1965

GEORGE MILLER: *Road Warrior,* 1983

VINCENTE MINNELLI: *Gigi,* 1958

KENJI MIZOGUCHI: *Ugetsu,* 1953

ERMANNO OLMI: *The Fiancés,* 1963

MAX OPHÜLS: *Letter from an Unknown Woman,* 1948; *The Earrings of Madame De,* 1953

YASUJIRO OZU: *Tokyo Story,* 1953

PEOPLE'S REPUBLIC OF CHINA: *Breaking with Old Ideas,* 1975

ROMAN POLANSKI: *Knife in the Water,* 1962; *Repulsion,* 1965; *Rosemary's Baby,* 1968; *Chinatown,* 1974; *The Tenant,* 1976

SAM PECKINPAH: *The Wild Bunch,* 1969; *Bring Me the Head of Alfredo Garcia,* 1974

GILLO PONTECORVO: *Burn!,* 1969

MICHAEL POWELL AND EMERIC PRESSBURGER: *The Life and Death of Colonel Blimp,* 1943; *Stairway to Heaven,* 1946

NICHOLAS RAY: *In a Lonely Place,* 1950

JEAN RENOIR: *A Day in the Country,* 1946; *Grand Illusion,* 1937; *The Rules of the Game,* 1939

JACQUES RIVETTE: *Out One Out Two/Out One: Spectre,* 1973

FRANCESCO ROSI: *Carmen,* 1985

ROBERT ROSSEN: *All the King's Men,* 1949

KEN RUSSELL: *The Music Lovers,* 1971

GENE SAKS: *The Odd Couple*, 1968

MARTIN SCORSESE: *Taxi Driver*, 1976; *Raging Bull*, 1979; *The King of Comedy*, 1982

SUSAN SEIDELMAN: *Desperately Seeking Susan*, 1985

GEORGE STEVENS: *Giant*, 1956

PRESTON STURGES: *Sullivan's Travels*, 1941; *The Miracle of Morgan's Creek*, 1944

ANDREI TARKOVSKY: *The Mirror*, 1975; *Nostalgia*, 1982

FRANÇOIS TRUFFAUT: *Jules and Jim*, 1961

ANDY WARHOL: *The Chelsea Girls*, 1966

ORSON WELLES: *Citizen Kane*, 1941; *The Magnificent Ambersons*, 1942

WIM WENDERS: *Kings of the Road*, 1976; *The American Friend*, 1977; *Paris, Texas*, 1984

BILLY WILDER: *Some Like It Hot*, 1959

FREDERICK WISEMAN: *Titicut Follies*, 1960

WILLIAM WYLER: *Wuthering Heights*, 1939

ROBERT YOUNG: *Nothing But a Man*, 1966

INDEX